Better Homes and Gardens®

Fast Fix
one-dish dinners

MORE THAN 400 EASY RECIPES YOUR FAMILY WILL LOVE

Meredith® Books
Des Moines, Iowa

Better Homes and Gardens® Fast Fix One-Dish Meals
Editor: Jessica Saari Christensen
Contributing Designers: Waterbury Publications, Inc. / Chad Jewell
Editorial Assistant: Diane Mason
Book Production Manager: Mark Weaver
Contributing Copy Editor: Sarah Oliver Watson
Contributing Proofreaders: Staci Scheurenbrand, Lynn Stratton, Stan West
Contributing Indexer: Elizabeth T. Parson
Test Kitchen Director: Lynn Blanchard
Test Kitchen Product Supervisor: Marilyn Cornelius
Test Kitchen Culinary Specialists: Juliana Hale, Maryellyn Krantz,
    Jill Moberly, Colleen Weeden, Lori Wilson
Test Kitchen Nutrition Specialists: Elizabeth Burt, R.D., L.D.;
    Laura Marzen, R.D., L.D.

Meredith® Books
Executive Editor: Jennifer Darling
Managing Editor: Kathleen Armentrout
Brand Manager: Janell Pittman
Group Editor: Jan Miller
Copy Chief: Doug Kouma
Senior Copy Editors: Kevin Cox, Jennifer Speer Ramundt,
    Elizabeth Keest Sedrel
Assistant Copy Editor: Metta Cederdahl

Executive Director, Sales: Ken Zagor
Director, Operations: George A. Susral
Director, Production: Douglas M. Johnston
Business Director: Janice Croat
Vice President and General Manager, SIM: Jeff Myers

Better Homes and Gardens® Magazine
Editor in Chief: Gayle Goodson Butler
Deputy Editor, Food and Entertaining: Nancy Hopkins

Meredith Publishing Group
President: Jack Griffin
Executive Vice President: Doug Olson

Meredith Corporation
Chairman of the Board: William T. Kerr
President and Chief Executive Officer: Stephen M. Lacy
In Memoriam: E. T. Meredith III (1933–2003)

All of us at Meredith® Books are dedicated to providing you with
the information and ideas you need to create delicious foods. We
welcome your comments and suggestions. Write to us at Meredith
Special Interest Media, 1716 Locust St., Des Moines, IA 50309-3023.

Our seal assures you
that every recipe in
*Fast Fix One-Dish
Meals* has been tested
in the Better Homes
and Gardens® Test
Kitchen. This means
that each recipe is
practical and reliable
and meets our high
standards of taste
appeal. We guarantee
your satisfaction with
this book for as long
as you own it.

table of
contents

Every night it's the same question—
"what's for dinner"? And not only do you
have to decide what to make, but you also
have to shop for it and find time to prepare
it! Weeknight meals can be difficult—but
one-dish dinners have it all. Everything
you need in one pan (or pot or casserole
dish). So when you're deciding what to
make for dinner tonight, check out the
more than 350 easy-to-prepare one-pan
options in *Fast Fix One-Dish Meals*. Your
family of hungry diners will be full and
satisfied in no time at all!

These rise-and-shine morning meals will fill you up and have you ready to face the world in no time. Every once in a while, turn dinner upside down and serve one of these morning meals at night!

early morning

brea

kfasts

ham-asparagus strata

Prep: 20 minutes Bake: 1 hour Stand: 10 minutes Chill: 2 hours
Oven: 325°F Makes: 6 servings

4   English muffins, torn
    or cut into bite-size
    pieces (4 cups)
2   cups cubed cooked
    ham or chicken
    (10 ounces)
1   10-ounce package
    frozen cut
    asparagus or frozen
    cut broccoli, thawed
    and well drained, or
    2 cups cut-up fresh
    cooked asparagus
    or broccoli
4   ounces process Swiss
    cheese, torn, or
    process Gruyère
    cheese, cut up
4   eggs, slightly beaten
¼   cup dairy sour cream
1¼ cups milk
2   tablespoons finely
    chopped onion
1   tablespoon Dijon-
    style mustard
⅛   teaspoon ground
    black pepper

1 In a greased 2-quart square baking dish spread half of the English muffin pieces. Top with the ham, asparagus, and cheese. Top with the remaining English muffin pieces.

2 In a medium bowl whisk together the eggs and sour cream. Stir in milk, onion, mustard, and pepper.* Pour evenly over the layers in dish. Cover and chill for 2 to 24 hours.

3 Preheat oven to 325°F. Bake, uncovered, in the preheated oven for 60 to 65 minutes or until heated through in center (170°F). Let stand for 10 minutes before serving.

*Note: If using chicken instead of ham, add ¼ teaspoon salt at this point.

Per serving: 349 cal., 16 g total fat (7 g sat. fat), 193 mg chol., 1,224 mg sodium, 25 g carbo., 2 g fiber, 26 g pro.

Strata is the ultimate make-ahead holiday brunch dish. This one achieves "favorite" status not only for its terrific flavors but also for the way the pink ham and green broccoli combine for a holiday look.

christmas morning strata

Prep: 20 minutes Bake: 1 hour Stand: 5 minutes Chill: 2 hours
Oven: 325°F Makes: 6 servings

1 cup broccoli florets
5 cups ½-inch French bread cubes (about 8 ounces)
2 cups shredded cheddar cheese (8 ounces)
1 cup cubed cooked ham (5 ounces)
3 eggs, beaten
1¾ cups milk
2 tablespoons finely chopped onion
1 teaspoon dry mustard
Dash ground black pepper

1 Grease a 2-quart square baking dish; set aside. In a 1-quart microwave-safe casserole combine broccoli florets and 1 tablespoon water. Cover with plastic wrap and microwave on 100% power (high) for 2 to 3 minutes or just until tender; drain well. (Or in a covered small saucepan cook broccoli in a small amount of boiling water for 4 to 6 minutes or just until tender; drain well.) Set aside.

2 Layer half of the bread cubes in the prepared baking dish. Top with cheese, ham, and broccoli. Top with the remaining bread cubes. In a medium bowl combine beaten eggs, milk, onion, mustard, and pepper. Pour egg mixture evenly over layers in baking dish. Cover and chill for 2 to 24 hours.

3 Preheat oven to 325°F. Bake strata, uncovered, in the preheated oven for 1 hour or until a knife inserted near the center comes out clean. Let stand for 5 minutes before serving.

Per serving: *377 cal., 20 g total fat (11 g sat. fat), 165 mg chol., 886 mg sodium, 25 g carbo., 2 g fiber, 24 g pro.*

Strata is Italian for "layers," but to American cooks strata translates roughly to "a terrific and terrifically easy crowd-pleasing brunch dish that you can make the night before." Here cranberries and maple syrup add irresistible sweet-tart layers.

cranberry strata

Prep: 25 minutes Bake: 65 minutes Stand: 10 minutes Chill: 8 hours
Oven: 350°F Makes: 9 to 12 servings

12 ounces crusty French
       bread or sourdough
       bread, torn into
       1-inch pieces
       (8 cups)
1   8-ounce package
       cream cheese
½ cup dried cranberries
6   eggs
2¼ cups milk
⅓ cup pure maple syrup
       or maple-flavored
       syrup
½ teaspoon ground
       cinnamon or ground
       nutmeg
    Pure maple syrup
       or maple-flavored
       syrup (optional)

1 In a greased 2-quart rectangular baking dish, arrange half of the bread pieces.

2 Cut the cream cheese into ½-inch slices. Arrange on bread pieces in baking dish. Sprinkle cranberries on bread; top with remaining bread pieces.

3 In a medium bowl beat together the eggs, milk, and ⅓ cup maple syrup. Pour over bread and cranberries in baking dish. Sprinkle with cinnamon. Lightly press down with back of spoon to saturate bread with egg mixture. Cover and chill for 8 to 24 hours.

4 Preheat oven to 350°F. Bake strata, covered, in the preheated oven for 45 minutes. Uncover; bake for 20 minutes more. Let stand for 10 minutes before serving. If desired, serve warm with additional maple syrup.

Per serving: 338 cal., 15 g total fat (8 g sat. fat), 177 mg chol., 403 mg sodium, 38 g carbo., 1 g fiber, 13 g pro.

Easy does it! There's no tricky flipping or folding needed with this Italian-style open-face omelet.

baked sunrise frittata

Prep: 20 minutes Bake: 25 minutes Stand: 5 minutes Oven: 350°F
Makes: 8 servings

1½	cups cubed potato
1	tablespoon cooking oil
1½	cups finely chopped cooked ham (8 ounces)
¾	cup shredded cheddar cheese (3 ounces)
8	eggs, slightly beaten
⅓	cup milk
1	4-ounce can diced green chile peppers, undrained
¼	cup thinly sliced green onion (2)
2	teaspoons snipped fresh oregano or ½ teaspoon dried oregano, crushed
¼	teaspoon salt
½	cup bottled roasted red sweet pepper strips
1½	cups bottled salsa Fresh cilantro (optional)

1 Preheat oven to 350°F. In a 10-inch ovenproof skillet cook potato in hot oil over medium heat for 5 minutes, stirring occasionally. Cook, covered, about 5 minutes more or until potato is tender, stirring once. Remove from heat. Sprinkle with ham and ½ cup of the cheddar cheese.

2 In a large bowl stir together eggs, milk, undrained green chile peppers, green onion, oregano, and salt. Pour over potato mixture in skillet. Arrange roasted pepper strips on top of frittata.

3 Bake in the preheated oven for 25 to 30 minutes or just until center is set and knife inserted in center comes out clean. Sprinkle top of frittata with remaining cheddar cheese. Let stand for 5 minutes.

4 Meanwhile, in small saucepan heat salsa. To serve, spoon salsa over frittata. If desired, garnish with cilantro.

Per serving: 226 cal., 14 g total fat (5 g sat. fat), 240 mg chol., 920 mg sodium, 12 g carbo., 2 g fiber, 15 g pro.

mediterranean frittata

Start to Finish: 25 minutes   Makes: 6 servings

1   cup chopped onion
     (1 large)
2   cloves garlic, minced
3   tablespoons olive oil
8   eggs
¼   cup half-and-half,
     light cream, or milk
½   cup crumbled feta
     cheese (2 ounces)
½   cup chopped bottled
     roasted red sweet
     peppers
½   cup sliced kalamata
     or pitted ripe olives
     (optional)
¼   cup slivered fresh
     basil
⅛   teaspoon ground
     black pepper
½   cup onion-and-garlic
     croutons, coarsely
     crushed
2   tablespoons finely
     shredded Parmesan
     cheese
     Fresh basil leaves
     (optional)

1 Preheat broiler. In a large broilerproof skillet cook onion and garlic in 2 tablespoons hot oil until onion is just tender.

2 Meanwhile, in a medium bowl beat together eggs and half-and-half. Stir in feta cheese, roasted peppers, olives (if desired), basil, and ground black pepper. Pour egg mixture over onion mixture in skillet. Cook over medium heat. As mixture sets, run a spatula around the edge of the skillet, lifting egg mixture so uncooked portion flows underneath. Continue cooking and lifting edges until egg mixture is almost set (surface will be moist). Reduce heat as necessary to prevent overcooking.

3 In a bowl combine crushed croutons, Parmesan cheese, and the remaining 1 tablespoon of oil; sprinkle over frittata.

4 Broil 4 to 5 inches from heat for 1 to 2 minutes or until top is set and crumbs are golden. Cut frittata in wedges to serve. If desired, garnish with fresh basil leaves.

Per serving: 246 cal., 19 g total fat (5 g sat. fat), 295 mg chol., 383 mg sodium, 8 g carbo., 1 g fiber, 11 g pro.

pepperoni pizza frittata

Start to Finish: 30 minutes Makes: 4 servings

6 eggs, slightly beaten
¾ teaspoon dried
    oregano, crushed
¼ teaspoon salt
¼ teaspoon ground
    black pepper
    Nonstick cooking
    spray
¾ cup chopped plum
    tomatoes
⅓ cup chopped
    pepperoni
½ cup shredded
    mozzarella cheese
    (2 ounces)

1 Preheat broiler. In a medium bowl combine eggs, oregano, salt, and pepper; set aside. Lightly coat a large broilerproof skillet with cooking spray. Heat skillet over medium heat.

2 Pour egg mixture into skillet. As mixture sets, run a spatula around edge of skillet, lifting egg mixture so uncooked portion flows underneath. Continue cooking and lifting edge until almost set (surface will be moist).

3 Remove skillet from heat. Sprinkle egg mixture with chopped tomatoes. Broil 4 to 5 inches from heat for 1 to 2 minutes or just until top is set. Remove from broiler; top with pepperoni and ¼ cup of the cheese. Return to broiler. Broil for 1 to 2 minutes more or until cheese melts. Sprinkle with remaining ¼ cup cheese. Cut into wedges.

Per serving: *212 cal., 15 g total fat (6 g sat. fat), 338 mg chol., 512 mg sodium, 3 g carbo., 1 g fiber, 15 g pro.*

asparagus, zucchini & yellow pepper frittata

Prep: 30 minutes Bake: 35 minutes Stand: 10 minutes Oven: 350°F Makes: 8 servings

1½ pounds fresh
asparagus, or two
9-ounce or 10-ounce
packages frozen cut
asparagus

1 medium yellow sweet
pepper, cut into
¼-inch strips

⅓ cup chopped onion
(1 small)

1 small zucchini,
halved lengthwise
and sliced ¼ inch
thick (about 1 cup)

10 eggs, slightly beaten

1 cup half-and-half,
light cream, or milk

2 tablespoons snipped
fresh Italian (flat-
leaf) parsley

1¼ teaspoons salt

¼ to ½ teaspoon ground
black pepper

1 Preheat oven to 350°F. Grease a 2-quart rectangular baking dish; set aside.

2 If using fresh asparagus, snap off and discard woody bases. If desired, scrape off scales. Cut into 1-inch pieces.

3 In a saucepan bring about 1 inch of water to boiling. Add asparagus, sweet pepper strips, and onion. Bring just to boiling; reduce heat. Simmer, covered, about 1 minute or until crisp-tender. Drain well. If desired, set aside some asparagus tips for garnish. Spread asparagus mixture evenly in baking dish. Layer zucchini slices over top.

4 In a medium bowl whisk together eggs, half-and-half, parsley, salt, and ground black pepper. Pour over vegetables in baking dish.

5 Bake, uncovered, in the preheated oven for 35 minutes or until a knife inserted near the center comes out clean. Let stand for 10 minutes before serving. If desired, garnish with asparagus tips.

Per serving: 160 cal., 10 g total fat (4 g sat. fat), 277 mg chol., 465 mg sodium, 6 g carbo., 1 g fiber, 11 g pro.

zucchini frittata

Start to Finish: 25 minutes Oven: 400°F Makes: 4 to 6 servings

6 eggs
2 tablespoons snipped fresh parsley
2 tablespoons water
½ teaspoon snipped fresh rosemary or ⅛ teaspoon dried rosemary, crushed
½ teaspoon salt
⅛ teaspoon ground black pepper
1 cup thinly sliced zucchini (1 small)
½ cup thinly sliced leek (1 medium)
1 tablespoon butter or margarine
½ of a 4½-ounce package Camembert cheese or 2 tablespoons freshly shredded Parmesan cheese

1 Preheat oven to 400°F. In a medium bowl beat together eggs, parsley, water, rosemary, salt, and pepper; set aside. In a large ovenproof skillet cook and stir zucchini and leek in hot butter just until tender.

2 Pour egg mixture over vegetables in skillet. Cook over medium heat. As mixture sets, run a spatula around edge of skillet, lifting the egg mixture so uncooked portion flows underneath. Continue cooking and lifting until egg mixture is almost set (surface will be moist).

3 Bake, uncovered, in the preheated oven about 4 minutes or just until top is set. Cut the half circle of Camembert (if using) horizontally; cut each half into 2 or 3 wedges and place on the frittata (or sprinkle frittata with Parmesan cheese). Allow cheese to melt slightly before serving.

Per serving: 201 cal., 14 g total fat (5 g sat. fat), 331 mg chol., 534 mg sodium, 5 g carbo., 1 g fiber, 13 g pro.

This no-fuss frittata is the perfect solution for a quick supper on a busy night or for a leisurely breakfast on the weekend.

cheese frittata with mushrooms & dill

Prep: 30 minutes Stand: 5 minutes Makes: 4 servings

6   eggs
⅓   cup shredded Gruyère or Swiss cheese (1½ ounces)
¼   cup water
¼   teaspoon salt
⅛   teaspoon freshly ground black pepper
2   tablespoons butter or margarine
1½ cups thinly sliced fresh mushrooms (such as shiitake, chanterelle, brown, or button)
¼   cup sliced green onions
1   tablespoon snipped fresh Italian (flat-leaf) parsley
1   tablespoon snipped fresh dill

1 In a medium bowl whisk together eggs, cheese, water, salt, and pepper; set aside.

2 In a 10-inch nonstick skillet melt butter over medium heat. Add mushrooms; cook and stir for 4 to 5 minutes or until tender. Stir in the green onions, parsley, and dill.

3 Pour the egg mixture over mushroom mixture. Cook, uncovered, over medium heat. As the egg mixture begins to set, run a spatula around edge of skillet, lifting egg mixture so the uncooked portion flows underneath. Continue cooking and lifting edge until the egg mixture is almost set (surface will be moist). Remove from heat.

4 Cover and let stand about 5 minutes or until top is set. Cut into wedges.

Per serving: 222 cal., 18 g total fat (8 g sat. fat), 347 mg chol., 341 mg sodium, 3 g carbo., 0 g fiber, 14 g pro.

corn frittata with cheese

Start to Finish: 25 minutes Makes: 4 servings

8 eggs, slightly beaten
1 tablespoon snipped
   fresh basil or
   1 teaspoon dried
   basil, crushed
2 tablespoons olive oil
1 cup frozen whole
   kernel corn or cut
   fresh corn
½ cup chopped zucchini
⅓ cup thinly sliced
   green onion
¾ cup chopped plum
   tomato
½ cup shredded
   cheddar cheese
   (2 ounces)

1 In a medium bowl combine eggs
and basil; set aside. Heat oil in a large
broilerproof skillet; add corn, zucchini, and
green onion. Cook and stir for 3 minutes;
add tomato. Cook, uncovered, over medium
heat about 5 minutes or until vegetables are
crisp-tender, stirring occasionally.

2 Pour egg mixture over vegetables
in skillet. Cook, uncovered, over
medium heat. As mixture sets, run a spatula
around edge of skillet, lifting egg mixture
so uncooked portion flows underneath.
Continue cooking and lifting edges until egg
mixture is almost set (surface will be moist).
Sprinkle with cheese.

3 Place the skillet under broiler 4 to 5 inches
from heat. Broil for 1 to 2 minutes or until
top is just set and cheese is melted.

Per serving: 313 cal., 22 g total fat (7 g sat. fat), 440 mg chol.,
220 mg sodium, 13 g carbo., 2 g fiber, 18 g pro.

Scrambled eggs, ham, and vegetables in a creamy cheese sauce—if anything can make you look forward to getting out of bed on a weekend morning, this is it. Toasted English muffins are easy serve-alongs.

oven-style eggs & ham

Prep: 30 minutes **Bake:** 45 minutes **Chill:** 4 hours
Oven: 350°F **Makes:** 6 servings

5 eggs
⅛ teaspoon salt
2 tablespoons butter
1 tablespoon all-purpose flour
⅛ teaspoon black pepper
¾ cup milk
¾ cup cut-up process Gruyère or Swiss cheese (3 ounces)
1 teaspoon prepared mustard
1 16-ounce package desired frozen loose-pack vegetable mix, such as corn, broccoli, and red sweet peppers
3 ounces cooked ham, cut into bite-size strips (about ½ cup)
¼ cup shredded process Gruyère or Swiss cheese (1 ounce)

1 In a medium bowl beat together eggs and salt. In a 10-inch skillet melt 1 tablespoon of the butter over medium heat; pour in egg mixture. Cook, without stirring, until mixture begins to set on the bottom and around the edges.

2 Using a spatula or large spoon lift and fold the partially cooked eggs so that the uncooked portion flows underneath. Continue cooking over medium heat for 2 to 3 minutes or until eggs are cooked through but are still glossy and moist. Remove from heat immediately; set aside.

3 For sauce, in a large saucepan melt the remaining 1 tablespoon butter over medium heat. Stir in flour and pepper. Add milk all at once. Cook and stir until mixture is thickened and bubbly. Add the ¾ cup cheese and the mustard, stirring until cheese melts.

4 Stir in vegetables and ham; gently fold in cooked eggs. Transfer mixture to a 3-quart rectangular baking dish. Cover and chill for 4 to 24 hours.

5 Preheat oven to 350°F. Bake, covered, in the preheated oven for 45 to 50 minutes or until heated through, stirring gently after 15 minutes. Stir gently again before serving. Sprinkle with the ¼ cup cheese.

Per serving: 261 cal., 15 g total fat (7 g sat. fat), 214 mg chol., 500 mg sodium, 13 g carbo., 2 g fiber, 15 g pro.

crustless mexican quiche

Prep: 15 minutes Bake: 30 minutes Stand: 10 minutes Oven: 325°F Makes: 6 servings

Nonstick cooking
    spray
½ pound bulk chorizo or
    spicy pork sausage
4 beaten eggs
1½ cups half-and-half or
    light cream
1½ cups shredded
    Monterey Jack
    cheese with
    jalapeño peppers
⅓ cup bottled salsa

1 Preheat oven to 325°F. Lightly coat a 9-inch pie plate with cooking spray; set aside.

2 In a medium skillet cook chorizo until brown; drain off fat. Meanwhile, in a medium bowl stir together eggs and half-and-half; stir in cooked chorizo. Add cheese; mix well. Pour egg mixture into the prepared pie plate.

3 Bake in the preheated oven for 30 minutes or until a knife inserted near the center comes out clean. Let stand for 10 minutes before serving. Top each serving with salsa.

Per serving: *406 cal., 33 g total fat (16 g sat. fat), 222 mg chol., 714 mg sodium, 4 g carbo., 0 g fiber, 22 g pro.*

crab quiche

Prep: 15 minutes Bake: 30 minutes Stand: 10 minutes Oven: 450°F/375°F Makes: 8 servings

½ of a 15-ounce
package rolled
refrigerated
unbaked piecrust
(1 crust)

3 tablespoons finely
chopped green
onion

1 tablespoon butter or
margarine

3 eggs

½ pound cooked
crabmeat (2 cups)
or one 6- to 8-ounce
package flake-style
imitation crabmeat

1 cup half-and-half,
light cream, or milk

3 tablespoons dry
vermouth (optional)

1 tablespoon tomato
paste

1 teaspoon salt*

¼ teaspoon ground
black pepper

½ cup shredded Swiss
cheese (2 ounces)

1 Preheat oven to 450°F. Unroll piecrust according to package directions. Line a 9-inch pie plate with crust. Bake according to package directions. Reduce oven temperature to 375°F.

2 In a small skillet cook green onion in hot butter until tender. Remove from heat. In a medium bowl beat eggs slightly with a fork. Stir in crabmeat, half-and-half, vermouth (if using), tomato paste, salt, and pepper. Stir in green onion mixture. Pour egg mixture into pastry shell. Sprinkle with cheese.

3 Bake the quiche in the 375°F oven for 30 minutes or until a knife inserted near the center comes out clean. Let stand for 10 minutes before serving. Cut into wedges to serve.

*Tip: You may want to cut the salt in the quiche filling to ½ teaspoon if using the imitation crabmeat option (which is higher in sodium).

Per serving: 279 cal., 18 g total fat (7 g sat. fat), 130 mg chol., 498 mg sodium, 16 g carbo., 1 g fiber, 13 g pro.

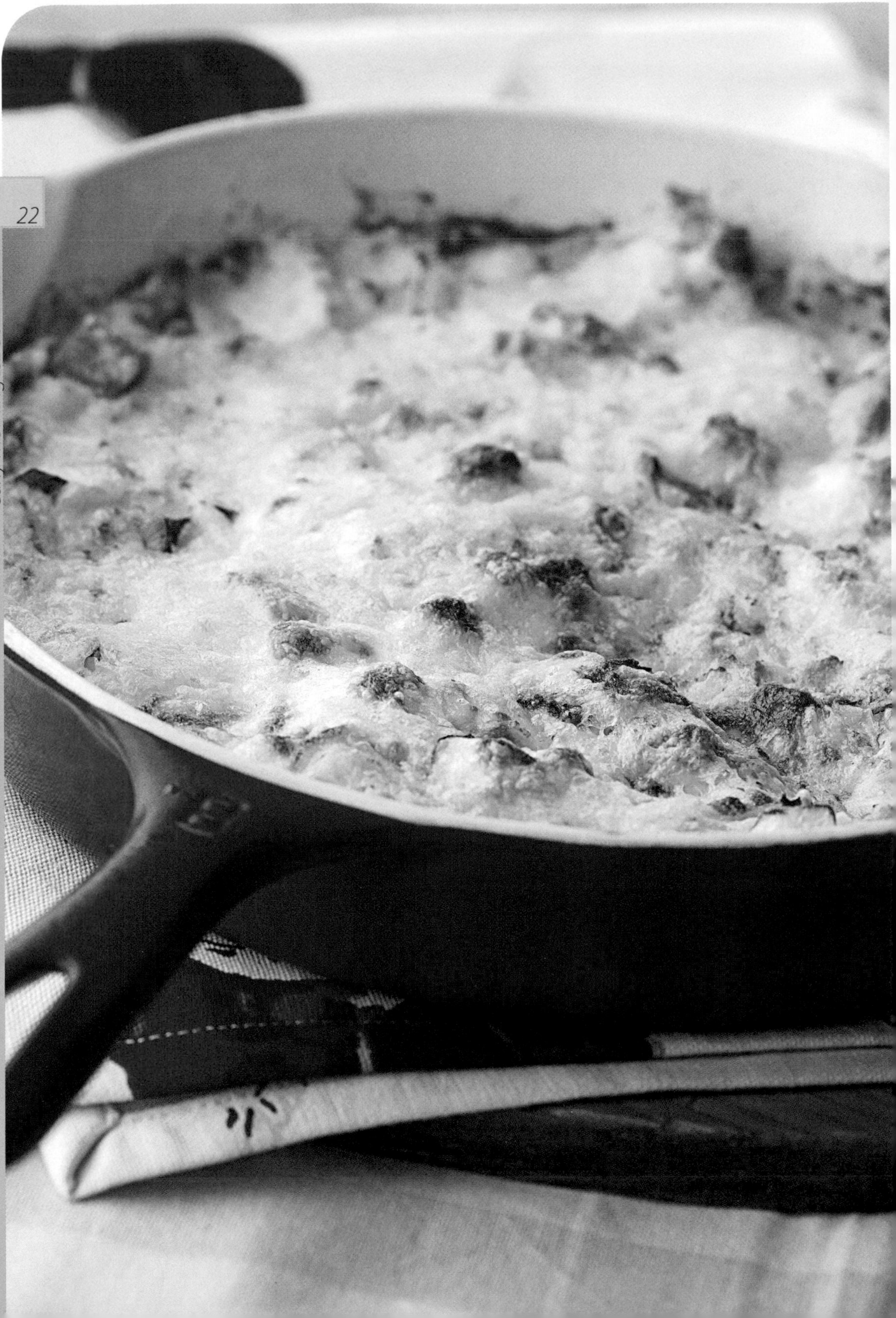

ham & swiss skillet

Start to Finish: 25 minutes Makes: 6 servings

12   eggs
½   teaspoon dried
     thyme, crushed
     Dash salt
     Dash black pepper
1   cup coarsely chopped
     zucchini or yellow
     summer squash
1   tablespoon butter or
     margarine
1½   cups coarsely
     chopped cooked
     ham
½   cup shredded Swiss
     cheese (2 ounces)
     Snipped chives
     (optional)

1 Preheat broiler. In a medium bowl combine eggs, thyme, salt, and pepper; set aside. In a 10-inch broilerproof skillet cook zucchini in hot butter until tender, stirring occasionally. Stir in ham.

2 Pour egg mixture over ham mixture in skillet. Cook over medium-low heat without stirring until mixture begins to set on the bottom and around the edge. As mixture sets, run a spatula around the edge of skillet, lifting egg mixture so uncooked portion flows underneath. Continue cooking and lifting edges until egg mixture is almost set (surface will be moist). Sprinkle with cheese.

3 Place the skillet under the broiler 4 to 5 inches from heat. Broil for 1 to 2 minutes or until top is just set and cheese melts. If desired, sprinkle with chives. Cut into wedges.

Per serving: 260 cal., 17 g total fat (7 g sat. fat), 456 mg chol., 638 mg sodium, 3 g carbo., 1 g fiber, 21 g pro.

Kicky Mexican-style eggs cook in a baking dish, perfect for serving at a buffet. The scent of cumin, garlic, and chili powder plus fresh cilantro lets you know what a delicious treat lies ahead.

easy huevos rancheros casserole

Prep: 15 minutes **Bake:** 38 minutes **Stand:** 10 minutes
Oven: 375°F **Makes:** 12 servings

Nonstick cooking
spray
1 32-ounce package
frozen fried potato
nuggets
12 eggs
1 cup milk
1½ teaspoons dried
oregano, crushed
1½ teaspoons ground
cumin
½ teaspoon chili
powder
¼ teaspoon garlic
powder
1 8-ounce package
shredded Mexican
cheese blend
1 16-ounce jar thick
and chunky salsa
1 8-ounce carton dairy
sour cream
Snipped fresh cilantro

1 Preheat oven to 375°F. Lightly coat a 3-quart rectangular baking dish with cooking spray. Arrange potato nuggets in dish.

2 In a large bowl combine eggs, milk, oregano, cumin, chili powder, and garlic powder. Beat with a wire whisk until combined. Pour egg mixture over potato nuggets.

3 Bake in the preheated oven for 35 to 40 minutes or until a knife inserted near center comes out clean. Sprinkle cheese evenly over egg mixture. Bake about 3 minutes more or until cheese melts. Let stand for 10 minutes before serving. Top with salsa, sour cream, and cilantro.

Per serving: 343 cal., 21 g total fat (9 g sat. fat), 238 mg chol., 823 mg sodium, 26 g carbo., 2 g fiber, 14 g pro.

horseradish
ham-potato bake

Prep: 20 minutes Bake: 55 minutes Stand: 5 minutes
Chill: 4 hours Oven: 350°F Makes: 8 servings

Nonstick cooking
  spray
1 28-ounce package
  frozen loose-pack
  diced hash brown
  potatoes with
  onions and peppers
1½ cups diced cooked
  ham (8 ounces)
1 cup shredded Swiss
  cheese (4 ounces)
⅓ cup finely chopped
  red onion
5 eggs, slightly beaten
1½ cups milk
3 tablespoons
  horseradish
  mustard
½ teaspoon salt
¼ teaspoon ground
  black pepper
½ cup dairy sour cream
1 to 2 tablespoons
  horseradish
  mustard
1 tablespoon snipped
  fresh chives

1 Coat a 3-quart rectangular baking dish with cooking spray. Arrange potatoes evenly in the bottom of the dish. Sprinkle with ham, cheese, and onion.

2 In a medium bowl whisk together eggs, milk, the 3 tablespoons horseradish mustard, the salt, and pepper. Pour egg mixture over potato mixture. Cover and chill for 4 to 24 hours.

3 Preheat oven to 350°F. Bake, uncovered, in the preheated oven for 55 to 60 minutes or until a knife inserted near center comes out clean. Let stand for 5 minutes before serving. Meanwhile, for the sauce, stir together sour cream, the 1 to 2 tablespoons horseradish mustard, and the chives. Serve with Horseradish Ham-Potato Bake.

Per serving: 270 cal., 14 g total fat (6 g sat. fat), 169 mg chol., 651 mg sodium, 21 g carbo., 2 g fiber, 16 g pro.

breakfast casserole

Prep: 25 minutes Bake: 50 minutes Stand: 10 minutes Chill: 2 hours
Oven: 325°F Makes: 10 servings

1½ pounds bulk pork
     sausage or bulk
     Italian sausage
     Nonstick cooking
     spray
2½ cups seasoned
     croutons
 2   cups shredded
     cheddar cheese
     (8 ounces)
2½ cups milk
 4   eggs, slightly beaten
 ¾   teaspoon dry mustard
 1   10.75-ounce can
     condensed cream of
     mushroom soup
 ½   cup milk

1 In a large skillet cook and stir sausage over medium heat until no pink remains; drain.

2 Meanwhile, lightly coat a 3-quart rectangular baking dish with cooking spray. Spread croutons evenly in bottom of prepared dish. Sprinkle half of the cheese over croutons. Top with sausage. In a large bowl combine the 2½ cups milk, the beaten eggs, and the dry mustard. Pour over layers in baking dish. Stir together soup and the ½ cup milk. Spoon soup mixture evenly over mixture in baking dish. Cover and chill for 2 to 24 hours.

3 To serve, preheat oven to 325°F. Bake, uncovered, for 45 minutes. Sprinkle remaining cheese over casserole. Bake for 5 to 10 minutes more or until a knife inserted near the center comes out clean. Let stand for 10 minutes before serving.

Per serving: 472 cal., 35 g total fat (15 g sat. fat), 154 mg chol., 883 mg sodium, 14 g carbo., 1 g fiber, 20 g pro.

Add some ham to this classic recipe for a family-friendly main dish that goes together in a flash.

hash brown casserole

Prep: 20 minutes Bake: 50 minutes Stand: 10 minutes
Oven: 350°F Makes: 6 servings

1   10.75-ounce can
      reduced-fat and
      reduced-sodium
      condensed cream
      of chicken soup
1   8-ounce carton light
      dairy sour cream or
      dairy sour cream
½   of a 30-ounce
      package frozen
      shredded hash
      brown potatoes
      (about 4 cups)
1   cup diced cooked
      ham (4 ounces)
1   cup cubed American
      cheese (4 ounces)
¼   cup chopped onion
⅛   teaspoon ground
      black pepper
1   cup cornflakes
3   tablespoons butter,
      melted

1 Preheat oven to 350°F. In a large bowl stir together soup and sour cream. Stir in frozen potatoes, ham, cheese, onion, and pepper. Evenly spread the mixture in a 2-quart square baking dish. In a small bowl combine cornflakes and butter. Sprinkle over potato mixture.

2 Bake, uncovered, in the preheated oven for 50 to 55 minutes or until hot and bubbly. Let stand for 10 minutes before serving.

Per serving: 351 cal., 19 g total fat (11 g sat. fat), 63 mg chol., 953 mg sodium, 35 g carbo., 2 g fiber, 13 g pro.

If you want a lighter dish, cut back on the fat in this strata by using reduced-fat cheese and nonfat milk.

waffle breakfast casserole

· Prep: 20 minutes Bake: 50 minutes Stand: 10 minutes
Chill: 4 hours Oven: 350°F Makes: 8 servings

1   pound bulk pork
    sausage
6   frozen waffles,
    toasted and cubed
1   cup shredded
    cheddar cheese
    (4 ounces)
6   eggs, slightly beaten
2   cups milk
1   teaspoon dry mustard
1/8 teaspoon ground
    black pepper
    Maple-flavor or
    pure maple syrup
    (optional)

1 In a large skillet cook sausage until brown. Drain off fat.

2 Arrange half of the cubed waffles in an ungreased 2-quart rectangular baking dish. Top with half of the sausage and about 2/3 cup of the cheddar cheese. Layer with remaining cubed waffles and sausage.

3 In a medium bowl combine eggs, milk, dry mustard, and pepper. Slowly pour over layers in baking dish. Press lightly with the back of a large spoon to moisten waffles. Cover and chill for 4 to 24 hours.

4 Preheat oven to 350°F. Uncover waffle mixture. Bake in the preheated oven for 50 to 60 minutes or until knife inserted near center comes out clean. Sprinkle with remaining 1/3 cup cheese. Let stand for 10 minutes before serving. If desired, drizzle with maple syrup.

Per serving: 413 cal., 28 g total fat (12 g sat. fat), 217 mg chol., 668 mg sodium, 15 g carbo., 1 g fiber, 19 g pro.

make-ahead french toast

Prep: 30 minutes Bake: 30 minutes Freeze: 3 hours
Oven: 350°F Makes: 10 servings

1   8-ounce package
      cream cheese,
      softened
¼   cup dairy sour cream
1   16-ounce loaf French
      bread
¾   cup orange
      marmalade
4   eggs
1   cup milk
1½ teaspoons vanilla
2½ cups finely chopped
      almonds
      (10 ounces)
      Maple syrup

1 In a medium mixing bowl combine cream cheese and sour cream. Beat with an electric mixer on medium speed until smooth; set aside. Trim off ends of bread; cut loaf crosswise in 20 slices. Spread half of the slices on one side with cheese mixture. Spread remaining slices on one side with marmalade. Sandwich slices together; set aside.

2 In a shallow dish use a fork to beat eggs, milk, and vanilla together. Place half of the almonds in another shallow dish. Dip both sides of sandwiches in egg mixture; allow excess to drip off. Coat both sides of sandwiches with almonds, adding more almonds to dish as needed.

3 Place coated sandwiches on baking sheet lined with waxed paper; cover and freeze about 3 hours or until firm. Transfer to freezer container or bag; seal, label, and freeze for up to 1 month.

4 To serve, preheat oven to 350°F. Place frozen French toast on a large greased baking sheet. Bake in the preheated oven for 30 to 35 minutes or until golden and heated through, turning once. Serve with maple syrup.

Per serving: 562 cal., 26 g total fat (8 g sat. fat), 114 mg chol., 402 mg sodium, 71 g carbo., 5 g fiber, 15 g pro.

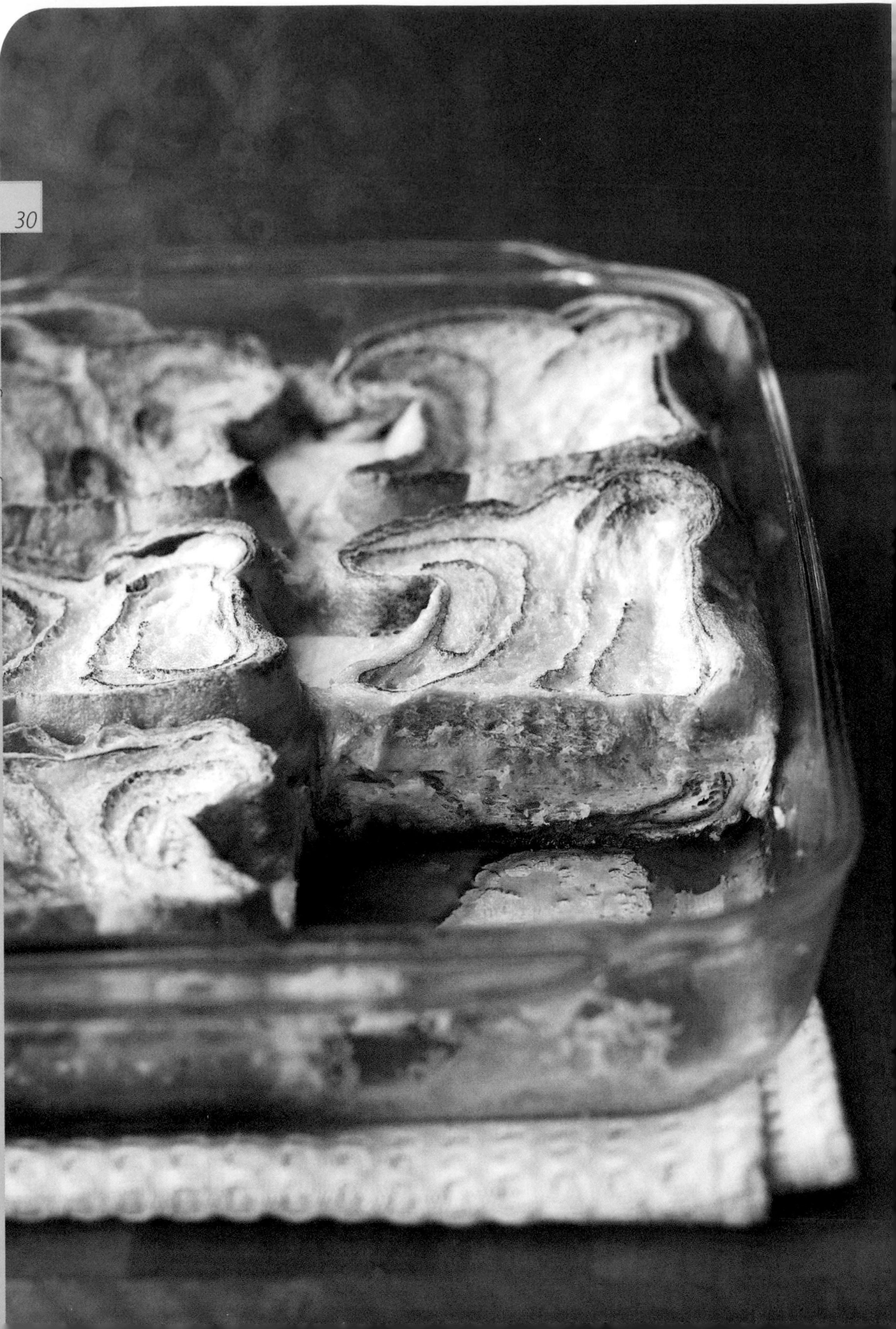

french toast casserole

Prep: 20 minutes Bake: 40 minutes Stand: 15 minutes Chill: 4 hours
Oven: 350°F Makes: 8 servings

1 cup packed brown
    sugar
½ cup butter
2 tablespoons light-
    colored corn syrup
1 1-pound loaf unsliced
    cinnamon bread
8 eggs, beaten
3 cups half-and-half or
    light cream
2 teaspoons vanilla
½ teaspoon salt
1 tablespoon orange
    liqueur (optional)

1 In a medium saucepan combine brown sugar, butter, and corn syrup; cook and stir until mixture comes to a boil. Boil for 1 minute. Pour into a 3-quart rectangular baking dish.

2 Cut cinnamon bread loaf into 1-inch slices. Arrange bread slices on top of brown sugar mixture. Combine eggs, half-and-half, vanilla, and salt; pour over bread slices. Cover and chill for 4 to 24 hours.

3 Preheat oven to 350°F. Let baking dish stand at room temperature while oven preheats. Bake, uncovered, in the preheated oven for 40 to 45 minutes or until top is brown and puffed and a knife inserted near center comes out clean. Let stand for 15 minutes before serving. If desired, drizzle with orange liqueur.

Per serving: 579 cal., 30 g total fat (16 g sat. fat), 279 mg chol., 692 mg sodium, 65 g carbo., 1 g fiber, 14 g pro.

This no-fry, hassle-free French toast makes everyone happy. Sweet orange-cinnamon syrup entices breakfast eaters, and the easy, one-batch preparation pleases the cook.

no-fry french toast

Prep: 15 minutes Bake: 13 minutes Oven: 450°F Makes: 4 servings

Nonstick cooking
  spray
1 egg, slightly beaten
⅓ cup milk
¼ teaspoon vanilla
  Dash ground
  cinnamon
4 slices Texas toast
½ cup orange juice
1 tablespoon honey
1 teaspoon cornstarch
⅛ teaspoon ground
  cinnamon
1 tablespoon sifted
  powdered sugar
  (optional)

1 Preheat oven to 450°F. Line a large baking sheet with foil; coat with cooking spray and set aside. In a pie plate combine the egg, milk, vanilla, and the dash of cinnamon. Cut each bread slice vertically into 3 sticks. Quickly dip sticks in egg mixture, turning to coat. Place on the prepared baking sheet.

2 Bake in the preheated oven for 8 minutes or until bread is light brown. Turn bread; bake for 5 to 8 minutes more or until golden brown.

3 Meanwhile, for the orange syrup, in a small saucepan stir together the orange juice, honey, cornstarch, and the ⅛ teaspoon cinnamon. Cook and stir over medium heat until thickened and bubbly. Reduce the heat. Cook and stir for 2 minutes more.

4 If desired, sprinkle the French toast with powdered sugar. Serve the toast with orange syrup.

Per serving: 178 cal., 4 g total fat (0 g sat. fat), 103 mg chol., 267 mg sodium, 29 g carbo., 0 g fiber, 9 g pro.

This isn't a classic soufflé (hence the "mock" in the title), but the top puffs up beautifully just like the real thing.

mock cheese soufflé

Prep: 15 minutes **Bake:** 45 minutes **Chill:** 2 hours **Oven:** 350°F
Makes: 6 servings

8 slices white bread, cubed (6 cups)

1½ cups shredded sharp cheddar cheese or Monterey Jack cheese with jalapeño peppers

4 eggs, slightly beaten

1½ cups milk

2 teaspoons Worcestershire sauce

½ teaspoon salt

1 Place half of the bread cubes in an ungreased 1½-quart soufflé dish. Top with half of the cheese. Repeat layers; press lightly.

2 In a medium bowl combine eggs, milk, Worcestershire sauce, and salt. Pour egg mixture over layers in dish. Cover and chill for 2 to 24 hours.

3 To serve, preheat oven to 350°F. Bake, uncovered, in the preheated oven for 45 to 50 minutes or until a knife inserted near center comes out clean. Serve immediately.

Per serving: *284 cal., 15 g total fat (8 g sat. fat), 176 mg chol., 639 mg sodium, 21 g carbo., 1 g fiber, 16 g pro.*

This hearty breakfast features a popular trio of meats—bacon, sausage, and ham.

meat lover's scrambled eggs

Start to Finish: 20 minutes Makes: 4 servings

8 eggs
½ cup water
¼ teaspoon salt
⅛ teaspoon ground
   black pepper
4 slices bacon, chopped
4 ounces bulk pork
   sausage
½ cup chopped cooked
   ham and/or Polish
   sausage
½ cup shredded
   cheddar cheese
   (2 ounces)
   Thinly sliced green
   onion (optional)

1 In a medium bowl beat together eggs, water, salt, and pepper with a fork or rotary beater; set aside.

2 In a large skillet cook and stir bacon and sausage over medium heat until bacon is crisp and pork is no longer pink. Drain, reserving 1 tablespoon drippings in skillet. Set bacon and sausage aside.

3 Add egg mixture to drippings in skillet. Cook over medium heat, without stirring, until mixture begins to set on the bottom and around edges. Sprinkle bacon, sausage, and ham over egg mixture.

4 Using a spatula or a large spoon, lift and fold the partially cooked egg mixture so the uncooked portion flows underneath. Continue cooking and folding for 2 to 3 minutes more or until egg mixture is cooked through but is still glossy and moist. Sprinkle with shredded cheese and, if desired, green onion. Remove from heat immediately. Let stand for 1 to 2 minutes or until cheese melts.

Per serving: 380 cal., 29 g total fat (11 g sat. fat), 473 mg chol., 707 mg sodium, 2 g carbo., 0 g fiber, 25 g pro.

This all-in-one skillet breakfast needs nothing more than a glass of orange juice or some fresh fruit to round out the menu.

ham & potato scramble

Start to Finish: 25 minutes Makes: 4 servings

8	eggs
¼	cup milk
¼	teaspoon garlic salt
¼	teaspoon ground black pepper
2	green onions, thinly sliced (¼ cup)
1	tablespoon butter or margarine
1	cup refrigerated shredded hash brown potatoes
½	cup diced cooked ham (about 2 ounces)
⅓	cup shredded cheddar cheese

1 In a medium bowl combine eggs, milk, garlic salt, and pepper; beat with a whisk until well mixed. Stir in green onions. Set aside.

2 In a large nonstick skillet melt butter over medium heat. Add potatoes and ham; cook for 6 to 8 minutes or until light brown, stirring occasionally. Add egg mixture. Cook over medium heat, without stirring, until mixture begins to set on the bottom and around edge.

3 Using a large spatula, lift and fold the partially cooked egg mixture so the uncooked portion flows underneath. Continue cooking and folding for 2 to 3 minutes more or until egg mixture is cooked through but is still glossy and moist. Remove from heat immediately. Sprinkle with cheese. Serve warm.

Per serving: 289 cal., 18 g total fat (8 g sat. fat), 453 mg chol., 540 mg sodium, 11 g carbo., 1 g fiber, 20 g pro.

tex-mex spinach omelet

Start to Finish: 25 minutes Makes: 2 servings

¼ cup chopped red
sweet pepper
¼ cup frozen whole
kernel corn, thawed
2 tablespoons chopped
red onion
1 tablespoon snipped
fresh cilantro
4 eggs
1 tablespoon snipped
fresh cilantro
Dash salt
Dash ground cumin
Nonstick cooking
spray
1 ounce cheddar
cheese, Swiss
cheese, or Monterey
Jack cheese with
jalapeño peppers,
shredded (¼ cup)
¾ cup fresh baby
spinach leaves

1 For relish, in a small bowl combine sweet pepper, corn, red onion, and 1 tablespoon cilantro; set aside.

2 In a medium bowl combine eggs, 1 tablespoon cilantro, salt, and cumin. Beat with a whisk until frothy.

3 Coat an unheated 10-inch nonstick skillet with flared sides with cooking spray. Heat skillet over medium heat.

4 Pour egg mixture into prepared skillet. Cook, without stirring, for 2 to 3 minutes or until egg mixture begins to set. Run a spatula around edge of skillet, lifting egg mixture so uncooked portion flows underneath.

5 Continue cooking and lifting edge until egg mixture is set but is still glossy and moist. Sprinkle with cheese. Top with three-fourths of the spinach and half of the relish. Using the spatula, lift and fold an edge of the omelet partially over filling. Top with remaining spinach and the remaining relish. Cut omelet in half; transfer to warm plates.

Per serving: 231 cal., 15 g total fat (6 g sat. fat), 438 mg chol., 311 mg sodium, 8 g carbo., 1 g fiber, 17 g pro.

scrambled eggs with
smoked salmon & chives

Start to Finish: 15 minutes Makes: 4 servings

6 eggs
⅓ cup water
3 tablespoons snipped
   fresh chives
1 tablespoon butter or
   margarine
1 3- to 4-ounce package
   thinly sliced
   smoked salmon
   (lox-style), cut into
   bite-size strips
   Fresh chives
   (optional)

1 In a medium bowl beat together eggs, water, and chives with a whisk. In a large skillet melt butter over medium heat; pour in egg mixture. Cook over medium heat without stirring until egg mixture begins to set on the bottom and around edges.

2 Using a spatula or large spoon lift and fold partially cooked egg mixture so the uncooked portion flows underneath. Fold in salmon; continue cooking over medium heat for 2 to 3 minutes or until egg mixture is cooked through but is still glossy and moist. If desired, garnish with fresh chives.

Per serving: 164 cal., 11 g total fat (4 g sat. fat), 332 mg chol., 551 mg sodium, 1 g carbo., 0 g fiber, 13 g pro.

brie & mushroom
scrambled eggs

Start to Finish: 30 minutes Makes: 6 servings

½ of a 4- to 5-ounce
round Brie or
Camembert cheese
8 eggs
2 tablespoons water
1 tablespoon snipped
fresh chives or
thinly sliced green
onion tops
¼ teaspoon salt
⅛ teaspoon ground
black pepper
2 ounces sliced
pancetta or 3 slices
bacon
Olive oil
1½ cups fresh
mushrooms, sliced
6 ounces fresh arugula
or fresh baby
spinach, lightly
steamed* (4½ cups)
(optional)

1 If desired, remove the rind from the cheese.
Cut cheese into bite-size pieces; set aside.

2 In a medium bowl beat together eggs,
water, chives, salt, and pepper with a
whisk; set aside. In a large skillet cook pancetta
over medium heat until crisp. Drain on paper
towels, reserving drippings in skillet. Crumble
pancetta and set aside. Measure 2 tablespoons
of drippings from skillet (add oil, if necessary,
to equal 2 tablespoons).

3 Add mushrooms to the 2 tablespoons of
drippings in skillet; cook over medium
heat until tender. Return pancetta to skillet.

4 Pour egg mixture over mushroom mixture
in skillet. Cook without stirring until
mixture begins to set on the bottom and
around edge. Using a large spatula, lift and
fold the partially cooked eggs so the uncooked
portion flows underneath.

5 Continue cooking over medium heat for
2 to 3 minutes or until egg mixture is
cooked through but is still glossy and moist.
Top with Brie. Remove from heat. Cover and
let stand for 1 to 2 minutes to soften cheese. If
desired, divide arugula among 4 plates. Spoon
egg mixture alongside.

*Note: To steam arugula, place in a steamer
basket in a skillet over a small amount of gently
boiling water. Add arugula to basket. Cover and
steam about 1 minute or until arugula is just
wilted. Drain well.

Per serving: 107 cal., 17 g total fat (5 g sat. fat), 298 mg chol.,
424 mg sodium, 1 g carbo., 0 g fiber, 12 g pro.

Instead of using the traditional hollandaise sauce, this speedy rendition of the breakfast classic saves time by substituting a sour cream sauce seasoned with mustard and lemon juice.

quick eggs benedict

Start to Finish: 20 minutes Makes: 4 servings

¼   cup dairy sour cream
      or crème fraîche
1   teaspoon lemon juice
¾   to 1 teaspoon dry
      mustard
3   to 4 teaspoons milk
4   eggs
4   ½-inch-thick slices
      crusty French bread
      or French bread,
      lightly toasted
4   ounces thinly sliced
      smoked salmon or
      4 slices Canadian-
      style bacon
      Diced red sweet
      pepper (optional)
      Salt
      Ground black pepper

1 In a small bowl combine sour cream, lemon juice, and dry mustard. Stir in enough of the milk to make desired consistency. Set aside.

2 Lightly grease a 2-quart saucepan. Fill the pan halfway with water; bring to boiling. Reduce heat to simmering. Break one egg into a measuring cup or custard cup. Carefully slide egg into water, holding the lip of the cup as close to the water as possible. Repeat with remaining eggs, spacing eggs equally. Simmer, uncovered, for 3 to 5 minutes or until egg whites are completely set and yolks begin to thicken but are not hard. Carefully remove eggs with a slotted spoon.

3 Top bread slices with smoked salmon. Top with poached eggs. Drizzle with mustard-sour cream mixture. If desired, sprinkle with sweet pepper. Season to taste with salt and black pepper.

Per serving: 206 cal., 10 g total fat (4 g sat. fat), 225 mg chol., 481 mg sodium, 14 g carbo., 1 g fiber, 14 g pro.

breakfast tortilla wraps

Start to Finish: 15 minutes Makes: 4 servings

2 slices bacon, chopped
½ cup chopped green
   sweet pepper
½ teaspoon ground
   cumin
¼ teaspoon salt
   (optional)
¼ teaspoon crushed red
   pepper (optional)
4 eggs, beaten, or
   1 cup refrigerated
   egg product
½ cup chopped tomato
   (1 medium)
   Few dashes bottled
   hot pepper sauce
   (optional)
4 8-inch flour tortillas,
   warmed*

1 In a large nonstick skillet cook bacon until crisp. Drain all but 1 tablespoon of the fat from skillet. Add sweet pepper, cumin, and, if desired, salt and crushed red pepper. Cook for 3 minutes. Add eggs. Using a spatula or a large spoon, lift and fold egg mixture so that uncooked portion flows underneath. Continue cooking over medium heat about 2 minutes or until egg is cooked through but is still glossy and moist. Stir in tomato and, if desired, hot pepper sauce. Spoon onto tortillas and roll up.

*Tip: To warm tortillas, wrap them tightly in foil and heat in 350°F oven for 10 minutes.

Per serving: 193 cal., 9 g total fat (3 g sat. fat), 216 mg chol., 285 mg sodium, 17 g carbo., 1 g fiber, 10 g pro.

breakfast pizza

Prep: 25 minutes Bake: 10 minutes Oven: 375°F Makes: 8 servings

Nonstick cooking
    spray
1½ cups loose-pack
    frozen diced hash
    brown potatoes
    with peppers and
    onion
1 clove garlic, minced
6 eggs, slightly beaten
⅓ cup milk
1 tablespoon snipped
    fresh basil
½ teaspoon salt
¼ teaspoon ground
    black pepper
1 tablespoon olive oil
1 14-ounce Italian
    bread shell (Boboli)
1 cup shredded
    mozzarella cheese
    (4 ounces)
2 plum tomatoes,
    halved lengthwise
    and sliced
¼ cup shredded fresh
    basil

1 Preheat oven to 375°F. Coat an unheated large skillet with cooking spray. Heat over medium heat. Add potatoes and garlic. Cook and stir about 4 minutes or until the vegetables are tender.

2 In a small bowl stir together eggs, milk, the 1 tablespoon snipped basil, salt, and pepper. Add oil to skillet; add egg mixture. Cook, without stirring, until mixture begins to set on the bottom and around the edge. Using a large spatula, lift and fold partially cooked egg mixture so uncooked portion flows underneath. Continue cooking and folding until egg mixture is cooked through but is still glossy and moist. Remove from heat.

3 To assemble pizza, place bread shell on a large baking sheet or a 12-inch pizza pan. Sprinkle half of the cheese over the bread shell. Top with egg mixture, tomato, and the remaining cheese.

4 Bake in the preheated oven for 10 minutes or until cheese melts. Sprinkle with the ¼ cup shredded basil. Cut into wedges to serve.

Per serving: *233 cal., 7 g total fat (2 g sat. fat), 11 mg chol., 579 mg sodium, 29 g carbo., 2 g fiber, 15 g pro.*

If you think cinnamon rolls are too much work, think again. You can have these little gems on the table in half an hour.

easy cinnamon rolls

Prep: 10 minutes Bake: 15 minutes Oven: 375°F Makes: 8 rolls

1 8-ounce package
   (8) refrigerated
   crescent rolls
1 tablespoon butter,
   melted
2 tablespoons
   granulated sugar
1 teaspoon ground
   cinnamon
½ cup powdered sugar
¼ teaspoon vanilla
1 to 2 teaspoons orange
   juice or milk

1 Preheat oven to 375°F. Grease an 8×1½- or 9×1½-inch round baking pan; set aside. Unroll dough (do not separate); press perforations to seal. Brush dough with melted butter. In a small bowl stir together the granulated sugar and cinnamon; sprinkle over dough. Starting from a long side, roll up dough into a spiral. Using a sharp knife, slice dough into 1½-inch pieces. Arrange pieces, cut side up, in prepared pan, flattening each roll slightly.

2 Bake in the preheated oven for 15 to 18 minutes or until golden brown. Remove and cool rolls slightly in pan on a wire rack. Remove from pan. In a small bowl stir together powdered sugar, vanilla, and enough orange juice to make an icing of drizzling consistency. Drizzle over warm rolls. Serve warm.

Per roll: 155 cal., 7 g total fat (2 g sat. fat), 4 mg chol., 241 mg sodium, 22 g carbo., 0 g fiber, 2 g pro.

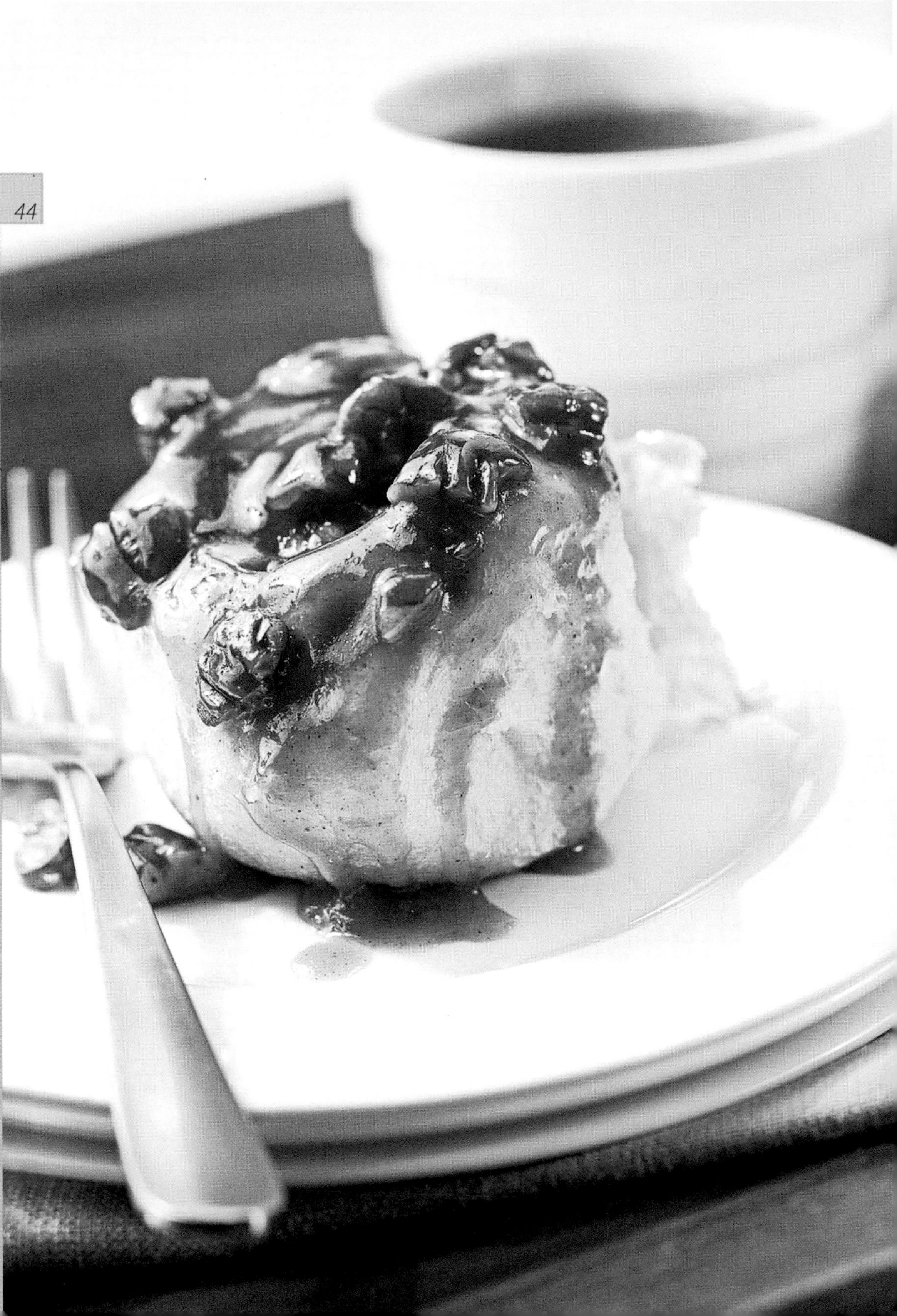

Mom made the dough from scratch and had to wait for two risings. You use frozen bread dough, which needs only one rising.

one-rise creamy
caramel-pecan rolls

Prep: 25 minutes Rise: 60 minutes Bake: 20 minutes Cool: 5 minutes
Oven: 375°F Makes: 24 rolls

1¼   cups powdered sugar
⅓   cup whipping cream
1   cup coarsely chopped
     pecans
½   cup packed brown
     sugar
1   tablespoon ground
     cinnamon
2   16-ounce loaves
     frozen white bread
     dough or sweet roll
     dough, thawed*
3   tablespoons butter or
     margarine, melted
¾   cup raisins (optional)

1 Generously grease two 9×1½-inch round baking pans. Line bottoms with a circle of parchment paper or nonstick foil; set pans aside. For topping, in a small bowl stir together powdered sugar and cream; divide sugar mixture evenly between prepared baking pans, gently spreading to edges. Sprinkle pecans evenly over sugar mixture in pans.

2 In another small bowl stir together brown sugar and cinnamon; set aside. On a lightly floured surface roll each loaf of dough into a 12×8-inch rectangle. Brush rectangles with melted butter; sprinkle evenly with the brown sugar-cinnamon mixture. If desired, sprinkle rectangles with raisins.

3 Roll up each rectangle starting from a long side. Pinch seams to seal. Slice each roll into 12 pieces; place pieces cut sides down in prepared pans. Cover rolls; let rise in a warm place until nearly double (about 1 hour).

4 Preheat oven to 375°F. Break any surface bubbles with a greased toothpick. Bake in the preheated oven for 20 to 25 minutes or until rolls sound hollow when gently tapped (if necessary, cover rolls with foil the last 10 minutes of baking to prevent overbrowning). Cool in pans on a wire rack for 5 minutes. Loosen edges of rolls and carefully invert rolls onto serving plates. Spoon any nut mixture in pan over rolls. Serve warm.

*Tip: Let dough thaw in the refrigerator overnight before making rolls.

Per roll: *183 cal., 6 g total fat (2 g sat. fat), 8 mg chol., 13 mg sodium, 27 g carbo., 1 g fiber, 3 g pro.*

monkey bread rolls

Prep: 20 minutes Bake: 40 minutes Cool: 15 minutes Chill: 8 hours
Oven: 350°F Makes: 12 servings

1	34.5-ounce package frozen cinnamon sweet roll dough or frozen orange sweet roll dough (12 rolls)
⅔	cup coarsely chopped pecans
⅓	cup butter or margarine, melted
1	cup sugar
⅓	cup caramel ice cream topping
1	tablespoon maple-flavor syrup

1 Place frozen rolls about 2 inches apart on a large greased baking sheet. Cover with plastic wrap. Refrigerate 8 hours or overnight to let dough thaw and begin to rise. Frosting packets, if present, can be set aside for another use.

2 Preheat oven to 350°F. Generously grease a 10-inch fluted tube pan. Sprinkle ⅓ cup of the pecans over the bottom of the tube pan.

3 Cut each roll into quarters. Dip pieces in melted butter, then roll in sugar. Layer pieces in prepared pan. (Or, dip and roll whole rolls; arrange rolls on their sides in the tube pan.) Drizzle with any remaining butter; sprinkle with any remaining sugar. Sprinkle the remaining ⅓ cup pecans on top.

4 Combine ice cream topping and syrup; drizzle over tops of rolls in pan. Bake in the preheated oven for 40 to 45 minutes or until golden brown. Let pan stand on a wire rack for 1 minute. Invert rolls onto a large serving platter. Spoon any topping and nuts in pan onto rolls. Cool slightly. Serve warm.

Per serving: 382 cal., 14 g total fat (4 g sat. fat), 13 mg chol., 302 mg sodium, 60 g carbo., 2 g fiber, 5 g pro.

apple bread

Prep: 30 minutes Bake: 45 minutes Oven: 325°F Makes: 30 servings

3   cups all-purpose flour
1   teaspoon baking soda
1   teaspoon salt
1   teaspoon ground
      cinnamon
¼   teaspoon baking
      powder
3   eggs, beaten
3   cups shredded,
      peeled cooking
      apples (4 medium)*
2   cups sugar
⅔   cup cooking oil
1   teaspoon vanilla

1 Preheat oven to 325°F. Grease and flour three 7½×3½×2-inch or two 8×4×2-inch loaf pans. Set aside. In a medium bowl combine flour, baking soda, salt, cinnamon, and baking powder; set aside.

2 In a large bowl combine eggs, apples, sugar, oil, and vanilla. Stir in flour mixture just until moistened. Pour batter into prepared pans.

3 Bake in the preheated oven for 45 to 55 minutes or until a toothpick inserted in center comes out clean. Cool in pans on wire racks for 10 minutes. Remove from pans. Cool on wire racks. Wrap and store overnight before slicing.

*Tip: Golden Delicious, Rome, Granny Smith or Jonathan are good choices for this bread.

Per serving: 152 cal., 6 g total fat (1 g sat. fat), 21 mg chol., 129 mg sodium, 24 g carbo., 1 g fiber, 2 g pro.

speedy

2

din

During the hectic workweek, making home-cooked dinners can be a real chore. But in 30 minutes or less, you can have an entire meal—all in one pan—ready to eat!

ners

Balsamic vinegar, an Italian staple with hallmark dark brown color, syrupy body, and slight sweetness, brings an out-of-the-ordinary touch to a recipe.

balsamic chicken & vegetables

Start to Finish: 30 minutes Makes: 4 servings

¼ cup bottled Italian salad dressing
2 tablespoons balsamic vinegar
1 tablespoon honey
⅛ to ¼ teaspoon crushed red pepper
2 tablespoons olive oil
12 ounces chicken breast tenderloins
10 ounces asparagus, cut into 2-inch pieces, or one 10-ounce package frozen cut asparagus, thawed and well drained
1 cup purchased shredded carrot
1 small tomato, seeded and chopped

1 For sauce, in a small bowl stir together salad dressing, vinegar, honey, and crushed red pepper. Set aside.

2 In a large skillet heat oil. Add chicken; cook over medium-high heat for 5 to 6 minutes or until chicken is tender and no longer pink, turning once. Transfer chicken from skillet to a serving platter; cover and keep warm.

3 Add asparagus and carrot to skillet. Cook and stir for 3 to 4 minutes or until asparagus is crisp-tender; transfer to serving platter.

4 Stir sauce; add to skillet. Cook and stir for 1 minute, scraping up brown bits. Drizzle sauce over chicken and vegetables. Sprinkle with tomato.

Per serving: 271 cal., 15 g total fat (2 g sat. fat), 49 mg chol., 174 mg sodium, 12 g carbo., 2 g fiber, 22 g pro.

This dish is packed with the flavor of fresh herbs and roasted red sweet peppers.

chicken with peppers & potatoes

Start to Finish: 30 minutes Makes: 4 servings

12 ounces skinless, boneless chicken breast halves
Nonstick cooking spray
2 cups chopped potato (2 medium)
1 7-ounce jar roasted red sweet peppers, drained and chopped
½ cup reduced-sodium chicken broth
4½ teaspoons snipped fresh basil or 1½ teaspoons dried basil, crushed
4½ teaspoons snipped fresh oregano or 1½ teaspoons dried oregano, crushed
⅛ teaspoon salt
⅛ teaspoon ground black pepper
2 tablespoons sliced pitted ripe olives

1 Cut chicken into 1-inch pieces. Coat a large skillet with cooking spray. Heat over medium-high heat. Add chicken. Cook and stir for 3 to 4 minutes or until chicken is no longer pink. Remove from skillet.

2 Add potato, roasted sweet peppers, broth, dried basil and oregano (if using), salt, and black pepper to skillet. Bring to boiling; reduce heat. Simmer, covered, for 7 minutes or just until potato is tender.

3 Stir the cooked chicken, fresh basil and oregano (if using), and olives into potato mixture; heat through.

Per serving: *183 cal., 4 g total fat (1 g sat. fat), 45 mg chol., 213 mg sodium, 20 g carbo., 2 g fiber, 19 g pro.*

High heat and thin pieces of chicken make for a quick cooking time. Use your favorite bottled stir-fry sauce.

fast chicken & rice

Start to Finish: 10 minutes   Makes: 4 servings

1   8.8-ounce package cooked brown or white rice
1   pound chicken breast tenders, halved crosswise
1   tablespoon cooking oil
½   cup frozen peas
¼   cup bottled stir-fry sauce
    Packaged oven-roasted sliced almonds

1 Heat rice in microwave oven according to package directions.

2 Meanwhile, in a large skillet cook and stir chicken in hot oil over medium-high heat for 2 to 3 minutes or until no longer pink. Stir rice and peas into skillet. Stir in stir-fry sauce; heat through. Sprinkle each serving with almonds.

Per serving: 311 cal., 9 g total fat (1 g sat. fat), 66 mg chol., 453 mg sodium, 25 g carbo., 2 g fiber, 31 g pro.

zesty chicken with black beans & rice

Start to Finish: 30 minutes Makes: 4 servings

1 pound skinless, boneless chicken breast halves, cut into 2-inch pieces
2 tablespoons cooking oil
1 6- to 7.4-ounce package Spanish rice mix
1¾ cups water
1 15-ounce can black beans, rinsed and drained
1 14.5-ounce can diced tomatoes, undrained
Dairy sour cream, sliced green onions, and lime wedges (optional)

1 In a 12-inch skillet brown the chicken pieces in 1 tablespoon of the oil over medium heat. Remove chicken from skillet.

2 Add rice mix and remaining 1 tablespoon oil to skillet; cook and stir for 2 minutes over medium heat. Stir in seasoning packet from rice mix, water, beans, and undrained tomatoes; add chicken. Bring to boiling; reduce heat. Simmer, covered, for 15 to 20 minutes or until rice is tender and chicken is no longer pink. Remove from heat and let stand, covered, for 5 minutes.

3 If desired, serve with sour cream, green onion, and lime wedges.

Per serving: 424 cal., 9 g total fat (2 g sat. fat), 66 mg chol., 1,080 mg sodium, 52 g carbo., 6 g fiber, 37 g pro.

Try this Tex-Mex-style combination with a crisp salad and warm tortillas or corn muffins.

simple salsa skillet

Start to Finish: 30 minutes   Makes: 4 to 6 servings

1   green sweet pepper, cut into thin bite-size strips (1 cup)
1   red sweet pepper, cut into thin bite-size strips (1 cup)
1   tablespoon cooking oil
2   cups cubed cooked potato
1½   cups cubed cooked chicken (8 ounces)
1   15.5-ounce can whole kernel corn, drained
1   15- or 16-ounce can black beans, rinsed and drained
1   16-ounce jar salsa
    Dairy sour cream (optional)

1 In a large skillet cook sweet pepper strips in hot oil for 2 minutes. Add potato, chicken, corn, beans, and salsa. Stir gently.

2 Cook, covered, over medium-low heat for 10 minutes or until mixture is heated through, stirring occasionally. If desired, serve with sour cream.

Per serving: 243 cal., 6 g total fat (1 g sat. fat), 31 mg chol., 744 mg sodium, 33 g carbo., 8 g fiber, 27 g pro.

chicken & pasta with pesto dressing

Start to Finish: 30 minutes Makes: 4 servings

6   ounces dried wagon
     wheel macaroni or
     rotini (about 2 cups)
12 ounces skinless,
     boneless chicken
     breast halves, cut
     into 1-inch pieces
½   cup dairy sour cream
¼   cup refrigerated
     pesto sauce
1   cup chopped fresh
     vegetables, such
     as red, yellow,
     or green sweet
     pepper; broccoli
     florets; zucchini; or
     cucumber
⅓   cup chopped tomato
     (1 small)
¼   cup pine nuts or
     chopped walnuts,
     toasted (optional)

1 Cook pasta according to package
directions, adding chicken the last 5 to
6 minutes of cooking. Cook until pasta is
tender but firm and chicken is no longer pink.
Drain pasta and chicken. Rinse with cold water;
drain again.

2 In a large bowl stir together sour cream
and pesto. Add pasta mixture, chopped
fresh vegetables, and tomato. Toss lightly to
coat. If desired, sprinkle with nuts.

Per serving: 392 cal., 14 g total fat (5 g sat. fat), 65 mg chol.,
218 mg sodium, 37 g carbo., 3 g fiber, 28 g pro.

Start to Finish: 20 minutes **Makes:** 4 servings

1 9-ounce package refrigerated red sweet pepper or plain fettuccine

¼ of a 7-ounce jar oil-packed dried tomato strips or pieces (¼ cup)

1 large zucchini or yellow summer squash, halved lengthwise and sliced (about 2 cups)

8 ounces packaged skinless, boneless chicken breast strips (stir-fry strips)

2 tablespoons olive oil

½ cup finely shredded Parmesan, Romano, or Asiago cheese (2 ounces)

Salt

Ground black pepper

1 Using kitchen scissors, cut fettuccine strands in half crosswise. Cook fettuccine according to package directions; drain. Return fettuccine to hot pan.

2 Meanwhile, drain dried tomatoes, reserving 2 tablespoons of the oil from the jar. Set drained tomatoes aside. In a large skillet heat 1 tablespoon of the reserved oil over medium-high heat. Add zucchini; cook and stir for 2 to 3 minutes or until crisp-tender. Remove from skillet. Add remaining 1 tablespoon reserved oil to skillet. Add chicken; cook and stir for 2 to 3 minutes or until no longer pink.

3 Add chicken, zucchini, drained tomatoes, and olive oil to cooked fettuccine; toss gently to combine. Sprinkle servings with cheese. Season to taste with salt and black pepper.

Per serving: 384 cal., 14 g total fat (4 g sat. fat), 93 mg chol., 356 mg sodium, 37 g carbo., 4 g fiber, 28 g pro.

easy turkey-pesto mock potpie

Prep: 15 minutes Bake: according to package directions Makes: 6 servings

1   11-ounce package (12) refrigerated breadsticks
1   12-ounce jar turkey gravy
½   cup dairy sour cream
⅓   cup purchased basil or dried tomato pesto
3   cups cubed, cooked turkey (about 1 pound)
1   16-ounce package frozen peas and carrots

1 Unroll and separate breadsticks; cut each breadstick into 3 pieces. Bake breadsticks according to package directions.

2 Meanwhile, in a large saucepan combine turkey gravy, sour cream, and pesto. Stir in turkey and peas and carrots. Bring to boiling, stirring frequently.

3 Spoon turkey mixture into 6 serving bowls. Top turkey mixture in each bowl with 6 baked breadsticks.

Per serving: 365 cal., 16 g total fat (5 g sat. fat), 52 mg chol., 964 mg sodium, 36 g carbo., 4 g fiber, 20 g pro.

Soft-style cream cheese makes an ultrarich sauce for this pasta dish.

herbed turkey & broccoli

Start to Finish: 30 minutes Makes: 4 servings

2 quarts water
8 ounces packaged dried linguine or spaghetti, broken in half
3 cups small broccoli florets
1 8-ounce container soft-style cream cheese with garlic and herbs
2/3 cup milk
1/4 teaspoon coarsely ground black pepper
6 ounces sliced smoked turkey breast, cut into bite-size strips

1 In a large saucepan or Dutch oven bring water to boiling. Add linguine a little at a time. Return to boiling. Reduce heat. Cook for 6 minutes. Add broccoli. Return to boiling. Cook for 2 to 3 minutes more or until pasta is tender and broccoli is crisp-tender. Drain.

2 In the same pan combine cream cheese, milk, and pepper. Cook and stir over low heat until cream cheese is melted. Add pasta-broccoli mixture and turkey. Toss until coated with the cheese mixture and heated through. If necessary, stir in additional milk to make desired consistency.

Per serving: 516 cal., 21 g total fat (11 g sat. fat), 81 mg chol., 675 mg sodium, 57 g carbo., 4 g fiber, 25 g pro.

Orzo is a tiny rice-shaped pasta, larger than a grain of rice, and slightly smaller than a pine nut. It makes a great alternative to rice for salads, sides, and pilafs.

creamy turkey & orzo

Start to Finish: 25 minutes   Makes: 4 servings

⅔ cup dried orzo pasta

2 tablespoons olive oil
  or cooking oil

12 ounces turkey breast
   tenderloin, cut into
   bite-size strips

8 ounces sliced fresh
  mushrooms

¼ cup sliced green
  onion (2)

1½ cups milk

3 tablespoons
  all-purpose flour

½ cup bottled blue
  cheese salad
  dressing

1 cup frozen peas
  Salt
  Ground black pepper

1 Cook pasta according to package directions; drain.

2 Meanwhile, in a large skillet heat oil over medium-high heat; add turkey, mushrooms, and green onion. Cook and stir for 4 to 5 minutes or until turkey is no longer pink.

3 Combine milk, flour, and salad dressing; add all at once to skillet along with cooked orzo. Cook and stir until thickened and bubbly. Stir in peas. Cook and stir for 2 minutes more. Season to taste with salt and pepper.

Per serving: 520 cal., 26 g total fat (5 g sat. fat), 65 mg chol., 515 mg sodium, 39 g carbo., 3 g fiber, 33 g pro.

speedy **dinners**

Start to Finish: 30 minutes **Makes:** 3 to 4 servings

1   tablespoon cooking
    oil
12 ounces turkey breast
    tenderloin, thinly
    sliced crosswise
1   small onion, cut into
    thin wedges
2   cloves garlic, minced
2   cups frozen cut
    broccoli or green
    beans
1   10-ounce container
    refrigerated light
    Alfredo pasta sauce
½   cup water
1   3-ounce package
    ramen noodles
    Ground black pepper

1 In a large skillet heat oil over medium heat. Add turkey, onion, and garlic; cook and stir about 4 minutes or until onion is crisp-tender. Stir in broccoli, Alfredo sauce, and ½ cup water.

2 Bring to boiling; reduce heat. Simmer, covered, for 5 minutes.

3 Break up noodles and discard seasoning packet. Add noodles to skillet. Cook, covered, for 2 to 3 minutes more or until noodles are just tender. Season to taste with pepper.

Per serving: 474 cal., 21 g total fat (7 g sat. fat), 101 mg chol., 713 mg sodium, 33 g carbo., 3 g fiber, 40 g pro.

This dish provides the heartiness and good flavor of Thanksgiving favorites—cranberries, turkey, apple cider, and pecans.

turkey cranberry fried rice

Start to Finish: 25 minutes Makes: 4 servings

Nonstick cooking
    spray
1 pound uncooked
    ground turkey
1 stalk celery, chopped
    (½ cup)
1 medium onion,
    chopped (½ cup)
1 8.8-ounce package
    cooked long grain
    and wild rice
½ cup apple cider or
    apple juice
⅓ cup dried cranberries
½ teaspoon dried
    thyme, crushed
⅓ cup chopped pecans,
    toasted
    Salt and ground black
    pepper

1 Coat a very large skillet with cooking spray. Add turkey, celery, and onion; cook and stir over medium heat until turkey is no longer pink and vegetables are tender.

2 Meanwhile, prepare long grain and wild rice according to package directions.

3 Stir rice, cider, cranberries, and thyme into the turkey mixture in skillet. Cook and stir until liquid is absorbed. Stir in pecans. Season to taste with salt and pepper.

Per serving: *385 cal., 18 g total fat (3 g sat. fat), 90 mg chol., 395 mg sodium, 34 g carbo., 2 g fiber, 23 g pro.*

tortellini with meat sauce

Start to Finish: 25 minutes Makes: 4 servings

8 ounces ground beef,
 ground lamb, or
 ground pork
1¾ cups bottled tomato
 and herb pasta
 sauce
1¼ cups water
¼ cup dry red wine or
 water
1 9-ounce package
 refrigerated cheese-
 filled tortellini or
 ½ of a 16-ounce
 package frozen
 cheese-filled
 tortellini
½ cup shredded
 mozzarella cheese
 (2 ounces)

1 In a large saucepan cook ground beef over medium-high heat until brown. Drain off fat.

2 Add pasta sauce, water, and wine to the beef. Bring to boiling. Stir in tortellini. Return to boiling. Simmer, uncovered, for 8 to 10 minutes or until tortellini are tender and sauce is of desired consistency. Sprinkle with mozzarella cheese. Let stand for 2 to 3 minutes or until cheese is slightly melted.

Per serving: 471 cal., 23 g total fat (9 g sat. fat), 80 mg chol., 784 mg sodium, 40 g carbo., 0 g fiber, 24 g pro.

Chipotle salsa adds a distinct, smoky flavor that complements any Mexican-style dish.

taco hash

Start to Finish: 25 minutes Makes: 4 servings

1 **In a large skillet cook ground beef over medium-high heat until brown; transfer to a colander to drain fat.**

1 pound lean ground beef or pork
2 tablespoons cooking oil
3 cups frozen diced hash brown potatoes with onions and peppers (½ of a 28-ounce package)
1 16-ounce jar chipotle salsa or desired salsa (1¾ cups)
1 11-ounce can whole kernel corn with sweet peppers, drained
1 cup shredded Mexican cheese blend (4 ounces)
2 cups shredded lettuce
1 tomato, chopped (1 cup)

2 **In the same skillet heat oil over medium heat. Add hash brown potatoes, spreading in a single layer. Cook, without stirring, over medium heat for 6 minutes. Stir potatoes; spread in an even layer. Cook, without stirring, for 3 to 4 minutes more or until brown.**

3 **Stir in ground beef, salsa, and drained corn. Heat through. Sprinkle with cheese, lettuce, and tomato. Serve from skillet.**

Per serving: *588 cal., 34 g total fat (13 g sat. fat), 102 mg chol., 1,303 mg sodium, 42 g carbo., 6 g fiber, 33 g pro.*

This recipe fits the bill for casual get-togethers. Spoon the mixture over pasta and serve with crusty bread or corn bread. Such a hearty and impressive main course calls for a simple finish such as a refreshing sorbet and sugar cookies.

beef-vegetable ragoût

Start to Finish: 30 minutes Makes: 4 servings

12 ounces beef
    tenderloin
1 tablespoon olive oil
1½ cups sliced fresh
    shiitake or button
    mushrooms
    (4 ounces)
½ cup chopped onion
    (1 medium)
2 cloves garlic, minced
3 tablespoons all-
    purpose flour
½ teaspoon salt
¼ teaspoon ground
    black pepper
1 14-ounce can beef
    broth
¼ cup port wine
2 cups sugar snap peas
    or one 10-ounce
    package frozen
    sugar snap peas,
    thawed
1 cup cherry tomatoes,
    halved
    Hot cooked bow tie
    pasta (optional)

1 Cut beef into ¾-inch pieces. In a large nonstick skillet heat oil. Cook and stir beef in hot oil for 2 to 3 minutes or until beef is of desired doneness. Remove beef; set aside. In the same skillet cook mushrooms, onion, and garlic until tender.

2 Stir in flour, salt, and pepper. Add broth and wine. Cook and stir until thickened and bubbly. Stir in peas; cook and stir for 2 to 3 minutes more or until peas are tender. Stir in beef and tomatoes; heat through. If desired, serve the beef and vegetable mixture over hot cooked bow tie pasta.

Per serving: *252 cal., 9 g total fat (3 g sat. fat), 48 mg chol., 647 mg sodium, 17 g carbo., 3 g fiber, 21 g pro.*

hamburger stroganoff

Start to Finish: 25 minutes Makes: 3 or 4 servings

12 ounces ground beef
1 clove garlic, minced,
    or ⅛ teaspoon
    garlic powder
1½ cups water
1½ cups half-and-half,
    light cream, or milk
1 4-ounce can (drained
    weight) sliced
    mushrooms,
    drained
1 1.5-ounce package
    stroganoff sauce
    mix
4 ounces dried medium
    egg noodles
    (2 cups)

1 In a large saucepan cook ground beef and garlic over medium heat until beef is brown. Drain off fat.

2 Stir the water, half-and-half, drained mushrooms, and dry stroganoff sauce mix into beef mixture in saucepan. Bring to boiling. Stir in noodles. Reduce heat. Simmer, covered, for 6 to 8 minutes or until noodles are tender, stirring occasionally.

Per serving: 528 cal., 34 g total fat (16 g sat. fat), 132 mg chol., 949 mg sodium, 31 g carbo., 1 g fiber, 23 g pro.

chili-burger supper

Start to Finish: 20 minutes Makes: 4 servings

1 cup dried elbow
   macaroni or penne
   pasta
1 pound ground beef
½ teaspoon chili
   powder
1 11.25-ounce can
   condensed chili
   beef soup
1 14.5-ounce can
   diced tomatoes,
   undrained
½ cup shredded
   cheddar cheese
   (2 ounces)
   Dairy sour cream
   (optional)
   Sliced green onion
   (optional)

1 Cook pasta according to package directions; drain well.

2 Meanwhile, in a large skillet cook ground beef over medium heat until beef is brown. Drain off fat. Add chili powder to beef in skillet; cook and stir for 1 minute.

3 Add soup, undrained tomatoes, and cooked pasta to beef mixture in skillet. Cook and stir over medium heat until the beef mixture is bubbly. Sprinkle with cheese. If desired, serve with sour cream and green onion.

Per serving: 501 cal., 23 g total fat (11 g sat. fat), 94 mg chol., 948 mg sodium, 38 g carbo., 7 g fiber, 33 g pro.

Want a more Asian flair? Substitute ¼ teaspoon five-spice powder for the ground ginger.

stir-fried beef & noodles

Start to Finish: 30 minutes Makes: 3 servings

1   3-ounce package beef-flavor ramen noodles

8   ounces beef sirloin steak, cut ¾ inch thick

1   tablespoon cooking oil

½   cup thinly sliced carrot (1 medium)

½   cup bias-sliced celery (1 stalk)

1   6-ounce package frozen pea pods, thawed

¼   cup water

1   tablespoon snipped fresh parsley

2   teaspoons teriyaki sauce

½   teaspoon ground ginger

¼   teaspoon crushed red pepper (optional)

1 Cook ramen noodles according to package directions, except drain the noodles and reserve the seasoning package.

2 Meanwhile, trim any separable fat from the steak. Cut the steak into thin bite-size strips; set aside.

3 Pour oil into a wok or large skillet. (Add more oil as necessary during cooking.) Preheat over medium-high heat. Add carrot and celery. Stir-fry for 2 to 3 minutes or until crisp-tender. Remove the vegetables from the wok or skillet.

4 Add the steak strips to the hot wok. Stir-fry for 2 to 3 minutes or to desired doneness. Return carrot and celery to the wok. Stir in noodles, reserved seasoning package, pea pods, water, parsley, teriyaki sauce, ginger, and, if desired, crushed red pepper. Cook over medium heat until heated through, stirring occasionally.

Per serving: 621 cal., 30 g total fat (3 g sat. fat), 50 mg chol., 1,724 mg sodium, 61 g carbo., 2 g fiber, 30 g pro.

cheesy
grilled ham
sandwiches

Start to Finish: 15 minutes Makes: 4 sandwiches

4 to 6 teaspoons Dijon-
style mustard
8 slices firm wheat
bread, white bread,
or sourdough bread
4 ounces thinly sliced
cooked ham
4 slices Swiss cheese
(4 ounces)
1 egg, slightly beaten
½ cup milk
Nonstick cooking
spray

1 Spread mustard on 4 of the bread
slices. Top with ham and cheese. Place
remaining bread slices over ham and cheese.
In a shallow bowl or pie plate beat together
egg and milk.

2 Coat an unheated nonstick griddle or
large skillet with cooking spray. Preheat
griddle or skillet over medium heat. Dip each
sandwich in milk mixture, turning to coat.
Place on griddle or in skillet; cook for 1 to
2 minutes on each side or until golden brown
and cheese melts.

Per sandwich: 323 cal., 14 g total fat (7 g sat. fat), 98 mg chol.,
839 mg sodium, 29 g carbo., 3 g fiber, 20 g pro.

If you have some extra time before serving, quick-chill the ham mixture in the freezer for 5 to 10 minutes.

ham & chutney pasta salad

Start to Finish: 25 minutes Makes: 4 servings

8   ounces packaged
     dried medium shell
     macaroni
½   cup chutney
½   cup mayonnaise or
     salad dressing
¼   cup sliced green
     onion (2)
⅛   teaspoon coarsely
     ground black
     pepper
1½ cups cubed cooked
     ham (8 ounces)
4   lettuce leaves
     Cherry tomato
     wedges (optional)

1 Cook macaroni according to package directions. Drain. Rinse with cold water. Drain again.

2 Meanwhile, cut up any large pieces of chutney. Stir together the chutney, mayonnaise, green onion, and pepper.

3 Toss together the chilled macaroni, the chutney mixture, and the ham. Line 4 salad plates with lettuce leaves. Spoon ham mixture on lettuce. If desired, garnish with cherry tomatoes.

Per serving: *580 cal., 26 g total fat (4 g sat. fat), 46 mg chol., 850 mg sodium, 66 g carbo., 2 g fiber, 20 g pro.*

cavatappi with tomatoes & ham

Start to Finish: 30 minutes Makes: 4 servings

- 1 medium onion, cut into 1/4-inch slices
- 12 red and/or yellow cherry and/or pear tomatoes, halved
- 8 ounces dried cavatappi or gemelli pasta
- 1/4 teaspoon crushed red pepper (optional)
- 2 ounces thinly sliced cooked ham, cut into strips
- 3 tablespoons thinly sliced fresh basil
- 2 tablespoons garlic-flavor olive oil or olive oil
- Fresh arugula leaves (optional)

1 Preheat broiler. Place onion slices on the foil-lined rack of an unheated broiler pan. Broil onion slices 4 inches from heat for 5 minutes. Add tomato halves to pan; broil about 5 minutes more or until edges are brown.

2 Meanwhile, cook pasta according to package directions, adding crushed red pepper (if desired) to water. Drain well. Return pasta to pan; cover and keep warm.

3 Cut up onion slices. Toss onion pieces and tomato halves with pasta, ham, basil, and olive oil. If desired, garnish with fresh arugula leaves.

Per serving: 341 cal., 11 g total fat (2 g sat. fat), 16 mg chol., 381 mg sodium, 47 g carbo., 2 g fiber, 13 g pro.

74

speedy dinners

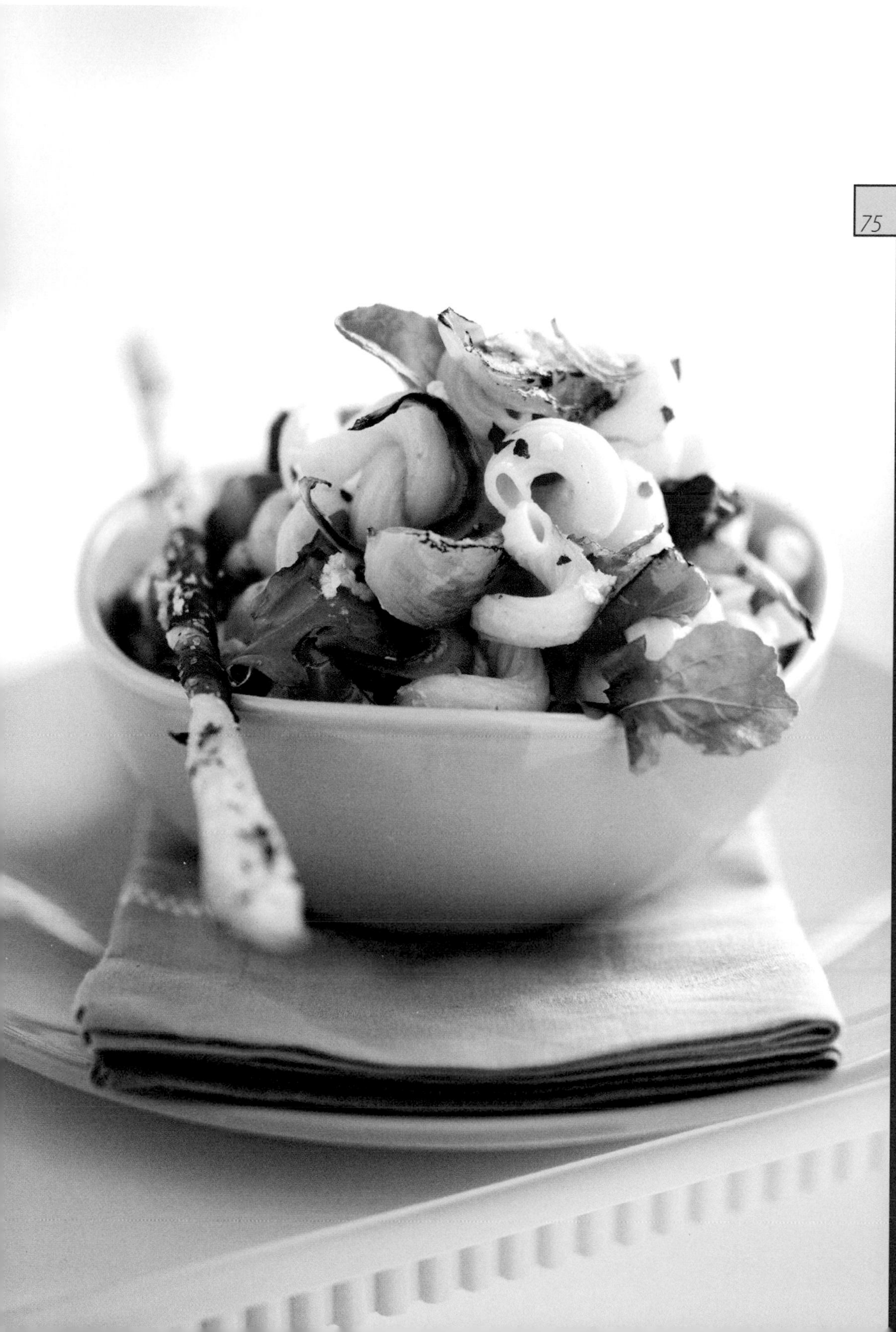

asian pork & vegetables

Prep: 15 minutes Cook: 8 minutes Makes: 4 servings

6   ounces rice stick
    noodles or two
    3-ounce packages
    ramen noodles (any
    flavor), broken,
    if desired
2   teaspoons sesame oil
    or olive oil
1   16-ounce package
    frozen stir-fry
    vegetables
1   12-ounce pork
    tenderloin, cut into
    ¼-inch-thick slices
¼   cup teriyaki sauce
2   tablespoons plum
    sauce

1 Discard spice packet from ramen noodles,
if using, or save for another use. Prepare
noodles as directed on package. Set aside and
keep warm.

2 Heat a very large nonstick skillet over
medium-high heat. Add 1 teaspoon of the
sesame oil. Cook and stir vegetables for 4 to
6 minutes or until crisp-tender. Remove from
skillet. Set aside and keep warm.

3 Add remaining sesame oil to skillet. Add
pork and cook over medium-high heat
for 4 to 6 minutes or until no longer pink,
turning slices once. Stir in vegetables (drained
if necessary), teriyaki sauce, and plum sauce.
Add noodles; toss to coat and heat through.

Per serving: *341 cal., 5 g total fat (1 g sat. fat), 55 mg chol.,
820 mg sodium, 48 g carbo., 3 g fiber, 22 g pro.*

A takeoff on Southern-style red beans and rice, this skillet main dish substitutes rice-shaped orzo pasta for the rice.

red beans & orzo

Start to Finish: 30 minutes   Makes: 4 servings

1   14-ounce can chicken
    broth
1½ cups water
1⅓ cups dried orzo pasta
¼   cup finely chopped
    onion
1   teaspoon herbes de
    Provence or dried
    Italian seasoning,
    crushed
1   15-ounce can red
    beans or pinto
    beans, rinsed and
    drained
1   ounce prosciutto or
    cooked ham, cut
    into thin strips
    (about ⅓ cup)
2   tablespoons snipped
    fresh Italian (flat-
    leaf) parsley
⅓   cup finely shredded
    Parmesan cheese

1 In a medium saucepan combine broth and water; bring to boiling. Stir in uncooked orzo, onion, and herbes de Provence. Return to boiling; reduce heat. Simmer, uncovered, for 12 to 15 minutes or just until orzo is tender and most of the liquid is absorbed, stirring often.

2 Stir in beans, prosciutto, and parsley; heat through. Top each serving with Parmesan cheese.

Per serving: 350 cal., 4 g total fat (1 g sat. fat), 11 mg chol., 1,118 mg sodium, 61 g carbo., 7 g fiber, 18 g pro.

Cook the spinach for this sausage-pasta salad quickly so it doesn't wilt too much.

pasta with spinach & smoked sausage

Start to Finish: 25 minutes Makes: 4 servings

speedy **dinners**

4 ounces cooked
smoked turkey or
chicken sausage
1 large leek, cut into
¼-inch slices
2 cloves garlic, minced
1 teaspoon olive oil
⅔ cup reduced-sodium
chicken broth
½ of a 7-ounce jar
roasted red sweet
peppers, drained
and cut into thin,
bite-size strips
8 cups torn fresh
spinach
6 ounces dried medium
bow tie pasta
¼ cup snipped
fresh basil or
1 tablespoon dried
basil, crushed
¼ cup finely shredded
Parmesan cheese
¼ teaspoon cracked
black pepper

1 Cut the sausage lengthwise into quarters. Slice into ¼-inch pieces. In a large skillet cook leek and garlic in hot oil until leek is tender. Stir in sausage, broth, and roasted sweet peppers. Bring to boiling; reduce heat. Add spinach. Cook, stirring frequently, for 1 to 2 minutes or just until spinach starts to wilt. Remove from heat.

2 Meanwhile, cook the pasta according to package directions, omitting any oil or salt; drain. Return pasta to saucepan. Add spinach mixture, basil, cheese, and cracked black pepper. Toss to coat. Serve immediately.

Per serving: 265 cal., 8 g total fat (2 g sat. fat), 61 mg chol., 440 mg sodium, 34 g carbo., 2 g fiber, 14 g pro.

Chorizo, a spicy sausage made of coarsely ground pork, can be found in stores specializing in Mexican foods. The Mexican version of the sausage, made of fresh pork, is what you want for this recipe; Spanish chorizo is made of smoked pork.

mexican skillet dinner

Start to Finish: 25 minutes Makes: 6 servings

12 ounces chorizo or pork sausage

2 cups frozen whole kernel corn

1 14.5-ounce can diced tomatoes, undrained

1 cup uncooked instant rice

½ cup water

2 teaspoons chili powder

½ teaspoon ground cumin

1 15-ounce can pinto beans, rinsed and drained

¾ cup shredded Mexican cheese blend or Colby and Monterey Jack cheese (3 ounces)

1 Remove casing from sausage, if present. In a large skillet cook sausage over medium heat for 10 to 15 minutes or until brown. Drain in a colander; set aside.

2 Add corn, undrained tomatoes, uncooked rice, water, chili powder, and cumin to skillet. Bring to boiling; reduce heat. Cover and simmer for 5 minutes or until liquid is absorbed and rice is tender. Stir in beans and cooked sausage; heat through. Sprinkle with cheese; cover and let stand for 2 to 3 minutes until cheese is slightly melted.

Per serving: 230 cal., 27 g total fat (11 g sat. fat), 13 mg chol., 585 mg sodium, 38 g carbo., 5 g fiber, 23 g pro.

white bean & sausage rigatoni

Start to Finish: 20 minutes Makes: 4 servings

8   ounces dried rigatoni
    pasta or medium
    shell pasta
1   15- to 19-ounce can
    cannellini beans
    (white kidney
    beans), Great
    Northern beans, or
    navy beans, rinsed
    and drained
1   14.5-ounce can
    Italian-style
    stewed tomatoes,
    undrained
6   ounces cooked
    smoked turkey
    sausage, halved
    lengthwise and cut
    into ½-inch slices
⅓   cup snipped fresh
    basil
1   ounce Asiago or
    Parmesan cheese,
    shaved or finely
    shredded (optional)

1 Cook pasta according to package
directions. Drain. Return pasta to
hot saucepan.

2 Add beans, undrained tomatoes, and
sausage; heat through. Add pasta and
basil; toss gently to combine. If desired,
sprinkle each serving with cheese.

Per serving: *378 cal., 6 g total fat (1 g sat. fat), 29 mg chol.,
760 mg sodium, 65 g carbo., 7 g fiber, 21 g pro.*

Escarole, a type of endive, is typically used in salads, but it makes a great addition to this hearty one-pot dish.

sausage, beans & greens

Start to Finish: 25 minutes Makes: 4 servings

8   ounces hot or mild Italian sausage links, bias-sliced into ½-inch pieces
½   cup chopped onion
2   19-ounce cans cannellini beans (white kidney beans), rinsed and drained
¾   cup reduced-sodium chicken broth
¼   cup dry white wine or reduced-sodium chicken broth
2   tablespoons snipped fresh thyme or 1 teaspoon dried thyme, crushed
2   cups coarsely chopped escarole or spinach
¼   cup finely shredded Parmesan cheese (optional)

1 In a large skillet cook Italian sausage and onion over medium heat about 5 minutes or until sausage is brown and onion is tender. Drain off fat. Stir in beans, broth, wine, and thyme.

2 Bring to boiling; reduce heat. Cover and simmer for 5 minutes. Stir in escarole; heat through. If desired, sprinkle each serving with Parmesan cheese.

Per serving: *309 cal., 12 g total fat (4 g sat. fat), 32 mg chol., 921 mg sodium, 39 g carbo., 13 g fiber, 24 g pro.*

tuna & pasta alfredo

Start to Finish: 25 minutes Makes: 4 servings

3   cups dried mini
    lasagna, broken
    mafalda, or medium
    noodles
2   cups chopped fresh
    broccoli
1   medium red sweet
    pepper, cut into thin
    strips
1   10-ounce container
    refrigerated light
    Alfredo sauce
¾   teaspoon dried dill
2   to 3 tablespoons milk
    (optional)
1   9.5-ounce can tuna
    (water pack),
    drained and broken
    into chunks

1 In a large saucepan cook pasta according to package directions, adding broccoli and sweet pepper for the last 5 minutes of cooking. Drain well. Return pasta and vegetables to hot pan.

2 Stir Alfredo sauce and dill into pasta mixture. If necessary, stir in enough of the milk to make sauce desired consistency. Gently stir tuna into pasta mixture. Heat through.

Per serving: 545 cal., 12 g total fat (7 g sat. fat), 47 mg chol., 821 mg sodium, 78 g carbo., 4 g fiber, 30 g pro.

shrimp & couscous jambalaya

Start to Finish: 25 minutes Makes: 4 servings

12 ounces fresh or
frozen medium
shrimp in shells
1 cup sliced celery
(2 stalks)
¾ cup chopped green
sweet pepper
(1 medium)
½ cup chopped onion
(1 medium)
½ teaspoon Cajun
seasoning
¼ teaspoon dried
oregano, crushed
2 tablespoons cooking
oil
1 14-ounce can
reduced-sodium
chicken broth
1 cup quick-cooking
couscous
½ cup chopped tomato
(1 medium)
Bottled hot pepper
sauce (optional)
Lemon wedges
(optional)

1 Thaw shrimp, if frozen. Peel and devein shrimp. Rinse shrimp and pat dry with paper towels; set aside. In a large skillet cook and stir celery, sweet pepper, onion, Cajun seasoning, and oregano in hot oil until vegetables are tender. Carefully add broth; bring to boiling.

2 Stir in the shrimp and remove from heat. Stir in the couscous and tomato. Cover and let stand for 5 minutes. To serve, fluff couscous mixture with a fork; transfer to a shallow serving bowl. If desired, serve with hot pepper sauce and lemon wedges.

Per serving: 317 cal., 8 g total fat (1 g sat. fat), 98 mg chol., 462 mg sodium, 42 g carbo., 9 g fiber, 18 g pro.

Dinner is 1-2-3 easy with ingredients cooked in the same pot. When dinner is over, there's only one pan to scrub.

lemony scallops & spaghettini

Start to Finish: 25 minutes Makes: 4 servings

12 ounces fresh or
    frozen scallops
 8 ounces spaghettini
    (thin spaghetti)
 3 cups small broccoli
    florets
 1 10-ounce container
    refrigerated light
    Alfredo sauce
 1 teaspoon finely
    shredded lemon
    peel

1 Thaw scallops, if frozen. Rinse scallops; drain. Cut any large scallops in half.

2 Cook pasta and broccoli according to pasta cooking directions or until broccoli is just crisp-tender, about 6 minutes. Add scallops; continue cooking for 1 to 2 minutes or until scallops are opaque. Drain well. Return to pan; stir in Alfredo sauce and lemon peel. Heat and stir about 2 minutes or until sauce is slightly thickened.

Per serving: *119 cal, 5 g total fat (0 g sat. fat), 11 mg chol., 759 mg sodium, 7 g carbo., 2 g fiber, 14 g pro.*

This fresh-tasting pasta dish is a delicious way to showcase the first tender spears of spring asparagus.

pasta with shrimp, asparagus & tomatoes

Start to Finish: 30 minutes   Makes: 4 servings

4   ounces dried
      spaghetti
12 ounces fresh or
      frozen peeled and
      deveined shrimp
16 thin spears fresh
      asparagus
1   teaspoon olive oil
4   cloves garlic, minced
2   cups chopped seeded
      plum tomato
      (6 medium)
¼   cup chicken broth
¼   teaspoon salt
¼   teaspoon ground
      black pepper
1   tablespoon butter or
      margarine
¼   cup shredded fresh
      basil

1 Cook pasta according to package directions; drain and return to pan to keep warm.

2 Meanwhile, thaw shrimp, if frozen. Set aside. Snap off and discard woody bases from asparagus. Remove tips; set aside. Bias-slice asparagus stalks into 1- to 1½-inch pieces; set aside.

3 In a large skillet heat oil over medium heat. Add garlic; cook and stir for 15 seconds. Add tomato; cook and stir for 2 minutes. Add asparagus stalks, broth, salt, and pepper. Cook, uncovered, for 3 minutes. Add asparagus tips and shrimp; cook, uncovered, for 2 to 3 minutes or until shrimp are opaque. Add butter; stir until melted.

4 Add asparagus mixture and basil to pasta in pan; toss to combine. Serve warm.

Per serving: 274 cal., 6 g total fat (2 g sat. fat), 137 mg chol., 362 mg sodium, 31 g carbo., 4 g fiber, 24 g pro.

trattoria-style spinach fettuccine

Start to Finish: 18 minutes Makes: 4 servings

1   9-ounce package
      refrigerated spinach
      fettuccine
1   medium carrot
1   tablespoon olive oil
¼   cup chopped green
      onion (2)
2   cups chopped
      red and/or
      yellow tomatoes
      (4 medium)
¼   cup oil-packed dried
      tomatoes, drained
      and snipped
½   cup crumbled
      garlic and herb or
      peppercorn feta
      cheese (2 ounces)

1 Using kitchen scissors, cut pasta strands in half. Cook the pasta according to package directions; drain. Return pasta to hot pan.

2 Meanwhile, using a vegetable peeler, slice carrot lengthwise into wide, flat "ribbons." Set carrot aside.

3 In a large skillet heat oil over medium heat. Add green onion; cook for 30 seconds. Stir in fresh tomato, carrot, and dried tomato. Cook, covered, for 5 minutes, stirring once.

4 Spoon tomato mixture over cooked pasta; toss gently. Sprinkle servings with cheese.

Per serving: 311 cal., 11 g total fat (4 g sat. fat), 73 mg chol., 250 mg sodium, 44 g carbo., 2 g fiber, 13 g pro.

ravioli with spinach pesto

Start to Finish: 20 minutes Makes: 4 servings

1   9-ounce package
    refrigerated four-
    cheese ravioli or
    tortellini
12 ounces baby
    pattypan squash,
    halved, or yellow
    summer squash,
    halved lengthwise
    and sliced ½ inch
    thick
3½ cups fresh baby
    spinach
½   cup torn fresh basil
¼   cup bottled Caesar
    Parmesan
    vinaigrette salad
    dressing
2   tablespoons water
    Shredded Parmesan
    cheese (optional)

1 Cook ravioli according to package directions, adding squash the last 2 minutes of cooking. Drain.

2 Meanwhile, for pesto, in a blender combine spinach, basil, salad dressing, and the water. Cover and process until smooth, stopping to scrape down blender as needed.

3 Toss ravioli mixture with pesto. If desired, sprinkle with cheese.

Per serving: 218 cal., 6 g total fat (2 g sat. fat), 27 mg chol., 525 mg sodium, 31 g carbo., 3 g fiber, 11 g pro.

pasta with three cheeses

Start to Finish: 30 minutes Makes: 4 servings

10 ounces dried medium
    shell macaroni
2   cups frozen
    cauliflower,
    broccoli, and carrots
    or other vegetable
    combination
1   cup milk
1   3-ounce package
    cream cheese, cut
    up
¼   teaspoon ground
    black pepper
¾   cup shredded Gouda,
    cheddar, or Swiss
    cheese (3 ounces)
¼   cup grated Parmesan
    cheese
    Grated Parmesan
    cheese (optional)

1 In a large saucepan cook pasta according
to package directions, adding the
frozen vegetables for the last 5 minutes of
cooking. Drain.

2 In the hot saucepan combine milk, cream
cheese, and pepper. Cook and stir over
low heat until cream cheese is melted.

3 Return pasta mixture to saucepan. Toss to
coat with cream cheese mixture. Gently
stir in the shredded Gouda cheese and the
¼ cup Parmesan cheese. If desired, sprinkle
servings with additional Parmesan cheese.

Per serving: *598 cal., 25 g total fat (14 g sat. fat), 86 mg chol.,
596 mg sodium, 66 g carbo., 3 g fiber, 28 g pro.*

Pumpkin and sage stirred into a purchased Alfredo sauce transform ravioli into an elegant dinner, just right for brisk autumn days.

cheese ravioli sauced with pumpkin & sage

Start to Finish: 25 minutes Makes: 4 servings

½ cup dry white wine or chicken broth

¼ cup finely chopped shallots

1⅓ cups purchased Alfredo pasta sauce

½ cup canned pumpkin

1½ teaspoons dried sage, crushed

2 9-ounce packages refrigerated four-cheese ravioli

2 tablespoons snipped fresh Italian (flat-leaf) parsley

2 tablespoons chopped hazelnuts (filberts), toasted

1 For sauce, in a large skillet combine wine and shallots. Cook over medium heat for 5 to 8 minutes or until most of the liquid is evaporated, stirring frequently. Stir in Alfredo sauce, pumpkin, and sage. Cook until sauce mixture is heated through, stirring occasionally.

2 Meanwhile, cook pasta according to package directions. Before draining pasta, remove ½ cup of the cooking water and set aside. Drain pasta; return to pan.

3 Stir the reserved cooking water into sauce. Stir in parsley. Pour the sauce over cooked pasta; toss gently to coat. Sprinkle each serving with hazelnuts.

Per serving: 687 cal., 38 g total fat (20 g sat. fat), 162 mg chol., 1,436 mg sodium, 69 g carbo., 6 g fiber, 22 g pro.

Twenty minutes is all it takes to build a healthful family dinner. Salsa, corn, beans, and cheese separate layers of tortillas in this hot Mexican-inspired casserole.

triple-decker tortilla

Prep: 15 minutes Bake: 15 minutes Oven: 450°F Makes: 4 servings

Nonstick cooking
  spray
1 cup canned pinto
  beans, rinsed and
  drained
1 cup bottled salsa
4 6-inch corn tortillas
¾ cup frozen whole
  kernel corn
½ cup shredded
  reduced-fat
  Monterey Jack or
  cheddar cheese
  (2 ounces)
½ of an avocado,
  seeded, peeled, and
  chopped
1 tablespoon fresh
  cilantro leaves

1 Preheat oven to 450°F. Lightly coat a 9-inch pie plate with cooking spray; set aside. Place beans in a small bowl; slightly mash the beans. In a small saucepan or skillet cook and stir beans over medium heat for 2 to 3 minutes to heat through. Set aside.

2 Spoon ¼ cup of the salsa into bottom of prepared pie plate. Layer ingredients in the following order: 1 tortilla, half of the mashed bean, 1 tortilla, all of the corn, ¼ cup of the cheese, ¼ cup salsa, 1 tortilla, remaining mashed bean mixture, remaining tortilla, and remaining ½ cup salsa.

3 Cover with foil; bake in the preheated oven for 12 minutes. Remove foil. Sprinkle with remaining ¼ cup cheese.

4 Bake, uncovered, for 3 minutes more. Top with avocado and cilantro.

Per serving: *219 cal., 5 g total fat (2 g sat. fat), 10 mg chol., 813 mg sodium, 38 g carbo., 6 g fiber, 10 g pro.*

Nutty-tasting barley and spicy beans provide a surprising and satisfying meatless topping for crisp tortillas.

bean-barley tostadas

Start to Finish: 20 minutes   Makes: 4 servings

1½   cups water
¾   cup quick-cooking
     barley
1   15-ounce can chili
     beans with chili
     gravy, undrained
½   cup bottled salsa
4   8-inch flour tortillas,
     fried*, or 4 cups
     tortilla chips
1   10-ounce package
     shredded iceberg
     lettuce
¾   cup shredded
     cheddar cheese
     (3 ounces)
     Dairy sour cream
     (optional)
     Bottled salsa
     (optional)

1 In a medium saucepan bring the water to boiling; add barley. Reduce heat. Cover and simmer for 10 to 12 minutes or until tender. Drain off any excess liquid. Stir undrained beans and gravy and the ½ cup salsa into barley; heat through.

2 Place a fried tortilla or 1 cup tortilla chips on each of four plates. Top with lettuce and barley mixture; sprinkle with cheese. If desired, top each serving with sour cream and additional salsa.

*Tip: To fry tortillas, in a heavy skillet heat about ¼ inch cooking oil. Fry tortillas, one at a time, in hot oil about 30 seconds on each side or until crisp and golden brown. Drain on paper towels.

Per serving: *437 cal., 14 g total fat (6 g sat. fat), 22 mg chol., 458 mg sodium, 63 g carbo., 14 g fiber, 17 g pro.*

minestrone

Start to Finish: 30 minutes Makes: 4 servings

2　14-ounce cans chicken broth
1　cup thinly sliced carrot (2 medium)
1　teaspoon dried basil, crushed
½　cup ditalini (tiny thimbles) or tiny bow tie pasta
1　medium zucchini, chopped (1¼ cups)
1　14.5-ounce can diced tomatoes with onions and garlic, undrained
1　15- to 15.5-ounce can cannellini (white kidney) beans or navy beans, rinsed and drained
¼　cup slivered fresh basil or spinach
　Bottled hot pepper sauce (optional)

1 In a large saucepan combine broth, carrot, and dried basil. Bring to boiling; reduce heat. Simmer, covered, for 5 minutes.

2 Stir in pasta and simmer, uncovered, for 8 minutes or just until pasta is tender. Add zucchini, undrained tomatoes, and beans; heat through. Ladle soup into bowls; sprinkle with fresh basil. If desired, pass bottled hot pepper sauce.

Per serving: 203 cal., 2 g total fat (0 g sat. fat), 0 mg chol., 1,328 mg sodium, 38 g carbo., 7 g fiber, 14 g pro.

Don't even worry about heating up the oven—
this chapter is full of one-pan plans just for the
stovetop and wok.

quick-fix
skillet

3

meals
& stir-fries

Braising—the method of cooking food slowly in a small amount of liquid in a tightly covered pan—results in moist and flavorful foods.

chicken braised with wine & tomatoes

Prep: 15 minutes Cook: 40 minutes Makes: 4 servings

8 small or 4 large chicken thighs (about 2 pounds)
1 tablespoon cooking oil
⅔ cup chicken broth
¼ cup dry white wine or chicken broth
2 cloves garlic, minced
2 teaspoons snipped fresh rosemary or ¾ teaspoon dried rosemary, crushed
¼ teaspoon salt
¼ teaspoon ground black pepper
2 cups chopped plum tomato (6 medium)
2 medium yellow and/or green sweet peppers, cut into ½-inch-wide strips (2 cups)
1½ cups sliced fresh mushrooms
2 tablespoons cornstarch
2 tablespoons cold water
 Hot cooked noodles or rice

1 Remove skin from chicken. In a large skillet heat oil. Brown chicken in hot oil over medium heat about 5 minutes, turning chicken to brown evenly. Drain off fat. Add broth, wine, garlic, dried rosemary (if using), salt, and ground black pepper to chicken in skillet. Bring to boiling; reduce heat. Simmer, covered, for 20 minutes.

2 Add tomato, sweet pepper, and mushrooms to skillet. Simmer, covered, for 15 minutes more or until chicken is tender and no longer pink. Transfer chicken to a serving dish, reserving vegetables and cooking liquid in skillet. Cover chicken with foil to keep warm.

3 In a small bowl combine the cornstarch, water, and fresh rosemary (if using); stir into vegetable mixture in skillet. Cook and stir until thickened and bubbly. Cook and stir for 2 minutes more. Return chicken pieces to sauce; spoon sauce over to coat and heat through. Serve with noodles.

Per serving: *355 cal., 10 g total fat (2 g sat. fat), 117 mg chol., 408 mg sodium, 34 g carbo., 3 g fiber, 29 g pro.*

The zesty flavors of the Mediterranean dominate this dish. Artichokes, oregano, kalamata olives, and feta cheese mingle with chicken pieces, garlic, and a splash of white wine.

mediterranean chicken & pasta

Start to Finish: 20 minutes Makes: 4 servings

1   6-ounce jar marinated artichoke hearts
1   tablespoon olive oil
12 ounces skinless, boneless chicken breasts, cut into bite-size pieces
3   cloves garlic, thinly sliced
¼   cup chicken broth
¼   cup dry white wine or chicken broth
1   teaspoon dried oregano, crushed
1   cup roasted red sweet peppers, drained and cut into strips
¼   cup pitted kalamata olives
    Hot cooked campanelle or penne pasta
¼   cup crumbled feta cheese (optional)
    Fresh basil leaves (optional)

1 Drain artichokes, reserving marinade. Cut up any large pieces. Set aside. In a large skillet heat oil over medium-high heat. Add chicken and garlic. Cook and stir until chicken is brown. Add the reserved artichoke marinade, broth, wine, and oregano.

2 Bring to boiling; reduce heat. Simmer, covered, for 10 minutes. Stir in artichokes, roasted sweet peppers, and olives. Heat through.

3 To serve, spoon the chicken mixture over hot cooked pasta. If desired, sprinkle with feta cheese and fresh basil leaves.

Per serving: 347 cal., 9 g total fat (1 g sat. fat), 49 mg chol., 323 mg sodium, 38 g carbo., 3 g fiber, 26 g pro.

For a delicious dinner entrée, begin with fruit juice plus a few simple ingredients. Red and green grapes add a light sweetness and a pretty color too.

chicken with grapes

Start to Finish: 20 minutes Makes: 4 servings

Nonstick cooking
   spray
4 skinless, boneless
   chicken breast
   halves (about
   1¼ pounds)
1 cup white grape
   juice, apple juice, or
   apple cider
2 teaspoons instant
   chicken bouillon
   granules
2 teaspoons cornstarch
1 cup seedless green
   and/or red grapes,
   halved
Hot cooked linguine
   (optional)
Fresh thyme or
   oregano sprigs
   (optional)

1 Coat a large skillet with cooking spray. Heat over medium-high heat. Add chicken and cook for 8 to 10 minutes or until chicken is no longer pink (170°F), turning once. If chicken browns too quickly, reduce heat to medium. Remove from skillet.

2 Meanwhile, for sauce, in a small bowl combine grape juice, bouillon granules, and cornstarch; add to skillet. Cook and stir until thickened and bubbly. Cook and stir for 2 minutes more. Stir in grapes. Return chicken to skillet. Cook, covered, for 2 to 3 minutes to heat through.

3 Serve the chicken with sauce. If desired, serve with hot cooked linguine and garnish with fresh thyme.

Per serving: 237 cal., 2 g total fat (1 g sat. fat), 82 mg chol., 632 mg sodium, 19 g carbo., 0 g fiber, 33 g pro.

The traditional Mediterranean flavors of tomato, wine, basil, and garlic go well with chicken.

chicken & olives

Prep: 30 minutes Cook: 35 minutes Makes: 4 servings

1½   to 2 pounds meaty
      chicken pieces
      (breast halves,
      thighs, and
      drumsticks)
      Nonstick cooking
      spray
  1   14.5-ounce can
      tomatoes,
      undrained and cut
      up
  ¼   cup dry red wine
  1   tablespoon snipped
      fresh basil or
      1 teaspoon dried
      basil, crushed
  1   teaspoon sugar
  1   bay leaf
  1   clove garlic, minced
  1   tablespoon cold
      water
  2   teaspoons cornstarch
      Hot cooked spaghetti
      (optional)
  ¼   cup sliced pimiento-
      stuffed green olives
      or pitted ripe olives

1 Remove skin from chicken; set chicken aside. Coat a very large skillet with cooking spray. Heat over medium heat. Add chicken pieces. Cook for 10 to 15 minutes or until brown, turning to brown evenly.

2 Add undrained tomatoes, wine, basil, sugar, bay leaf, and garlic. Bring to boiling; reduce heat. Simmer, covered, for 35 to 40 minutes or until chicken is no longer pink (170°F for breasts, 180°F for thighs and drumsticks). Remove chicken from skillet; cover and keep warm. Discard bay leaf.

3 For sauce, in a small bowl stir together water and cornstarch; stir into tomato mixture. Cook and stir until thickened and bubbly. Cook and stir for 2 minutes more. Return chicken to skillet; spoon sauce over chicken.

4 If desired, serve the chicken and sauce over hot cooked spaghetti. Sprinkle with olives.

Per serving: 194 cal., 7 g total fat (2 g sat. fat), 69 mg chol., 401 mg sodium, 8 g carbo., 1 g fiber, 23 g pro.

This recipe, which leans on three prepared foods, will ease the what's-for-dinner anxiety.

chicken & vegetables alfredo with rice

Start to Finish: 25 minutes Makes: 4 servings

4 skinless, boneless chicken breast halves (about 1 pound) or 8 skinless boneless chicken thighs
1 tablespoon butter or margarine
2½ cups frozen stir-fry vegetables (such as broccoli, carrots, onions, and red sweet peppers)
1⅓ cups uncooked instant white rice
1 10-ounce container refrigerated light Alfredo pasta sauce
1 cup milk
2 tablespoons grated or finely shredded Parmesan cheese (optional)

1 In a large skillet cook chicken in hot butter over medium heat for 6 to 8 minutes or until chicken is brown, turning once. Remove chicken from skillet.

2 Add frozen vegetables, rice, Alfredo sauce, and milk to skillet. Bring to boiling, stirring occasionally; reduce heat. Top with chicken.

3 Cover and cook over medium-low heat for 6 to 8 minutes or until chicken is tender and no longer pink (170°F for breasts, 180°F for thighs), stirring once or twice. If desired, sprinkle with Parmesan cheese.

Per serving: 433 cal., 13 g total fat (8 g sat. fat), 105 mg chol., 638 mg sodium, 39 g carbo., 2 g fiber, 38 g pro.

chicken veneto

Start to Finish: 30 minutes Makes: 4 servings

8 ounces dried
    fettuccine or
    linguine
12 ounces skinless,
    boneless chicken
    breast halves
2 tablespoons olive oil
¼ cup butter
3 cloves garlic, minced
1 9-ounce package
    frozen artichoke
    hearts, thawed and
    halved
¼ cup coarsely chopped
    pistachios
¾ cup dry white wine
¼ teaspoon salt
2 tablespoons snipped
    fresh Italian (flat-
    leaf) parsley
    Cracked black pepper

1 Cook pasta according to package directions. Drain; keep warm.

2 Meanwhile, cut chicken into bite-size strips. In a very large skillet cook chicken in hot oil over medium-high heat for 3 to 4 minutes or until chicken is no longer pink. Remove chicken from skillet with a slotted spoon; discard pan drippings.

3 In the same skillet melt butter over medium heat. Add garlic; cook and stir for 15 seconds. Remove from heat. Add artichokes, pistachios, and wine. Return to heat. Bring to boiling; reduce heat. Simmer, uncovered, for 5 minutes. Stir in salt. Return chicken to the skillet. Cook for 1 to 2 minutes more or until heated through. Add pasta and toss to coat.

4 Sprinkle with parsley and cracked black pepper to taste. Serve immediately.

Per serving: 583 cal., 25 g total fat (8 g sat. fat), 82 mg chol., 325 mg sodium, 51 g carbo., 6 g fiber, 31 g pro.

Imagine a comforting pot roast dinner in only 30 minutes. Thanks to precooked meat, all you have to do is add a few ingredients to give it a personal touch.

quick honey-garlic pot roast

Prep: 10 minutes Cook: 20 minutes Makes: 4 servings

1 **17-ounce package refrigerated cooked beef roast au jus or beef pot roast with juices**

2 **tablespoons honey**

1 **tablespoon Worcestershire sauce**

1 **to 1½ teaspoons bottled roasted minced garlic**

¼ **teaspoon ground black pepper**

2 **cups packaged peeled baby carrots, halved lengthwise**

12 **ounces small red potatoes, quartered**

1 **medium red onion, cut into thin wedges**

1 Remove beef from package, reserving juices. In a medium bowl combine reserved juices, honey, Worcestershire sauce, roasted garlic, and pepper. Place beef in a large nonstick skillet. Arrange carrots, potatoes, and onion wedges around beef. Pour honey mixture over beef and vegetables. Bring to boiling; reduce heat. Simmer, covered, for 20 to 25 minutes or until vegetables are tender.

2 Transfer beef and vegetables to a serving platter. Spoon sauce over beef and vegetables.

Per serving: 305 cal., 9 g total fat (4 g sat. fat), 64 mg chol., 502 mg sodium, 35 g carbo., 4 g fiber, 26 g pro.

skillet pot roast with mushrooms & cherries

Start to Finish: 30 minutes Makes: 4 to 6 servings

1   12-ounce package
    frozen unsweetened
    pitted dark sweet
    cherries

8   ounces fresh button
    mushrooms, halved
    (3 cups)

1   medium red sweet
    pepper, cut into
    bite-size strips
    (¾ cup)

1   cup chopped onion
    (1 large)

2   tablespoons snipped
    fresh herb, such as
    sage or thyme or
    2 teaspoons dried
    sage or thyme

1   tablespoon olive oil or
    cooking oil

2   16- to 17-ounce
    packages
    refrigerated cooked
    beef pot roast with
    juices

2   tablespoons balsamic
    vinegar

1 Place frozen cherries in a colander. Run cold water over cherries to partially thaw. Set aside; drain well.

2 In a very large skillet cook mushrooms, sweet pepper, onion, and 1 tablespoon of the fresh herb or 1 teaspoon of the dried herb in hot oil for 7 minutes or until tender. Add pot roasts and juices, cherries, and balsamic vinegar to skillet. Bring to boiling; reduce heat. Simmer, uncovered, for 10 minutes or until heated through and juices thicken slightly, stirring occasionally. Sprinkle with remaining herb; stir to combine.

Per serving: 420 cal., 17 g total fat (5 g sat. fat), 104 mg chol., 1,174 mg sodium, 31 g carbo., 3 g fiber, 40 g pro.

Save a step and use leftover baked or boiled potatoes in this hearty stir-fry.

beef curry & potatoes

Start to Finish: 30 minutes Makes: 4 servings

12 ounces boneless beef top round steak
½ cup beef broth
2 teaspoons cornstarch
¼ teaspoon salt
2 medium potatoes, halved lengthwise and thinly sliced
Nonstick cooking spray
¾ cup chopped onion
¾ cup chopped green or red sweet pepper (1 medium)
1 tablespoon cooking oil
1 to 3 teaspoons curry powder
½ cup coarsely chopped tomato (1 medium)

1 Trim fat from beef. If desired, partially freeze beef for easier slicing. Thinly slice beef across the grain into bite-size strips. For sauce, in a small bowl stir together broth, cornstarch, and salt. Set aside.

2 In a small saucepan cook potatoes in boiling, lightly salted water for 5 minutes or until tender; drain.

3 Meanwhile, coat a large skillet or wok with cooking spray. Heat over medium-high heat. Stir-fry onion in hot skillet for 2 minutes. Add sweet pepper; stir-fry for 2 minutes more or until vegetables are crisp-tender. Remove vegetables from skillet.

4 Add oil to hot skillet. Stir-fry beef and curry powder in hot oil for 2 to 3 minutes or until beef is slightly pink in center. Push beef from center of skillet.

5 Stir sauce; add to center of skillet. Cook and stir until thickened and bubbly. Add cooked potatoes, onion mixture, and tomato. Stir all ingredients together to coat with sauce. Cook and stir about 1 minute more or until heated through.

Per serving: 268 cal., 8 g total fat (2 g sat. fat), 54 mg chol., 282 mg sodium, 26 g carbo., 2 g fiber, 24 g pro.

saucy pizza skillet dinner

Start to Finish: 30 minutes Makes: 4 servings

1   6.4-ounce package
     lasagna dinner mix
3   cups water
1   4-ounce can (drained
     weight) mushroom
     stems and pieces,
     undrained
½   cup chopped green
     sweet pepper
½   cup sliced pitted ripe
     olives (optional)
½   cup shredded
     mozzarella cheese
     (2 ounces)

1 If the noodles in the dinner mix are large, break them into bite-size pieces. In a large skillet combine noodles and seasoning from the dinner mix, the water, undrained mushrooms, and sweet pepper.

2 Bring to boiling, stirring occasionally; reduce heat. Simmer, covered, for 13 minutes or until pasta is tender. Uncover and cook for 2 to 3 minutes more or until sauce is of desired consistency.

3 If desired, sprinkle with olives. Top with cheese. Remove from heat; let stand for 1 to 2 minutes or until cheese melts.

Per serving: 318 cal., 14 g total fat (5 g sat. fat), 28 mg chol., 1,774 mg sodium, 37 g carbo., 3 g fiber, 14 g pro.

Talk about quick! The most time-consuming part of this recipe is boiling the water for the pasta. After that, a hearty lasagna is just minutes away.

quick skillet lasagna

Start to Finish: 30 minutes Makes: 6 servings

3 cups dried mafalda (mini lasagna) noodles (6 ounces)

12 ounces lean ground beef or bulk pork sausage

1 26- to 27.75-ounce jar tomato-base pasta sauce

1½ cups shredded mozzarella cheese (6 ounces)

¼ cup grated Parmesan cheese (1 ounce)

1 Cook pasta according to package directions; drain.

2 Meanwhile, in a large nonstick skillet cook beef until brown; drain off fat. Set beef aside. Wipe skillet with paper towels.

3 Spread about half of the cooked pasta in the skillet. Cover with about half of the pasta sauce. Spoon cooked beef over sauce. Sprinkle with 1 cup of the mozzarella cheese. Top with remaining pasta and pasta sauce. Sprinkle remaining mozzarella cheese and Parmesan cheese over top.

4 Cook, covered, over medium heat for 5 to 7 minutes or until heated through and cheese melts.

Per serving: *375 cal., 17 g total fat (6 g sat. fat), 50 mg chol., 1,046 mg sodium, 30 g carbo., 2 g fiber, 25 g pro.*

A jar of picante sauce makes an easy yet flavor-packed sauce for this stir-fry dish.

southwest
beef & linguine toss

Start to Finish: 25 minutes Makes: 4 servings

4   ounces packaged
    dried linguine
12 ounces beef top
    round steak
1   tablespoon cooking
    oil
2   teaspoons chili
    powder
1   clove garlic, minced
1   small onion, sliced
    and separated into
    rings
1   red or green sweet
    pepper, cut into
    strips
1   10-ounce package
    frozen whole kernel
    corn
¼   cup picante sauce
    Fresh cilantro
    (optional)
    Chili powder
    (optional)

1 Cook linguine according to package directions. Drain. Rinse with warm water. Set aside.

2 Meanwhile, trim fat from steak. Cut steak into thin, bite-size strips. Set aside.

3 Pour oil into a wok or large skillet. (Add more oil as necessary during cooking.) Preheat over medium-high heat. Stir-fry the 2 teaspoons chili powder and the garlic in hot oil for 15 seconds. Add onion and stir-fry for 1 minute. Add sweet pepper; stir-fry for 1 to 2 minutes more or until vegetables are crisp-tender. Remove vegetables from wok.

4 Add the beef to the hot work; stir-fry for 2 to 3 minutes or to desired doneness. Return vegetables to the wok. Stir in corn and picante sauce. Add the cooked linguine. Toss together to coat with sauce. Cook and stir until heated through. If desired, garnish with fresh cilantro and sprinkle with additional chili powder.

Per serving: *351 cal., 9 g total fat (2 g sat. fat), 54 mg chol., 166 mg sodium, 43 g carbo., 1 g fiber, 27 g pro.*

Once relegated to home-style cooking, pork chops are appearing more on the menus of upscale restaurants. In this sophisticated recipe, the chop is enhanced by two of winter's best flavors—sweet pears and aromatic fennel.

pork with pear, fennel & cabbage

Start to Finish: 30 minutes   Makes: 4 servings

2	fennel bulbs
4	boneless pork loin chops, cut $1\frac{1}{2}$ inches thick
	Salt
	Ground black pepper
1	tablespoon olive oil
1	small onion, sliced
$2\frac{1}{2}$	cups coarsely chopped cabbage ($\frac{1}{2}$ of small head)
$\frac{1}{2}$	cup pear nectar
$\frac{1}{4}$	cup balsamic vinegar
$\frac{1}{2}$	teaspoon caraway seed
$\frac{1}{2}$	teaspoon dried thyme, crushed
$\frac{1}{4}$	teaspoon salt
$\frac{1}{4}$	teaspoon ground black pepper
$\frac{1}{8}$	teaspoon ground nutmeg
1	tablespoon cornstarch
2	tablespoons water
1	large pear, cored and sliced

1 Trim fennel, discarding the upper stalks, which tend to be tough. Remove feathery leaves; trim bottoms. Cut fennel into thin wedges. Season pork with salt and pepper. In a large skillet heat oil. Brown pork with onion in hot oil about 4 minutes per side. Drain off fat.

2 Arrange fennel wedges and chopped cabbage on top of pork. In a small bowl stir together the pear nectar, the vinegar, caraway seeds, thyme, the $\frac{1}{4}$ teaspoon salt, the $\frac{1}{4}$ teaspoon pepper, and the nutmeg; pour into skillet. Simmer, covered, for 12 to 15 minutes or until tender and pork is no longer pink. Using a slotted spoon, transfer pork and vegetables to platter. Cover with foil to keep warm.

3 Measure pan juices. If necessary, add enough additional pear nectar to equal $1\frac{1}{4}$ cups. Return juices to skillet. In a small bowl stir cornstarch into water until smooth. Stir into skillet juices. Cook and stir over medium heat until thickened and bubbly. Stir in pear; heat through. Spoon sauce over pork and vegetables.

Per serving: 344 cal., 15 g total fat (4 g sat. fat), 77 mg chol., 229 mg sodium, 25 g carbo., 2 g fiber, 26 g pro.

thyme pork chops with cauliflower

Start to Finish: 30 minutes Makes: 4 servings

4   pork rib chops, cut
    ¾ inch thick
4   teaspoons snipped
    fresh thyme or
    1 teaspoon dried
    thyme or Italian
    seasoning, crushed
¼   teaspoon salt
¼   teaspoon ground
    black pepper
    Nonstick cooking
    spray
6   cups packaged
    cauliflower florets
2   small onions, cut into
    wedges
2   tablespoons olive oil

1 Trim fat from chops. In a small bowl stir together thyme, salt, and pepper; sprinkle evenly on both sides of chops. Set chops aside.

2 Coat an unheated very large nonstick skillet with cooking spray. Preheat over medium-high heat. Add cauliflower and onion; cook and stir for 5 minutes or until almost tender. Remove skillet from heat.

3 Push cauliflower and onion to the edge of the skillet. Add oil to the skillet. Arrange the seasoned chops in a single layer in skillet. Return skillet to heat and cook over medium heat for 10 to 15 minutes or until pork chops are 160°F and vegetables are tender, turning chops to brown evenly and stirring the vegetable mixture often.

Per serving: 296 cal., 14 g total fat (3 g sat. fat), 70 mg chol., 389 mg sodium, 11 g carbo., 4 g fiber, 32 g pro.

pork & sweet potato stir-fry

Start to Finish: 25 minutes   Makes: 4 servings

1½   cups uncooked
       instant white rice
¼   cup thinly sliced
       green onion (2)
1   large sweet potato
       (about 12 ounces)
1   medium tart apple
       (such as Granny
       Smith), cored
12   ounces packaged
       pork stir-fry strips
2   to 3 teaspoons
       Jamaican jerk
       seasoning
1   tablespoon cooking
       oil
⅓   cup water

1 Prepare rice according to package directions. Stir half of the green onion into the cooked rice.

2 Meanwhile, peel sweet potato. Cut into quarters lengthwise, then thinly slice crosswise. Place in a microwave-safe pie plate or shallow dish. Cover with vented plastic wrap. Microwave on 100% power (high) for 3 to 4 minutes or until tender, stirring once. Cut apple into 16 wedges. Sprinkle pork strips with Jamaican jerk seasoning; toss to coat.

3 In a wok or large skillet heat oil over medium-high heat. Add pork and stir-fry for 2 minutes (add more oil if necessary during cooking). Add apple and remaining green onion. Stir-fry for 1 to 2 minutes more or until no pink remains in pork strips.

4 Stir in sweet potato and water. Bring to boiling; reduce heat. Simmer, uncovered, for 1 minute. Spoon over hot cooked rice mixture.

Per serving: 365 cal., 9 g total fat (2 g sat. fat), 38 mg chol., 131 mg sodium, 54 g carbo., 3 g fiber, 16 g pro.

tex-mex skillet

Start to Finish: 30 minutes Makes: 4 servings

8 ounces ground pork
4 ounces uncooked
   chorizo sausage
1 10-ounce can diced
   tomatoes and green
   chile peppers,
   undrained
1 cup frozen whole
   kernel corn
¾ cup water
½ cup chopped red
   sweet pepper
1 cup uncooked instant
   rice
½ cup shredded
   cheddar cheese
   or Monterey Jack
   cheese (2 ounces)
   Flour tortillas,
   warmed* (optional)
   Dairy sour cream
   (optional)

1 In a large skillet cook pork and sausage over medium-high heat until brown. Drain off fat. Stir undrained tomatoes, corn, water, and sweet pepper into pork mixture in skillet. Bring to boiling.

2 Stir uncooked rice into pork mixture in skillet. Remove from heat. Top with cheese. Cover and let stand for 5 minutes or until rice is tender. If desired, serve in flour tortillas and top with sour cream.

*Tip: To warm tortillas, wrap them in white microwave-safe paper towels; microwave on 100% power (high) for 15 to 30 seconds or until tortillas are softened. (Or preheat oven to 350°F. Wrap tortillas in foil. Heat in preheated oven for 10 to 15 minutes or until warmed.)

Per serving: 395 cal., 20 g total fat (9 g sat. fat), 66 mg chol., 748 mg sodium, 33 g carbo., 1 g fiber, 21 g pro.

This creamy one-dish meal will be a sure hit with your family. Use strips of chicken in place of the pork, if you like.

pork & noodle skillet dinner

Prep: 15 minutes Cook: 12 minutes Makes: 4 servings

12	ounces lean boneless pork
½	cup chopped onion (1 medium)
1	tablespoon cooking oil
3	cups frozen broccoli, cauliflower, and carrots
4	ounces dried plain or curly medium noodles (3 cups)
1	10.75-ounce can reduced-sodium condensed cream of celery soup
1	cup reduced-sodium chicken broth
¾	cup water
½	teaspoon dried marjoram or thyme, crushed
¼	teaspoon ground black pepper

1 Trim fat from pork. Cut pork into bite-size strips. In a very large skillet cook and stir pork and onion in hot oil over medium-high heat for 3 to 4 minutes or until meat is slightly pink in center.

2 Stir in frozen vegetables, uncooked noodles, soup, broth, water, marjoram, and pepper. Bring to boiling; reduce heat. Simmer, covered, for 12 to 15 minutes or until noodles are tender, stirring occasionally.

Per serving: 317 cal., 12 g total fat (3 g sat. fat), 64 mg chol., 531 mg sodium, 33 g carbo., 3 g fiber, 19 g pro.

sausage & vegetables
with polenta

Start to Finish: 30 minutes Makes: 4 servings

1 tablespoon olive oil
1 1-pound tube
   refrigerated cooked
   polenta, cut into
   12 slices and
   quartered
8 ounces light smoked
   turkey sausage,
   halved lengthwise
   and cut into ½-inch
   slices
2 medium red, green,
   and/or yellow sweet
   peppers, cut into
   bite-size pieces
1 medium onion, cut
   into bite-size pieces
1 cup packaged sliced
   fresh mushrooms
½ cup bottled pasta
   sauce

1 In a very large nonstick skillet heat the oil over medium heat. Add polenta in a single layer; cook for 10 to 12 minutes or until light brown, stirring occasionally. Remove polenta from skillet; keep warm.

2 Add sausage, sweet pepper, onion, and mushrooms to skillet. Cook and stir until sausage is brown and vegetables are crisp-tender. Stir in pasta sauce. Add polenta; gently toss to combine ingredients. Heat through.

Per serving: 260 cal., 9 g total fat (2 g sat. fat), 38 mg chol., 1,088 mg sodium, 32 g carbo., 5 g fiber, 14 g pro.

quick-fix **skillet meals and stir-fries**

pasta with sausage & sweet peppers

Start to Finish: 25 minutes   Makes: 4 servings

8   ounces dried large
     farfalle (bow ties)
12 ounces spicy Italian
     sausage links
2   medium red sweet
     peppers, cut into
     ¾-inch pieces
½   cup vegetable broth
     or beef broth
¼   teaspoon coarsely
     ground black
     pepper
¼   cup snipped fresh
     Italian (flat-leaf)
     parsley

1 Cook pasta according to package directions; drain. Return pasta to saucepan.

2 Meanwhile, cut the sausage into 1-inch pieces. In a large skillet over medium-high heat cook sausage and sweet pepper until sausage is brown. Drain off fat.

3 Stir broth and black pepper into skillet. Bring to boiling. Reduce heat; simmer, uncovered, for 5 minutes. Remove from heat. Pour over pasta; add parsley. Toss gently to mix.

Per serving: 397 cal., 18 g total fat (6 g sat. fat), 94 mg chol., 713 mg sodium, 38 g carbo., 3 g fiber, 24 g pro.

sausage & cavatelli skillet

Start to Finish: 20 minutes Makes: 4 servings

8 ounces dried cavatelli
   (about 1¾ cups)
1 pound bulk Italian
   sausage or ground
   beef
¾ cup chopped green
   sweet pepper
   (1 medium)
1 20-ounce jar pasta
   sauce with
   mushrooms
1 cup shredded
   mozzarella cheese
   (4 ounces)

1 Cook pasta according to package
directions; drain well. Return pasta to pan;
cover and keep warm.

2 Meanwhile, in a large skillet cook sausage
and sweet pepper over medium heat until
sausage is brown. Drain off fat. Stir in pasta
sauce; cook about 2 minutes or until heated
through. Stir in drained pasta. Sprinkle with
cheese. Cook, covered, for 2 minutes more or
until cheese is melted.

Per serving: 677 cal., 32 g total fat (13 g sat. fat), 93 mg chol.,
1,469 mg sodium, 60 g carbo., 4 g fiber, 32 g pro.

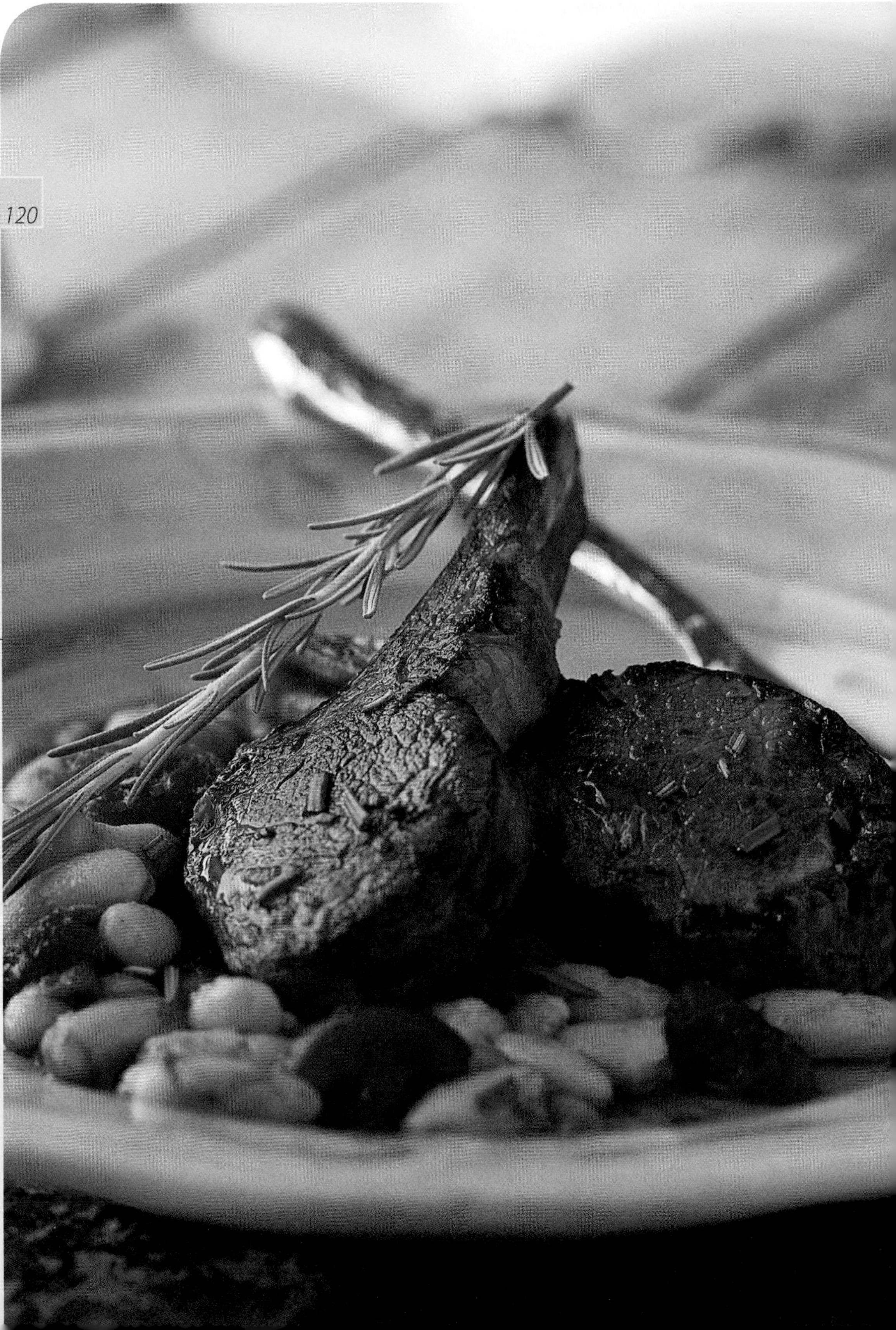

In recent years, Americans have embraced Tuscan-style cooking. Its stylish simplicity and quick-cooking techniques mesh well with a fast-paced lifestyle.

tuscan lamb chop skillet

Start to Finish: 25 minutes Makes: 4 servings

8   lamb rib chops, cut
      1 inch thick (about
      1½ pounds)
    Salt
    Ground black pepper
1   tablespoon olive oil
3   cloves garlic, minced
1   15- to 19-ounce can
      cannellini (white
      kidney) beans,
      rinsed and drained
1   14.5-ounce can
      Italian-style
      stewed tomatoes,
      undrained
2   tablespoons balsamic
      vinegar
2   teaspoons dried
      rosemary, crushed
    Fresh rosemary
      sprigs (optional)

1 Trim fat from lamb chops. Season chops with salt and pepper. In a very large skillet heat oil over medium heat. Add chops; cook for 8 minutes or until medium doneness (160°F), turning once. Transfer chops to a serving plate; keep warm.

2 Stir garlic into drippings in skillet. Cook and stir for 1 minute. Stir in beans, undrained tomatoes, balsamic vinegar, and dried rosemary. Bring to boiling; reduce heat. Simmer, uncovered, for 5 minutes.

3 Return chops to skillet; cover and cook for 2 to 3 minutes to heat through. If desired, garnish with rosemary sprigs.

Per serving: *266 cal., 11 g total fat (3 g sat. fat), 48 mg chol., 576 mg sodium, 24 g carbo., 6 g fiber, 22 g pro.*

easy salmon pasta

Start to Finish: 20 minutes Makes: 4 servings

1½	cups dried rotini, cut ziti, or gemelli pasta
2	cups frozen mixed vegetables
1	10.75-ounce can condensed cheddar cheese soup
½	cup milk
1	tablespoon Dijon-style mustard
½	teaspoon dried dill or 1½ teaspoons fresh snipped dill
⅛	teaspoon ground black pepper
2	6-ounce cans skinless, boneless salmon or tuna, drained
	Fresh dill sprigs (optional)

1 In a large saucepan cook pasta according to package directions, adding mixed vegetables for the last 3 minutes of cooking. Drain well; return to saucepan.

2 Stir soup, milk, mustard, dill, and pepper into pasta mixture. Cook over low heat until heated through, stirring occasionally. Gently fold in salmon; heat through. If desired, garnish with fresh dill sprigs.

Per serving: 315 cal., 10 g total fat (3 g sat. fat), 58 mg chol., 1,049 mg sodium, 34 g carbo., 4 g fiber, 25 g pro.

Feta, the world's favorite Greek cheese, shares its tangy flavor with fish in this colorful combo.

salmon with feta & pasta

Start to Finish: 25 minutes Makes: 5 servings

12 ounces fresh or frozen skinless salmon fillet

8 ounces dried rotini pasta

2 teaspoons olive oil
   Nonstick cooking spray

2 cloves garlic, minced
   Salt

2 cups chopped plum tomato (4 large)

1 cup sliced green onion (8)

⅓ cup sliced pitted ripe olives

3 tablespoons snipped fresh basil

½ teaspoon coarsely ground black pepper

1 4-ounce package crumbled feta cheese

1 Thaw salmon, if frozen. Rinse salmon; pat dry with paper towels. Cut into 1-inch pieces. Cook pasta according to package directions. Drain well. Return pasta to hot pan; add olive oil and toss to coat. Cover to keep warm.

2 Meanwhile, lightly coat an unheated very large nonstick skillet with cooking spray. Preheat skillet over medium-high heat. Add garlic. Cook and stir for 15 seconds. Lightly season salmon pieces with salt. Add salmon to skillet. Cook salmon for 4 to 6 minutes or until salmon begins to flake when tested with a fork, turning salmon pieces occasionally. Stir in tomato, green onion, olives, basil, and pepper. Heat through. Add pasta; toss to mix.

Per serving: 373 cal., 13 g total fat (5 g sat. fat), 56 mg chol., 443 mg sodium, 41 g carbo., 3 g fiber, 24 g pro.

mediterranean
shrimp & couscous

Start to Finish: 25 minutes Makes: 4 servings

1 pound fresh or frozen
    medium shrimp
1 14.5-ounce can diced
    tomatoes with
    garlic and onion,
    undrained
¾ cup water
1 5.6-ounce package
    toasted pine nut
    couscous mix
½ cup golden raisins

1 Thaw shrimp, if frozen. Peel and devein shrimp. Rinse shrimp; pat dry with paper towels. Set aside.

2 In a large skillet combine undrained tomatoes, water, and the seasoning packet from the couscous mix; bring to boiling. Stir in shrimp; cook over high heat for 2 to 3 minutes or until shrimp are opaque. Stir in couscous mix and raisins. Remove from heat. Cover and let stand for 5 minutes or until liquid is absorbed.

Per serving: 338 cal., 4 g total fat (1 g sat. fat), 129 mg chol., 967 mg sodium, 53 g carbo., 6 g fiber, 25 g pro.

The sprightly marriage of lemon and dill is a match made in heaven, and three certainly isn't a crowd when sweet pink shrimp are added to the mix. Rely on the convenience of purchased fully cooked, peeled shrimp to get this dish to the table in less than half an hour.

dilled shrimp with rice

Start to Finish: 25 minutes Makes: 4 servings

1 tablespoon butter or margarine
²⁄₃ cup thinly sliced leek (2 medium)
1½ cups shredded carrot (3 medium)
1 cup fresh pea pods, cut in half
1 teaspoon instant chicken bouillon granules
¼ cup water
12 ounces fully cooked peeled shrimp
2 cups hot cooked rice
1 teaspoon finely shredded lemon peel
1 tablespoon snipped fresh dill or ½ teaspoon dried dill
Dill sprigs (optional)

1 In a large skillet melt butter over medium-high heat. Cook and stir leek, carrot, and pea pods in hot butter for 2 to 3 minutes or until vegetables are crisp-tender.

2 Dissolve bouillon granules in water. Stir shrimp, rice, lemon peel, and dissolved bouillon into skillet. Cook about 5 minutes or until heated through, stirring occasionally. Stir in the snipped dill. To serve, divide rice mixture among 4 bowls. If desired, garnish with dill sprigs.

Per serving: 268 cal., 4 g total fat (1 g sat. fat), 166 mg chol., 478 mg sodium, 35 g carbo., 5 g fiber, 22 g pro.

spicy jalapeño shrimp pasta

Start to Finish: 30 minutes Makes: 4 servings

12 ounces fresh or
   frozen large shrimp
   in shells
8 ounces dried linguine
2 tablespoons olive oil
1 or 2 fresh jalapeño
   chile peppers, finely
   chopped*
2 cloves garlic, minced
½ teaspoon salt
⅛ teaspoon ground
   black pepper
2 cups chopped tomato
   and/or cherry
   tomatoes, halved or
   quartered
   Finely shredded
   Parmesan cheese
   (optional)

1 Thaw shrimp, if frozen. Peel and devein shrimp. Rinse shrimp; pat dry with paper towels. Cook linguine according to package directions; drain well. Return to pan. Cover and keep warm.

2 In a large skillet heat oil over medium-high heat. Add jalapeño pepper, garlic, salt, and black pepper; cook and stir for 1 minute. Add shrimp; cook for 3 minutes more or until shrimp are opaque. Stir in tomato; heat through.

3 Toss cooked linguine with shrimp mixture. If desired, sprinkle with cheese.

*Note: Because chile peppers contain volatile oils that can burn your skin and eyes, avoid direct contact with them as much as possible. When working with chile peppers, wear plastic or rubber gloves. If your bare hands do touch the peppers, wash your hands well with soap and warm water.

Per serving: 363 cal., 9 g total fat (1 g sat. fat), 97 mg chol., 396 mg sodium, 48 g carbo., 3 g fiber, 21 g pro.

Traditional risotto requires a cook's full attention, an ideal not always possible for a busy cook. This simplified main-dish version cooks on its own.

shortcut shrimp risotto

Prep: 10 minutes Cook: 26 minutes Makes: 4 servings

2   14-ounce cans reduced-sodium chicken broth
1⅓ cups Arborio rice or short grain white rice
½   cup finely chopped onion (1 medium)
¾   teaspoon dried basil, crushed
1   10- to 12-ounce package frozen peeled and cooked shrimp, thawed
1½ cups frozen peas, thawed
¼   cup grated Parmesan cheese

1 In a large saucepan combine broth, rice, onion, and dried basil (if using). Bring rice mixture to boiling; reduce heat. Simmer, covered, for 18 minutes.

2 Stir in shrimp and peas. Cook, covered, for 3 minutes more (do not lift lid). Stir in fresh basil (if using). Sprinkle with Parmesan cheese.

Per serving: *325 cal., 3 g total fat (1 g sat. fat), 171 mg chol., 842 mg sodium, 45 g carbo., 3 g fiber, 29 g pro.*

spanish-style rice with seafood

Start to Finish: 25 minutes Makes: 4 servings

1 5.6- to 6.2-ounce
   package Spanish-
   style rice mix
1¾ cups water
1 tablespoon butter or
   margarine
   Several dashes
   bottled hot pepper
   sauce
1 12-ounce package
   frozen peeled,
   deveined shrimp
1 cup frozen peas
½ cup chopped, seeded
   tomato (1 medium)

1 In a large skillet stir together rice mix, water, butter, and hot pepper sauce. Bring to boiling; reduce heat. Simmer, covered, for 5 minutes.

2 Stir shrimp into rice mixture. Return to boiling; reduce heat. Simmer, covered, for 2 to 3 minutes more or until shrimp are opaque. Remove from heat. Stir in peas. Cover and let stand for 10 minutes. Sprinkle with chopped tomato before serving.

Per serving: 282 cal., 5 g total fat (2 g sat. fat), 137 mg chol., 897 mg sodium, 36 g carbo., 3 g fiber, 23 g pro.

ravioli skillet lasagna

Start to Finish: 30 minutes Makes: 4 servings

2 cups bottled tomato-
base pasta sauce
⅓ cup water
1 9-ounce package
refrigerated cheese-
or meat-filled ravioli
1 egg, slightly beaten
1 15-ounce carton
ricotta cheese
¼ cup grated Romano
or Parmesan cheese
1 10-ounce package
frozen chopped
spinach, thawed
and well drained
Grated Romano or
Parmesan cheese

1 Preheat broiler. In a large broilerproof
skillet combine pasta sauce and water.
Bring to boiling. Stir in ravioli. Cook, covered,
over medium heat for 5 minutes or until
ravioli is nearly tender, stirring once to
prevent sticking.

2 Meanwhile, in a medium bowl combine
egg, ricotta cheese, and the ¼ cup
Romano cheese. Dot the ravioli mixture with
small amounts of spinach. Top with spoonfuls
of the ricotta mixture.

3 Cook, covered, over low heat for
10 minutes more or just until ravioli is
tender and ricotta mixture is set.

4 Uncover. Broil 4 to 5 inches from the heat
for 4 to 5 minutes or until top is light
brown. Sprinkle each serving with additional
Romano cheese.

Per serving: 505 cal., 27 g total fat (15 g sat. fat), 171 mg chol.,
910 mg sodium, 38 g carbo., 4 g fiber, 30 g pro.

italian rice skillet

Start to Finish: 20 minutes Makes: 4 servings

1   19-ounce can ready-
    to-serve hearty
    tomato soup
1   15- to 19-ounce can
    cannellini (white
    kidney) beans,
    rinsed and drained
2   cups frozen cut green
    beans
1   cup uncooked instant
    white rice
½   cup water
⅓   cup finely shredded
    Parmesan cheese

1 In a large skillet combine soup, cannellini beans, green beans, uncooked rice, and water. Bring to boiling; reduce heat. Simmer, covered, for 10 minutes or until rice and green beans are tender, stirring frequently.

2 Sprinkle with Parmesan cheese before serving.

Per serving: 271 cal., 4 g total fat (2 g sat. fat), 8 mg chol., 685 mg sodium, 51 g carbo., 9 g fiber, 14 g pro.

mixed bean
& portobello ragoût

Start to Finish: 20 minutes Makes: 4 servings

1 10-ounce package
   frozen baby lima
   beans
1½ cups frozen cut green
   beans
1 tablespoon olive oil or
   cooking oil
3 cups packaged sliced
   fresh portobello
   mushrooms or
   sliced button
   mushrooms
1 15-ounce can
   chickpeas
   (garbanzo beans),
   rinsed and drained
1 14.5-ounce can
   Italian-style
   stewed tomatoes,
   undrained and cut
   up
1 8-ounce can tomato
   sauce

1 In a large saucepan cook lima beans and green beans according to package directions; drain and return to the pan.

2 Meanwhile, in a large skillet heat oil over medium-high heat. Add mushrooms; cook for 5 minutes or until tender, stirring occasionally. Stir in chickpeas, undrained tomatoes, and tomato sauce; heat through. Add mushroom mixture to lima beans and green beans in saucepan. Stir to combine.

Per serving: 289 cal., 5 g total fat (1 g sat. fat), 0 mg chol., 934 mg sodium, 50 g carbo., 12 g fiber, 14 g pro.

thai chicken pasta

Start to Finish: 25 minutes Makes: 4 servings

6 ounces dried angel
   hair pasta
3 cups cooked chicken
   cut into strips
   (about 1 pound)
1 14-ounce can
   unsweetened
   coconut milk
⅓ cup thinly sliced
   green onion
⅓ cup packaged
   shredded carrot
   (1 small)
2 teaspoons Thai
   seasoning
½ cup chopped dry-
   roasted peanuts
   Fresh cilantro leaves
   (optional)

1 Cook pasta according to package
directions; drain well. Return pasta to pan;
keep warm.

2 Meanwhile, in a large skillet combine
chicken, coconut milk, green onion,
carrot, and Thai seasoning. Cook and gently
stir over medium heat until heated through.
Pour hot chicken mixture over cooked pasta
in pan. Toss gently to coat. Sprinkle servings
with peanuts and, if desired, cilantro leaves.

Per serving: 653 cal., 36 g total fat (20 g sat. fat), 93 mg chol.,
287 mg sodium, 41 g carbo., 3 g fiber, 42 g pro.

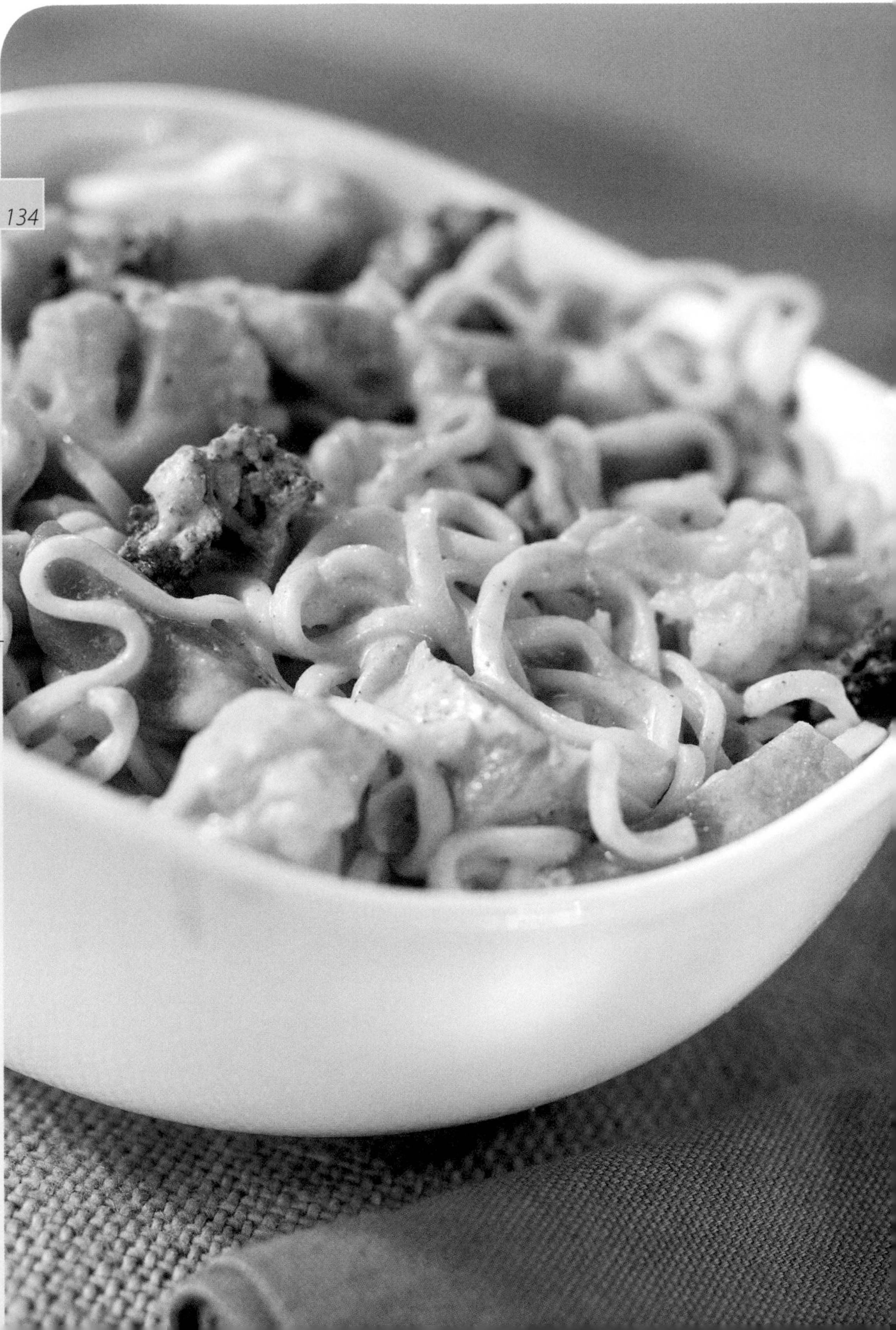

curried chicken & noodles

Start to Finish: 15 minutes Makes: 4 servings

5   cups water
2   3-ounce packages
    chicken-flavor
    ramen noodles
2   cups frozen broccoli,
    cauliflower, and
    carrots
½   cup coconut milk
1   to 2 teaspoons curry
    powder
    Dash cayenne pepper
1   cup cubed cooked
    chicken breast
    (5 ounces)

1 In a large saucepan bring water to boiling. Add ramen noodles with seasoning packets and frozen vegetables to saucepan. Cook, uncovered, for 3 minutes or until noodles and vegetables are tender. Drain. Return noodle mixture to saucepan.

2 Stir together coconut milk, curry powder, and cayenne pepper. Stir coconut milk mixture and chicken into noodle mixture in saucepan. Heat through.

Per serving: 333 cal., 15 g total fat (10 g sat. fat), 30 mg chol., 934 mg sodium, 32 g carbo., 3 g fiber, 18 g pro.

Thanks to bottled stir-fry sauce, this is a meal you can whip up during the busy workweek. If you like, substitute regular button mushrooms for shiitakes.

ginger noodle bowl

Start to Finish: 25 minutes   Makes: 3 servings

2   cups dried Chinese
     egg noodles or
     fine egg noodles
     (4 ounces)
¼   teaspoon ground
     ginger
⅓   cup bottled stir-fry
     sauce
2   teaspoons peanut oil
     or cooking oil
1   cup fresh sugar snap
     peas or pea pods,
     tips and stems
     removed and cut up
1   cup sliced fresh
     shiitake mushrooms
1   small red sweet
     pepper, cut into
     bite-size strips
5   ounces cooked
     chicken breast, cut
     into strips (about
     1 cup)
2   tablespoons cashews,
     broken

1 Cook noodles according to package
directions. Drain; set aside. Stir ginger into
the stir-fry sauce; set aside.

2 In a large skillet heat oil over medium-
high heat. Add sugar snap peas,
mushrooms, and sweet pepper; cook and stir
for 3 to 5 minutes or until crisp-tender. Stir in
cooked noodles, chicken, cashews, and stir-fry
sauce mixture; heat through.

Per serving: 362 cal., 10 g total fat (2 g sat. fat), 77 mg chol.,
734 mg sodium, 42 g carbo., 4 g fiber, 25 g pro.

orange chicken & fried rice

Start to Finish: 25 minutes Makes: 4 servings

1   6-ounce package
     Oriental-flavored
     fried rice mix
2   tablespoons butter or
     margarine
1   pound packaged
     chicken breast stir-
     fry strips
8   green onions, bias-
     cut into 1-inch
     pieces
2   cloves garlic, minced,
     or ¼ teaspoon garlic
     powder
1   teaspoon ground
     ginger
1   tablespoon frozen
     orange juice
     concentrate,
     thawed
¼   cup chopped
     cashews (optional)

1 Cook rice according to package directions.

2 Meanwhile, in a large skillet melt butter over medium-high heat. Add chicken strips, green onion, garlic, and ginger; cook and stir for 3 to 5 minutes or until chicken is no longer pink.

3 Stir orange juice concentrate into cooked rice. Stir rice mixture into chicken mixture in skillet. Cook and stir until heated through. If desired, sprinkle servings with cashews.

Per serving: 396 cal., 13 g total fat (5 g sat. fat), 82 mg chol., 985 mg sodium, 38 g carbo., 2 g fiber, 32 g pro.

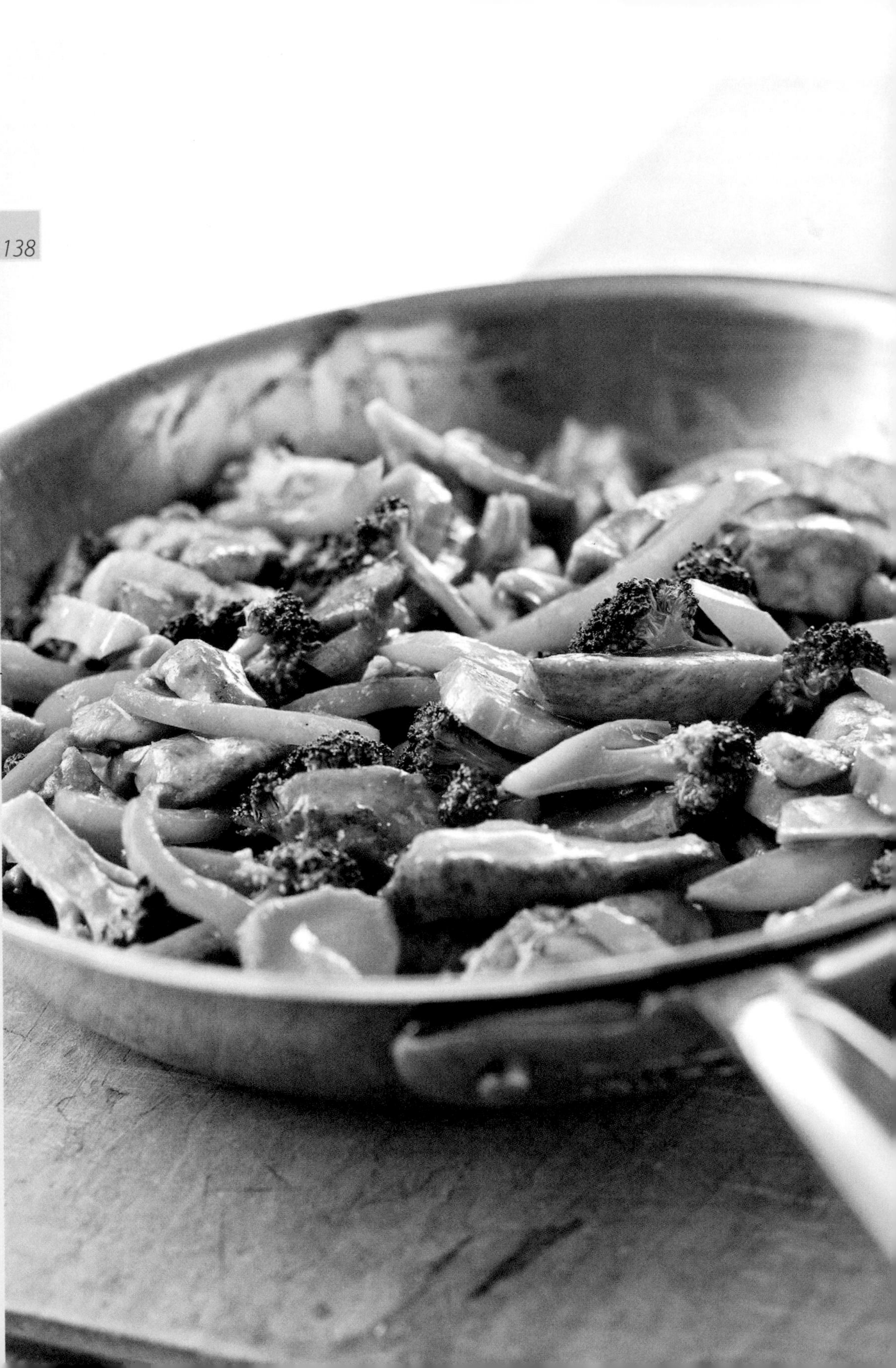

Thirty minutes to a fresh, homemade stir-fry that beats takeout any day! This is especially true when the results are seasoned with hoisin sauce and sesame oil—two super-convenient ways to bring complex, aromatic flavors to a dish.

chicken & broccoli stir-fry

Start to Finish: 30 minutes Makes: 4 servings

½ cup water
2 tablespoons soy sauce
2 tablespoons hoisin sauce
2 teaspoons cornstarch
1 teaspoon grated fresh ginger
1 teaspoon toasted sesame oil
1 pound broccoli
1 yellow sweet pepper
2 tablespoons cooking oil
12 ounces skinless, boneless chicken, cut into bite-size pieces
Chow mein noodles or hot cooked rice
Toasted sesame seeds (optional)
Hoisin sauce (optional)

1 For sauce, in a small bowl stir together water, soy sauce, the 2 tablespoons hoisin sauce, the cornstarch, ginger, and sesame oil. Set aside.

2 Cut florets from broccoli stems and separate florets into small pieces. Cut broccoli stems crosswise into ¼ inch slices. Cut sweet pepper into short, thin strips.

3 In a wok or large skillet heat 1 tablespoon of the cooking oil over medium-high heat. Cook and stir broccoli stems in hot oil for 1 minute. Add broccoli florets and sweet pepper; cook and stir for 3 to 4 minutes or until crisp-tender. Remove from wok; set aside.

4 Add remaining cooking oil to wok or skillet. Add chicken; cook and stir for 2 to 3 minutes or until no longer pink. Push chicken from center of wok. Stir sauce; pour into center of wok. Cook and stir until thickened and bubbly. Return cooked vegetables to wok. Stir together to coat all ingredients with sauce. Cook and stir for 1 minute more or until heated through. Serve over chow mein noodles or rice. If desired, garnish with toasted sesame seeds and serve with additional hoisin sauce.

Per serving: *378 cal., 16 g total fat (3 g sat. fat), 49 mg chol., 877 mg sodium, 31 g carbo., 6 g fiber, 29 g pro.*

If you're preparing this dish for guests, you can roll the turkey bundles ahead; cover and refrigerate.

asparagus-stuffed
turkey rolls

Prep: 25 minutes Cook: 8 minutes Makes: 4 servings

2	turkey breast tenderloin steaks (about 1 pound)
16	asparagus spears, woody ends removed
	Nonstick cooking spray
²/₃	cup reduced-sodium chicken broth
2	tablespoons lemon juice
2	tablespoons orange juice
¼	teaspoon salt-free seasoning blend
⅛	teaspoon ground black pepper
1	tablespoon cold water
2	teaspoons cornstarch
	Slivered orange or lemon peel (optional)
	Hot cooked pasta or rice (optional)

1 Cut turkey breast tenderloins in half horizontally to make 4 steaks. Place each turkey steak between two pieces of plastic wrap. Working from the center to edges, pound lightly with the flat side of a meat mallet to ¼-inch thickness. Remove plastic wrap. Arrange 4 asparagus spears on the short end of each turkey piece. Roll up turkey; if necessary, secure with wooden toothpicks.

2 Coat a large nonstick skillet with cooking spray. Heat over medium heat. Add turkey rolls and cook, turning to brown evenly. Add chicken broth, lemon juice, orange juice, seasoning blend, and pepper. Bring to boiling; reduce heat. Simmer, covered, for 8 to 10 minutes or until turkey is no longer pink. Transfer to a platter; remove toothpicks.

3 For sauce, in a small bowl stir together water and cornstarch; add to liquid in skillet. Cook and stir until thickened and bubbly. Cook and stir for 2 minutes more. Return turkey rolls to skillet; cook, covered, for 2 to 3 minutes to heat through. Serve the turkey rolls with sauce. If desired, sprinkle with slivered peel and serve with hot cooked pasta.

Per serving: *137 cal., 3 g total fat (1 g sat. fat), 50 mg chol., 154 mg sodium, 4 g carbo., 1 g fiber, 23 g pro.*

five-spice turkey stir-fry

Start to Finish: 25 minutes Makes: 4 servings

1 4.4-ounce package
     beef lo-mein noodle
     mix
12 ounces turkey breast
     tenderloin, cut into
     thin bite-size strips
¼ teaspoon five-spice
     powder
¼ teaspoon salt
¼ teaspoon ground
     black pepper
2 tablespoons cooking
     oil
½ of a 16-ounce
     package frozen
     sweet pepper
     and onion stir-fry
     vegetables
2 tablespoons chopped
     honey-roasted
     peanuts or plain
     peanuts

1 Prepare noodle mix according to package directions; set aside. In a small bowl toss together turkey strips, five-spice powder, salt, and pepper; set aside.

2 Pour 1 tablespoon of the oil into a wok or large skillet. Heat over medium-high heat. Carefully add frozen vegetables to wok; cook and stir for 3 minutes. Remove vegetables from wok. Add remaining 1 tablespoon oil to hot wok. Add turkey mixture; cook and stir for 2 to 3 minutes or until turkey is no longer pink. Return vegetables to wok. Cook and stir about 1 minute more or until heated through. Add noodles; toss gently to coat.

3 To serve, sprinkle each serving with peanuts.

Per serving: 314 cal., 11 g total fat (2 g sat. fat), 76 mg chol., 670 mg sodium, 26 g carbo., 3 g fiber, 27 g pro.

All the ingredients for this apple-studded pilaf simmer in a single skillet.

smoked turkey & wild rice pilaf

Prep: 15 minutes   Cook: 43 minutes   Makes: 4 servings

1	tablespoon butter or margarine
1	cup sliced celery (2 stalks)
¼	cup chopped onion
⅓	cup uncooked wild rice, rinsed and drained
1	14-ounce can reduced-sodium chicken broth
⅓	cup uncooked long grain rice
12	ounces cooked smoked turkey, cubed
1⅓	cups chopped red-skinned apple (2 medium)
1	large carrot, peeled and cut into matchstick-size strips
2	tablespoons snipped fresh parsley

1 In a large skillet melt butter. Add celery and onion; cook about 10 minutes or until tender. Add uncooked wild rice; cook and stir for 3 minutes. Add broth. Bring to boiling; reduce heat. Simmer, covered, for 20 minutes. Stir in long grain rice. Return to boiling; reduce heat. Simmer, covered, for 20 minutes more or until wild rice and long grain rice are tender and most of the liquid is absorbed.

2 Stir in turkey, apple, and carrot. Cook, uncovered, for 3 to 4 minutes more or until heated through and liquid is absorbed. Stir in parsley.

Per serving: 289 cal., 7 g total fat (2 g sat. fat), 44 mg chol., 1,231 mg sodium, 37 g carbo., 3 g fiber, 21 g pro.

blackened beef stir-fry

Start to Finish: 25 minutes Makes: 4 servings

12 ounces packaged
      beef stir-fry strips
2¼ teaspoons blackened
      steak seasoning
⅔ cup water
2 tablespoons tomato
      paste
2 teaspoons cornstarch
½ teaspoon instant beef
      bouillon granules
1 tablespoon cooking
      oil
1 16-ounce package
      frozen stir-fry
      vegetables (any
      combination)

1 Sprinkle steak strips with 2 teaspoons of the blackened steak seasoning; toss to coat well. Set beef strips aside.

2 For sauce, in a small bowl stir together the remaining ¼ teaspoon blackened steak seasoning, the water, tomato paste, cornstarch, and bouillon granules. Set aside.

3 In a wok or large skillet heat oil over medium-high heat. Add stir-fry vegetables. Cook and stir for 2 to 3 minutes or until crisp-tender. Remove vegetables from wok. Add beef strips to hot wok. (Add more oil as necessary during cooking.) Cook and stir for 2 to 3 minutes or until beef is slightly pink in center.

4 Push beef from center of wok. Stir sauce; add to center of wok. Cook and stir until thickened and bubbly. Return vegetables to wok. Stir together to coat all ingredients with sauce. Heat through.

Per serving: 190 cal., 6 g total fat (2 g sat. fat), 40 mg chol., 373 mg sodium, 10 g carbo., 3 g fiber, 21 g pro.

This version of the classic Szechwan recipe is a bit less pungent than you might find at a Chinese restaurant. We've also added spinach and water chestnuts for extra color and crunch.

orange-beef stir-fry

Prep: 30 minutes Cook: 6 minutes Makes: 4 servings

12	ounces beef top round steak
1	teaspoon finely shredded orange peel
½	cup orange juice
1	tablespoon cornstarch
1	tablespoon soy sauce
1	teaspoon sugar
1	teaspoon instant beef bouillon granules
2	tablespoons cooking oil
4	green onions, bias-sliced into 1-inch pieces
1	clove garlic, minced
5	cups coarsely shredded fresh spinach (5 to 6 ounces)
½	of an 8-ounce can sliced water chestnuts, drained
	Hot cooked rice

1 Trim fat from beef. Thinly slice beef across the grain into bite-size strips. Set aside. For sauce, in a small bowl stir together finely shredded orange peel, orange juice, cornstarch, soy sauce, sugar, and bouillon granules. Set aside.

2 In a wok or large skillet heat 1 tablespoon of the oil over medium-high heat. Add green onion and garlic; cook and stir in hot oil for 1 minute. Remove onion mixture from wok using a slotted spoon. Carefully add remaining 1 tablespoon oil to wok. Add beef to hot wok. (Add more oil as necessary during cooking.) Cook and stir for 2 to 3 minutes or to desired doneness. Push beef from center of wok.

3 Stir sauce. Add sauce to center of wok. Cook and stir until thickened and bubbly. Return green onion mixture to wok. Add spinach and drained water chestnuts. Stir all ingredients together to coat with sauce. Cook, covered, about 1 minute more or until heated through. Serve over hot cooked rice. If desired, garnish with slivered *orange peel*.

Per serving: *366 cal., 9 g total fat (2 g sat. fat), 37 mg chol., 527 mg sodium, 45 g carbo., 3 g fiber, 25 g pro.*

beef & asparagus sauté

Start to Finish: 20 minutes Makes: 4 servings

12   ounces fresh
      asparagus
2   teaspoons olive oil
1   pound packaged beef
      stir-fry strips
      Salt and ground black
      pepper
½   cup shredded carrot
      (1 medium)
1   teaspoon dried
      herbes dc Provence,
      crushed
½   cup dry Marsala
¼   teaspoon finely
      shredded lemon
      peel

1 Snap off and discard woody bases from asparagus. Bias-slice asparagus into 2-inch pieces; set aside.

2 In a large nonstick skillet heat 1 teaspoon of the oil over medium-high heat. Add half of the beef to hot oil. Sprinkle with salt and black pepper. Cook and stir for 3 minutes. Remove beef from skillet. Repeat with the remaining 1 teaspoon oil and the remaining beef.

3 Return all of the beef to the skillet. Add asparagus, carrot, and herbes de Provence; cook and stir for 2 minutes more. Add Marsala and lemon peel; reduce heat. Cook for 3 to 5 minutes more or until beef is desired doneness and asparagus is crisp-tender.

Per serving: 327 cal., 7 g total fat (2 g sat. fat), 69 mg chol., 209 mg sodium, 29 g carbo., 2 g fiber, 28 g pro.

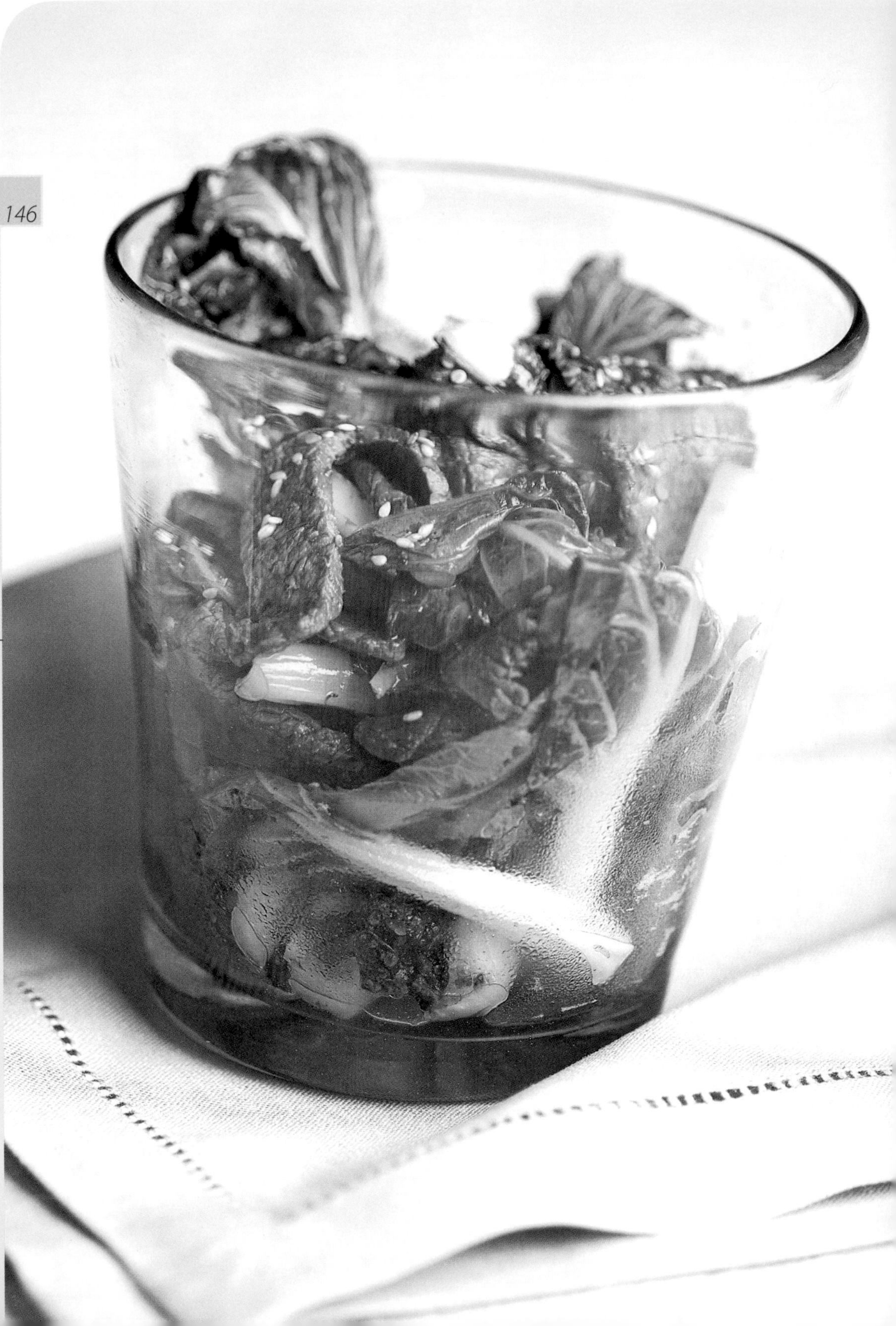

beef & bok choy

Start to Finish: 20 minutes Makes: 4 servings

4 teaspoons toasted
   sesame oil
12 ounces packaged
   beef stir-fry strips
1 teaspoon red chili
   pepper paste
6 cups sliced bok choy
2 cloves garlic, minced
1 tablespoon reduced-
   sodium soy sauce
2 teaspoons sesame
   seeds, toasted

1 In a very large nonstick skillet heat
2 teaspoons of the oil over medium-high
heat. Add beef and chili paste to hot oil.
Stir-fry for 3 minutes or until beef is desired
doneness. Remove skillet from heat. Reduce
heat to medium. Remove beef from pan with
a slotted spoon, reserving liquid in pan; cover
beef to keep warm.

2 Add remaining 2 teaspoons oil to skillet.
Add bok choy and garlic; stir-fry for 2 to
3 minutes or until bok choy is crisp-tender.
Transfer to serving dish. Top with warm beef
mixture. Drizzle with soy sauce and sprinkle
with sesame seeds.

Per serving: 179 cal., 9 g total fat (2 g sat. fat), 52 mg chol.,
271 mg sodium, 4 g carbo., 1 g fiber, 20 g pro.

4

fireside

When winter rolls around, nothing hits the spot like a piping hot bowl of soup. These picks will keep you warm straight through to spring!

soups

& stews

fireside **soups & stews**

chicken & dumpling soup

Start to Finish: 30 minutes Makes: 6 servings

5 cups reduced-sodium
 chicken broth
1 cup sliced carrot
 (2 medium)
1 cup chopped celery
 (2 stalks)
⅛ teaspoon ground
 black pepper
1½ cups chopped cooked
 chicken (8 ounces)
1½ cups packaged
 biscuit mix
½ cup milk

1 In a medium saucepan combine broth, carrot, celery, and pepper. Bring to boiling; reduce heat. Simmer, covered, for 10 minutes. Stir in chicken.

2 Meanwhile, for dumplings, in a medium bowl combine biscuit mix and milk. Stir just until combined.

3 Spoon dough in 12 mounds on top of hot chicken mixture. Cook, covered, for 10 minutes or until a toothpick inserted into dumplings comes out clean.

Per serving: 222 cal., 8 g total fat (2 g sat. fat), 33 mg chol., 916 mg sodium, 23 g carbo., 1 g fiber, 15 g pro.

pasta & bean chicken soup

Start to Finish: 25 minutes Makes: 5 servings

3½ cups reduced-sodium
    chicken broth
1 19-ounce can
    cannellini beans
    (white kidney
    beans) or one
    15-ounce can Great
    Northern beans,
    rinsed and drained
1 14.5-ounce can diced
    tomatoes with
    onion and garlic or
    diced tomatoes with
    basil, oregano, and
    garlic, undrained
2 cups chopped cooked
    chicken (10 ounces)
1½ cups thinly sliced
    carrot (3 medium)
1 cup water
1 cup dried ditalini or
    tiny bow tie pasta
    (4 ounces)
¼ cup purchased pesto

1 In a large saucepan combine broth, beans, undrained tomatoes, chicken, carrot, water, and pasta.

2 Bring to boiling; reduce heat. Simmer, covered, for 10 minutes or until pasta is tender. Stir in pesto.

Per serving: 323 cal., 12 g total fat (1 g sat. fat), 46 mg chol., 914 mg sodium, 33 g carbo., 5 g fiber, 25 g pro.

chicken & salsa soup

Start to Finish: 25 minutes Makes: 4 servings

1¾ cups water
1 14-ounce can
  reduced-sodium
  chicken broth
8 ounces skinless,
  boneless chicken
  breast halves or
  thighs, cut into
  bite-size pieces
1 to 2 teaspoons chili
  powder
1 11-ounce can whole
  kernel corn with
  sweet peppers,
  drained
1 cup chunky salsa
3 cups broken tortilla
  chips
½ cup shredded
  Monterey Jack
  cheese with
  jalapeño peppers
  (2 ounces)

1 In a 3-quart saucepan combine water, broth, chicken, and chili powder. Bring to boiling; reduce heat. Simmer, covered, for 8 minutes. Add corn. Simmer, uncovered, for 5 minutes more or until chicken is no longer pink. Stir in salsa; heat through.

2 To serve, ladle soup into bowls. Top with tortilla chips and sprinkle with cheese.

Per serving: *284 cal., 6 g total fat (3 g sat. fat), 45 mg chol., 1,153 mg sodium, 27 g carbo., 3 g fiber, 22 g pro.*

easy oriental chicken soup

Start to Finish: 20 minutes Makes: 3 servings

1 tablespoon cooking
   oil
8 ounces packaged
   chicken breast stir-
   fry strips
3 cups water
½ of a 16-ounce
   package frozen
   broccoli, carrots,
   and water
   chestnuts (2 cups)
1 3-ounce package
   chicken-flavor
   ramen noodles
2 tablespoons reduced-
   sodium soy sauce

1 In a large saucepan heat oil over medium-high heat. Add chicken; cook and stir for 2 to 3 minutes or until no longer pink. Remove from heat. Drain off fat.

2 Carefully add water, vegetables, and seasoning packet from ramen noodles to chicken in saucepan. Bring to boiling. Break up noodles; stir noodles into soup. Reduce heat. Simmer, covered, for 3 minutes. Stir in soy sauce.

Per serving: 254 cal., 8 g total fat (1 g sat. fat), 63 mg chol., 829 mg sodium, 22 g carbo., 5 g fiber, 22 g pro.

chicken soup with spinach & orzo

Start to Finish: 20 minutes Makes: 6 servings

4 14-ounce cans
   reduced-sodium
   chicken broth
1 cup dried orzo pasta
12 ounces fresh
   asparagus spears,
   trimmed and bias-
   sliced into 1½-inch
   pieces
3 cups chopped fresh
   spinach, Swiss
   chard, or kale,
   or one 10-ounce
   package frozen
   chopped spinach,
   thawed and well
   drained
1½ cups chopped fresh
   tomato (3 medium)
1½ cups shredded
   cooked chicken
   (8 ounces)
⅓ cup cubed cooked
   ham
   Salt
   Ground black pepper
   Snipped fresh chives
   and/or parsley
   (optional)

1 In a covered 5- to 6-quart Dutch oven bring broth to boiling. Add orzo. Return to boiling; reduce heat. Simmer, uncovered, for 6 minutes. Add asparagus; simmer about 2 minutes more or until orzo is tender and asparagus is crisp-tender.

2 Stir in spinach, tomato, chicken, and ham; heat through. Season to taste with salt and pepper. If desired, sprinkle with chives.

Per serving: 221 cal., 4 g total fat (1 g sat. fat), 35 mg chol., 837 mg sodium, 28 g carbo., 3 g fiber, 20 g pro.

If you can, seek out the less common varieties of mushrooms, such as the meaty shiitake or the earthy porcini. They'll add an exotic richness to the soup. Serve with crisp breadsticks.

turkey & mushroom soup

Start to Finish: 35 minutes Makes: 4 servings

2	cups sliced fresh mushrooms (such as crimini, shiitake, porcini, or button)
½	cup thinly sliced celery (1 stalk)
½	cup thinly sliced carrot (1 medium)
⅓	cup chopped onion (1 small)
1	tablespoon butter or margarine
4½	cups water
1	tablespoon instant chicken bouillon granules
⅛	teaspoon ground black pepper
½	cup dried orzo pasta
1½	cups chopped cooked turkey (8 ounces)
2	tablespoons snipped fresh parsley
1	teaspoon snipped fresh thyme

1 In a large saucepan cook mushrooms, celery, carrot, and onion in hot butter until crisp-tender. Add water, bouillon granules, and pepper.

2 Bring to boiling; stir in orzo. Return to boiling; reduce heat. Simmer, uncovered, for 5 to 8 minutes or until orzo is tender but still firm. Stir in turkey, parsley, and thyme; heat through.

Per serving: 199 cal., 6 g total fat (2 g sat. fat), 40 mg chol., 767 mg sodium, 17 g carbo., 2 g fiber, 19 g pro.

turkey ravioli soup

Start to Finish: 25 minutes Makes: 6 servings

6 cups reduced-sodium
   chicken broth
¾ cup chopped red
   sweet pepper
   (1 medium)
½ cup chopped onion
   (1 medium)
1½ teaspoons dried
   Italian seasoning,
   crushed
1½ cups chopped cooked
   turkey (8 ounces)
1 9-ounce package
   refrigerated light
   cheese ravioli
2 cups shredded fresh
   spinach
   Finely shredded
   Parmesan cheese
   (optional)

1 In a Dutch oven combine broth, sweet pepper, onion, and Italian seasoning. Bring to boiling; reduce heat. Simmer, covered, for 5 minutes.

2 Add turkey and ravioli to broth mixture. Return to boiling; reduce heat. Simmer, uncovered, about 6 minutes or just until ravioli is tender. Stir in spinach. If desired, sprinkle servings with cheese.

Per serving: 246 cal., 7 g total fat (3 g sat. fat), 48 mg chol., 879 mg sodium, 24 g carbo., 2 g fiber, 22 g pro.

quick-fix turkey & rice soup

Start to Finish: 25 minutes Makes: 6 servings

4 cups chicken broth
1 cup water
¼ teaspoon dried Italian
   seasoning, crushed
¼ teaspoon ground
   black pepper
2 cups frozen mixed
   vegetables
1 cup uncooked instant
   rice
2 cups chopped cooked
   turkey or chicken
   (10 ounces)
1 14.5-ounce can
   diced tomatoes,
   undrained

1 In a large saucepan or Dutch oven, combine broth, water, Italian seasoning, and pepper. Bring to boiling.

2 Stir mixed vegetables and rice into broth mixture in saucepan. Return to boiling; reduce heat. Simmer, covered, for 8 to 10 minutes or until vegetables are tender. Stir in turkey and undrained tomatoes; heat through.

Per serving: *213 cal., 4 g total fat (1 g sat. fat), 35 mg chol., 687 mg sodium, 24 g carbo., 2 g fiber, 20 g pro.*

italian beef soup

Start to Finish: 25 minutes Makes: 6 servings

1 pound ground beef
2 14-ounce cans beef
   broth
1 16-ounce package
   frozen broccoli and/
   or cauliflower
1 14.5-ounce can
   diced tomatoes,
   undrained
1 5.5-ounce can tomato
   juice (¾ cup)
1 cup dried rotini,
   wagon wheel, or
   other small pasta
½ cup purchased basil
   pesto

1 In a 4-quart Dutch oven cook ground beef over medium heat until brown. Drain off fat. Stir in broth, frozen vegetables, undrained tomatoes, and tomato juice.

2 Bring to boiling; stir in pasta. Reduce heat. Simmer, covered, for 10 minutes or until vegetables and pasta are tender. Stir in pesto.

Per serving: 317 cal., 16 g total fat (5 g sat. fat), 54 mg chol., 905 mg sodium, 20 g carbo., 4 g fiber, 21 g pro.

Keep the ingredients for this recipe on hand and you can whip up a hearty Italian soup for your family in no time.

meatball soup with tiny pasta

Prep: 10 minutes Cook: 10 minutes Makes: 4 servings

1 14.5-ounce can diced tomatoes with onion and garlic, undrained
1 14-ounce can beef broth
1½ cups water
½ teaspoon dried Italian seasoning, crushed
½ of a 16-ounce package frozen cooked Italian-style meatballs
1 cup frozen Italian blend vegetables (zucchini, carrots, cauliflower, lima beans, and Italian beans) or desired frozen mixed vegetables
½ cup small dried pasta (such as tripolini, farfallini, ditalini, stellini, or orzo)
2 tablespoons finely shredded or grated Parmesan cheese

1 In a large saucepan stir together undrained tomatoes, broth, water, and Italian seasoning; bring to boiling.

2 Add meatballs, frozen vegetables, and uncooked pasta. Return to boiling; reduce heat. Simmer, covered, for 10 minutes or until pasta and vegetables are tender. Sprinkle servings with Parmesan cheese.

Per serving: 280 cal., 14 g total fat (6 g sat. fat), 38 mg chol., 1,335 mg sodium, 23 g carbo., 4 g fiber, 15 g pro.

easy beef & noodle soup

Start to Finish: 25 minutes Makes: 4 servings

1   pound ground beef
2½ cups water
1   10.75-ounce can
      condensed cream of
      onion soup
1   10.5-ounce can
      condensed beef
      broth
1½ cups dried medium
      noodles
2   tablespoons dried
      parsley flakes
    Finely shredded
      Parmesan cheese
      (optional)

1 In a large saucepan cook ground beef over medium-high heat until brown. Drain off fat. Stir in water, onion soup, broth, uncooked noodles, and parsley flakes.

2 Bring to boiling; reduce heat. Simmer, covered, for 5 minutes or until noodles are tender, stirring occasionally. If desired, sprinkle servings with cheese.

Per serving: 357 cal., 19 g total fat (7 g sat. fat), 98 mg chol., 1,218 mg sodium, 19 g carbo., 1 g fiber, 27 g pro.

The recipe is much like Mexico's famed posole—a hominy and pork soup often served around Christmastime.

mexican pork & hominy soup

Prep: 20 minutes Cook: 1 hour 20 minutes Makes: 6 servings

12 ounces lean boneless pork
1   tablespoon cooking oil
1   cup chopped onion (1 large)
2   cloves garlic, minced
3   cups chicken broth
1   14.5-ounce can tomatoes, undrained and cut up
2   teaspoons dried oregano, crushed
¼   teaspoon ground cumin
¼   teaspoon ground black pepper
1   14.5-ounce can golden hominy, drained, or one 10-ounce package frozen whole kernel corn, thawed
1   cup sliced carrot (2 medium)
½   cup sliced celery (1 stalk)
    Shredded Mexican cheese or Monterey Jack cheese with jalapeño peppers (optional)

1 Trim fat from pork. Cut pork into ½-inch pieces. In a large saucepan heat oil. Brown pork in hot oil over medium-high heat. Remove pork from saucepan; set aside. Add onion and garlic to drippings in pan. Cook over medium heat until tender. Drain fat. Return pork to saucepan.

2 Stir in broth, undrained tomatoes, oregano, cumin, and pepper. Bring to boiling; reduce heat. Simmer, covered, for 1 hour. Stir in hominy, carrot, and celery. Return to boiling; reduce heat. Simmer, covered, for 20 to 30 minutes more or until vegetables are tender. If desired, garnish servings with cheese.

Per serving: 205 cal., 10 g total fat (3 g sat. fat), 32 mg chol., 680 mg sodium, 15 g carbo., 2 g fiber, 14 g pro.

Tender chunks of baked potato and a liberal sprinkling of shredded cheese transform ordinary cream of potato soup into an irresistible, company-special dish.

baked potato soup

Prep: 20 minutes Bake: 40 minutes Cook: 15 minutes Oven: 425°F
Makes: 4 servings

2 large baking potatoes (about 8 ounces each)
3 tablespoons thinly sliced green onion
3 tablespoons butter or margarine
3 tablespoons all-purpose flour
2 teaspoons snipped fresh dill or chives or ¼ teaspoon dried dill
¼ teaspoon salt
¼ teaspoon ground black pepper
4 cups milk
1¼ cups shredded American cheese (5 ounces)
3 tablespoons thinly sliced green onion
4 slices bacon, crisp-cooked, drained, and crumbled

1 Preheat oven to 425°F. Scrub potatoes thoroughly with a brush; pat dry with paper towels. Prick potatoes with a fork. Bake for 40 to 60 minutes or until tender. Let cool. Cut potatoes in half lengthwise; gently scoop out each potato. Break up any large pieces of potato. Discard potato skins.

2 In a large saucepan cook 3 tablespoons green onion in hot butter until tender; stir in flour, dill, salt, and pepper. Add milk all at once. Cook and stir for 12 to 15 minutes or until thickened and bubbly. Add the potato pulp and 1 cup of the shredded cheese; stir until cheese melts. Top servings with the remaining ¼ cup shredded cheese, 3 tablespoons green onion, and bacon.

Make-Ahead Directions: Prepare as directed in Step 1. Place potato pulp in an airtight container. Cover and refrigerate for up to 24 hours. Continue as directed in Step 2.

Per serving: *505 cal., 28 g total fat (17 g sat. fat), 85 mg chol., 1,027 mg sodium, 42 g carbo., 2 g fiber, 22 g pro.*

A subtle touch of tarragon enhances the flavor of this chunky pea soup, which becomes a hearty spring meal when topped with a slice of French bread, prosciutto, and feta cheese.

spring pea soup

Prep: 25 minutes Cook: 10 minutes Makes: 6 servings

5	cups shelled peas
2	14-ounce cans chicken broth
2	small heads Boston or Bibb lettuce, torn into small pieces
12	green onions, sliced
3	tablespoons snipped fresh tarragon
1½	to 2 cups half-and-half, light cream, or milk
	Salt
	Ground black pepper
6	slices French bread, toasted
2	ounces prosciutto, cut into thin strips
⅓	cup crumbled feta cheese
	Fresh tarragon sprigs (optional)

1 In a 4-quart Dutch oven combine peas and broth. Bring to boiling; reduce heat. Simmer, covered, for 6 minutes. Add lettuce and green onion. Return to boiling; reduce heat. Simmer, covered, for 4 to 6 minutes more or until peas are tender. If desired, use a slotted spoon to remove ⅓ cup peas; reserve for garnish. Stir tarragon into pea mixture in Dutch oven. Cool slightly.

2 Transfer one-fourth of the soup to a blender or food processor. Cover and blend or process until nearly smooth. Repeat with remaining soup, blending or processing one-fourth at a time. Return all of the soup to Dutch oven. Stir in half-and-half to reach desired consistency; heat through. Do not boil. Season to taste with salt and pepper.

3 Top each serving with a slice of French bread, some prosciutto, and some feta cheese. If desired, garnish with reserved peas and a tarragon sprig.

Per serving: *341 cal., 12 g total fat (6 g sat. fat), 36 mg chol., 1,120 mg sodium, 41 g carbo., 9 g fiber, 20 g pro.*

black bean & kielbasa soup

Start to Finish: 20 minutes Makes: 5 servings

2 15- to 18.5-ounce
   cans ready-to-serve
   black bean soup
1 14.5-ounce can diced
   tomatoes with
   garlic and onion,
   undrained
12 ounces cooked,
   smoked Polish
   sausage, halved
   lengthwise and cut
   into $1/2$-inch slices
1 cup frozen whole
   kernel corn

1 In a large saucepan stir together soup, undrained tomatoes, sausage, and corn. Bring to boiling; reduce heat. Simmer, covered, for 10 minutes or until heated through.

Per serving: 414 cal., 22 g total fat (7 g sat. fat), 48 mg chol., 1,624 mg sodium, 36 g carbo., 13 g fiber, 18 g pro.

To sliver the basil that flavors this robust Tuscan-style soup, stack basil leaves on a cutting board, roll lengthwise, and thinly slice crosswise with a knife. Measure the ¼ cup basil after slicing.

sausage-tortellini soup

Prep: 15 minutes Cook: 20 minutes Makes: 8 servings

Nonstick cooking
   spray
12 ounces smoked,
   cooked chicken
   sausage, halved
   lengthwise and
   sliced crosswise
   into 1-inch pieces
1 large onion, cut into
   thin wedges
2 cloves garlic, minced
3 14-ounce cans
   reduced-sodium
   chicken broth
1 14.5-ounce can diced
   tomatoes with basil,
   garlic and oregano,
   undrained
1 10-ounce package
   frozen baby lima
   beans
1 cup water
2 9-ounce packages
   refrigerated cheese
   or mushroom
   tortellini
¼ cup slivered fresh
   basil
2 tablespoons finely
   shredded Parmesan
   cheese (optional)

1 Lightly coat an unheated Dutch oven with cooking spray. Heat over medium heat. Add sausage, onion, and garlic to hot Dutch oven; cook until sausage is brown and onion is tender. Drain off fat.

2 Add broth, undrained tomatoes, lima beans, and water. Bring to boiling; reduce heat. Simmer, covered, for 10 minutes. Add tortellini. Return to boiling; reduce heat. Simmer, uncovered, for 5 minutes or until pasta and beans are tender.

3 Serve at once. Sprinkle servings with basil. If desired, sprinkle with cheese.

Per serving: *336 cal., 6 g total fat (2 g sat. fat), 65 mg chol., 1,182 mg sodium, 46 g carbo., 3 g fiber, 24 g pro.*

Braising the lamb shanks, which are relatively tough cuts of meat, transforms them into fork-tender morsels that add flavor and richness to soups.

lamb-orzo soup

Prep: 30 minutes Cook: 1½ hours Makes: 6 servings

2½	pounds lamb shanks
3	14-ounce cans chicken broth or vegetable broth
2¾	cups water
2	bay leaves
1	tablespoon snipped fresh oregano or 1 teaspoon dried oregano, crushed
1½	teaspoons snipped fresh marjoram or ½ teaspoon dried marjoram, crushed
¼	teaspoon ground black pepper
2	medium carrots, peeled into thin ribbons or cut into short thin strips
1	cup sliced celery (2 stalks)
¾	cup dried orzo pasta
3	cups torn fresh spinach or ½ of a 10-ounce package frozen chopped spinach, thawed and well drained
	Finely shredded Parmesan cheese (optional)

1 In a large Dutch oven combine lamb shanks, broth, water, bay leaves, oregano, marjoram, and pepper. Bring to boiling; reduce heat. Simmer, covered, for 1¼ to 1½ hours or until lamb shanks are tender.

2 Remove lamb shanks from Dutch oven. When cool enough to handle, cut meat off bones; coarsely chop meat. Discard bones. Strain broth through a large sieve or colander lined with 2 layers of 100-percent-cotton cheesecloth; discard bay leaves and herbs. Skim fat; return broth to Dutch oven.

3 Stir chopped lamb, carrot, celery, and orzo into Dutch oven. Return to boiling; reduce heat. Simmer, covered, for 15 minutes or until vegetables and orzo are tender. Stir in spinach. Cook for 1 to 2 minutes more or just until fresh spinach wilts or frozen spinach is heated through. If desired, serve with Parmesan cheese.

Per serving: 240 cal., 9 g total fat (4 g sat. fat), 54 mg chol., 513 mg sodium, 19 g carbo., 3 g fiber, 20 g pro.

chunky fish soup

Prep: 25 minutes Cook: 20 minutes Makes: 6 servings

½ cup chopped onion
    (1 medium)
½ cup chopped celery
    (1 stalk)
½ cup chopped carrot
    (1 medium)
1 clove garlic, minced
2 tablespoons olive oil
5 cups vegetable broth
1 14.5-ounce can
    diced tomatoes,
    undrained
1½ pounds assorted
    white fish, cut into
    bite-size pieces
    (such as halibut, red
    snapper, or cod)
2 tablespoons snipped
    fresh Italian (flat-
    leaf) parsley
6 slices country-style
    bread, toasted

1 In a Dutch oven cook onion, celery, carrot, and garlic in hot oil over medium-high heat about 5 minutes or until tender. Add broth and undrained tomatoes. Heat to boiling; reduce heat. Simmer, covered, for 15 minutes. Stir in fish. Simmer, covered, for 5 minutes more or until fish begins to flake when tested with a fork. Stir in parsley. Serve with toasted bread.

Per serving: 286 cal., 8 g total fat (1 g sat. fat), 36 mg chol., 1,146 mg sodium, 23 g carbo., 2 g fiber, 27 g pro.

shrimp & greens soup

Start to Finish: 30 minutes Makes: 4 servings

12 ounces peeled and
deveined fresh or
frozen shrimp
1 large leek, sliced
2 cloves garlic, minced
1 tablespoon olive oil
3 14-ounce cans
reduced-sodium
chicken broth or
vegetable broth
1 tablespoon snipped
fresh parsley
1 tablespoon snipped
fresh marjoram or
thyme
¼ teaspoon lemon-
pepper seasoning
2 cups shredded bok
choy or spinach
leaves

1 Thaw shrimp, if frozen.

2 In a large saucepan cook leek and garlic in hot oil over medium heat until leek is tender. Carefully add broth, parsley, marjoram, and lemon-pepper seasoning. Bring to boiling; add shrimp. Return to boiling; reduce heat.

3 Simmer, uncovered, for 2 minutes. Stir in bok choy. Cook for 1 minute more or until shrimp are opaque.

Per serving: 159 cal., 6 g total fat (1 g sat. fat), 132 mg chol., 1,642 mg sodium, 6 g carbo., 1 g fiber, 21 g pro.

tomato-tortellini soup

Start to Finish: 15 minutes Makes: 4 servings

2 14-ounce cans
    reduced-sodium
    chicken broth or
    vegetable broth
1 9-ounce package
    refrigerated
    tortellini
½ of an 8-ounce tub
    cream cheese
    spread with chive
    and onion
1 10.75- or 11-ounce
    can condensed
    tomato or tomato
    bisque soup
    Snipped fresh chives
    (optional)

1 In a medium saucepan bring broth to boiling. Add tortellini; reduce heat. Simmer, uncovered, for 5 minutes. In a bowl whisk ⅓ cup of the hot broth into the cream cheese spread until smooth. Return all to saucepan. Stir in tomato soup; heat through. If desired, garnish with chives.

Per serving: 363 cal., 14 g total fat (8 g sat. fat), 57 mg chol., 1,264 mg sodium, 44 g carbo., 1 g fiber, 14 g pro.

vegetable pasta soup

Start to Finish: 35 minutes Makes: 6 servings

6   cloves garlic, minced
2   teaspoons olive oil
1½   cups coarsely
        shredded carrot
        (3 medium)
1   cup chopped onion
        (1 large)
1   cup thinly sliced
        celery (2 stalks)
1   32-ounce box
        reduced-sodium
        chicken broth
4   cups water
1½   cups dried ditalini
        pasta
¼   cup shaved Parmesan
        cheese
2   tablespoons snipped
        fresh Italian (flat-
        leaf) parsley

1 In a 5- to 6-quart Dutch oven cook garlic in hot oil over medium heat for 15 seconds. Add carrot, onion, and celery; cook for 5 to 7 minutes or until tender, stirring occasionally. Add broth and water; bring to boiling. Add uncooked pasta; simmer, uncovered, for 7 to 8 minutes or until pasta is tender.

2 To serve, ladle soup into bowls; top with Parmesan cheese and parsley.

Per serving: 172 cal., 4 g total fat (0 g sat. fat), 2 mg chol., 454 mg sodium, 28 g carbo., 2 g fiber, 8 g pro.

potato soup

Prep: 25 minutes Cook: 15 minutes Makes: 6 servings

6 slices bacon,
    halved crosswise
    (about 4 ounces)
½ cup chopped onion
    (1 medium)
½ cup chopped celery
    (1 stalk)
3 cups coarsely
    chopped, peeled
    potato
    (2 large)
1 cup water
1 teaspoon mustard
    seed or Dijon-style
    mustard
1½ cups half-and-half,
    light cream, or milk
1 10.75-ounce can
    condensed cream of
    chicken or golden
    mushroom soup
    Snipped fresh parsley
    (optional)

1 In a large saucepan cook bacon over medium heat until crisp. Remove bacon, reserving 1 tablespoon drippings in pan. Drain bacon on paper towels. Crumble bacon and set aside, reserving several pieces for garnish, if desired.

2 Add onion and celery to saucepan. Cook until tender. Stir in potato, water, and mustard. Bring to boiling; reduce heat. Simmer, covered, about 15 minutes or just until the potato is tender.

3 Stir in half-and-half and soup. Heat through; do not boil. Stir in bacon. If desired, garnish servings with parsley and reserved bacon.

Per serving: 317 cal., 22 g total fat (9 g sat. fat), 44 mg chol., 728 mg sodium, 20 g carbo., 2 g fiber, 11 g pro.

This hearty chowder lives up to its name. It's easy—only takes about 30 minutes to make—and with a cup of cheddar cheese, it's definitely cheesy!

easy cheesy vegetable-chicken chowder

Start to Finish: 30 minutes Makes: 4 servings

1	cup small broccoli florets
1	cup frozen whole kernel corn
½	cup water
¼	cup chopped onion
½	teaspoon dried thyme, crushed
2	cups milk
1½	cups chopped cooked chicken (about 8 ounces)
1	10.75-ounce can condensed cream of potato soup
1	cup shredded cheddar cheese (4 ounces)

1 In a large saucepan combine broccoli, corn, water, onion, and thyme. Bring to boiling; reduce heat. Simmer, covered, for 8 to 10 minutes or until vegetables are tender. Do not drain.

2 Stir milk, chicken, soup, and ¾ cup of the cheese into vegetable mixture. Cook and stir over medium heat until cheese melts and mixture is heated through. Sprinkle servings with remaining cheese.

Per serving: *374 cal., 18 g total fat (9 g sat. fat), 92 mg chol., 858 mg sodium, 24 g carbo., 2 g fiber, 29 g pro.*

Chopped red sweet pepper and green spinach give this creamy chicken chowder its festive name.

confetti chicken chowder

Start to Finish: 25 minutes Makes: 6 servings

¼ cup butter or
   margarine
½ cup chopped red
   sweet pepper
½ cup all-purpose flour
6 cups chicken broth
2 cups chopped cooked
   chicken
1 10-ounce package
   frozen chopped
   spinach, thawed
   and drained
¼ teaspoon ground
   nutmeg
1 cup half-and-half or
   light cream
   Croutons (optional)

1 In a large saucepan melt butter over medium heat. Add sweet pepper; cook and stir for 2 to 3 minutes or until tender. Stir in flour; cook and stir for 1 minute more. Stir in broth; cook and stir until thickened and bubbly.

2 Add chicken, spinach, and nutmeg. Stir in half-and-half; heat through. If desired, top each serving with croutons.

Per serving: *292 cal., 18 g total fat (9 g sat. fat), 78 mg chol., 1,205 mg sodium, 12 g carbo., 2 g fiber, 19 g pro.*

This hearty soup is brimming with corn and chunks of pork sausage. Slices of garlic toast make perfect partners.

corn-sausage chowder

Start to Finish: 30 minutes Makes: 6 servings

1 pound bulk pork sausage
1 cup coarsely chopped onion (1 large)
3 cups ½-inch pieces red potato (3 medium)
2 cups water
1 teaspoon salt
½ teaspoon dried marjoram, crushed
⅛ teaspoon ground black pepper
1 15.25-ounce can whole kernel corn, drained
1 14.75-ounce can cream-style corn, undrained
1 12-ounce can evaporated milk (1½ cups)

1 In a Dutch oven cook sausage and onion until sausage is brown and onion is tender. Drain well.

2 Return sausage mixture to Dutch oven. Stir in potato, water, salt, marjoram, and pepper. Bring to boiling; reduce heat. Simmer, covered, for 10 minutes or until potato is tender.

3 Stir in the whole kernel corn, undrained cream-style corn, and evaporated milk. Cook and stir until heated through.

Per serving: 491 cal., 27 g total fat (12 g sat. fat), 60 mg chol., 1,135 mg sodium, 43 g carbo., 4 g fiber, 17 g pro.

If you love the flavor of Reuben sandwiches, you'll enjoy this chowder. Be sure to use process Swiss cheese—it melts more smoothly than natural Swiss.

reuben chowder

Prep: 15 minutes Bake: 15 minutes Oven: 325°F Makes: 4 servings

1   tablespoon butter or
      margarine, softened
4   slices rye bread
½   teaspoon caraway
      seeds
3   cups milk
1   10.75-ounce can
      condensed cream of
      celery soup
2   ounces process Swiss
      cheese slices, torn
      into pieces
1   14- or 16-ounce
      can sauerkraut,
      rinsed, drained, and
      snipped
2   5-ounce packages
      sliced corned beef,
      chopped

1 Preheat oven to 325°F. Butter both sides of each slice of the bread; sprinkle with caraway seeds. Cut bread into triangles; place on a baking sheet. Bake 15 minutes or until toasted.

2 Meanwhile, in a large saucepan combine milk, soup, and cheese. Cook and stir just until boiling. Stir in sauerkraut and corned beef; heat through. Serve soup with toasted bread.

Per serving: *456 cal., 23 g total fat (11 g sat. fat), 77 mg chol., 2,696 mg sodium, 35 g carbo., 5 g fiber, 27 g pro.*

fish chowder

Prep: 30 minutes Cook: 20 minutes Makes: 6 servings

1   pound fresh or frozen
    skinless whitefish
    fillets or other white
    fleshed fish (such as
    cod, orange roughy,
    or haddock)
2   large potatoes, cut
    into ½-inch cubes
1½ cups coarsely
    chopped carrot
    (3 medium)
1½ cups chopped celery
    with leaves
    (3 stalks)
1   cup chopped onion
    (1 large)
1   clove garlic, minced
½   teaspoon salt
½   teaspoon lemon-
    pepper seasoning
2   cups water
1   10-ounce can whole
    baby clams, rinsed
    and drained
1   cup half-and-half or
    light cream
1   cup milk
    Freshly ground black
    pepper (optional)

1 Thaw fish, if frozen. In a 4-quart Dutch oven or saucepan combine potato, carrot, celery, onion, garlic, salt, and lemon-pepper seasoning. Add the water. Bring to boiling, reduce heat. Simmer, covered, for 12 to 15 minutes or until potato is tender, stirring occasionally.

2 Meanwhile, rinse fish; pat dry. Cut fish into 1-inch pieces. Stir fish into vegetable mixture; cook, covered, for 5 to 10 minutes more or until fish begins to flake when tested with a fork. Stir in clams, half-and-half, and milk. Cook and stir until heated through.

3 Ladle soup into bowls. If desired, garnish each serving with freshly ground pepper.

Per serving: 297 cal., 10 g total fat (4 g sat. fat), 80 mg chol., 440 mg sodium, 24 g carbo., 3 g fiber, 27 g pro.

If you prefer, use purchased bacon pieces from a jar instead of regular bacon. Cook the celery, onion, and carrot in 2 tablespoons olive or cooking oil.

manhattan clack chowder

Start to Finish: 40 minutes Makes: 4 servings

1 pint shucked clams or two 6.5-ounce cans minced clams
2 slices bacon
1 cup chopped celery (2 stalks)
⅓ cup chopped onion (1 small)
¼ cup chopped carrot
1 8-ounce bottle clam juice or 1 cup chicken broth
2 cups cubed red potato
1 teaspoon dried thyme, crushed
⅛ teaspoon cayenne pepper
⅛ teaspoon ground black pepper
1 14.5-ounce can diced tomatoes, undrained

1 Chop fresh clams (if using), reserving juice; set clams aside. Strain clam juice to remove bits of shell. (Or, drain canned clams, reserving juice.) If necessary, add enough water to reserved clam juice to equal 1½ cups. Set juice aside.

2 In a large saucepan cook bacon over medium heat until crisp. Remove bacon and drain on paper towels; crumble. Reserve 2 tablespoons drippings in pan.

3 Heat bacon drippings over medium heat. Add celery, onion, and carrot; cook and stir until tender. Stir in the reserved 1½ cups clam juice and the 8 ounces clam juice. Stir in potato, thyme, cayenne pepper, and ground black pepper. Bring to boiling; reduce heat. Simmer, covered, for 10 minutes. Stir in clams, bacon, and undrained tomatoes. Return to boiling; reduce heat. Cook for 1 to 2 minutes more or until heated through.

Per serving: *254 cal., 9 g total fat (1 g sat. fat), 41 mg chol., 507 mg sodium, 24 g carbo., 3 g fiber, 19 g pro.*

seafood chowder

Start to Finish: 25 minutes Makes: 4 servings

12 ounces fresh or
frozen fish fillets
(such as salmon,
orange roughy, or
cod)

3 cups loose-pack
frozen diced hash
brown potatoes
with onions and
peppers

1 cup water

1 12-ounce can
evaporated milk
(1½ cups)

1 10.75-ounce can
condensed cream of
shrimp or cream of
potato soup

⅓ of a 3-ounce can
cooked bacon
pieces (⅓ cup)

2 teaspoons snipped
fresh dill or ¾
teaspoon dried dill

¼ teaspoon ground
black pepper

1 2-ounce jar diced
pimiento, drained

1 Thaw fish, if frozen. Rinse fish; pat dry with
paper towels. Cut fish into 1-inch pieces.
Set aside.

2 Meanwhile, in a large saucepan combine
hash brown potatoes and water. Bring
to boiling; reduce heat. Simmer, covered, for
5 minutes or until tender.

3 Stir in evaporated milk, soup, bacon, dill,
and pepper. Return to boiling. Add fish
and pimiento; reduce heat. Simmer, covered,
for 3 to 5 minutes or until fish begins to flake
when tested with a fork.

Per serving: 366 cal., 15 g total fat (7 g sat. fat), 86 mg chol.,
1,045 mg sodium, 27 g carbo., 2 g fiber, 30 g pro.

macaroni & cheese chowder

Start to Finish: 30 minutes Makes: 4 to 6 servings

1 14-ounce can
   reduced-sodium
   chicken broth
1 cup water
1 cup dried elbow
   macaroni
1 cup frozen whole
   kernel corn
1 cup chopped sliced
   cooked ham
   (5 ounces)
6 ounces American
   cheese, cubed
1 cup milk
   Shredded cheddar
   cheese (optional)

1 In a large saucepan bring broth and water to boiling. Add macaroni; reduce heat. Simmer, covered, for 12 minutes or until macaroni is tender, stirring occasionally.

2 Stir in corn, ham, American cheese, and milk. Cook and stir over medium heat until cheese melts. Ladle into bowls. If desired, top servings with cheese.

Per serving: 393 cal., 18 g total fat (10 g sat. fat), 64 mg chol., 1,338 mg sodium, 35 g carbo., 2 g fiber, 23 g pro.

jalapeño corn chowder

Prep: 15 minutes Cook: 5 minutes Makes: 4 servings

3 cups frozen whole kernel corn
1 14-ounce can vegetable broth or chicken broth
⅔ cup dried small pasta (such as ditalini or tiny shell macaroni)
1 cup milk, half-and-half, or light cream
¼ cup bottled roasted red sweet peppers, drained and chopped
1 or 2 fresh jalapeño chile peppers, seeded and finely chopped (see note, page 126)
½ cup shredded cheddar cheese (optional)

1 In a blender or food processor combine 1 ½ cups of the corn and all of the broth. Cover and blend or process until nearly smooth.

2 In a large saucepan combine the broth mixture and the remaining corn. Bring to boiling; add pasta. Reduce heat; simmer, uncovered, for 5 to 7 minutes or until pasta is tender. Stir in milk, roasted sweet peppers, and jalapeño peppers; heat through. Ladle soup into bowls. If desired, sprinkle with cheese.

Per serving: 219 cal., 2 g total fat (1 g sat. fat), 5 mg chol., 419 mg sodium, 45 g carbo., 3 g fiber, 8 g pro.

smoky cheese & corn chowder

Start to Finish: 25 minutes Makes: 4 servings

1	10-ounce package frozen whole kernel corn (2 cups)
½	cup chopped onion (1 medium)
½	cup water
1	teaspoon instant chicken bouillon granules
¼	teaspoon ground black pepper
2½	cups milk
3	tablespoons all-purpose flour
4	ounces smoked process cheddar cheese, shredded (1 cup)
1	tablespoon chopped pimiento, drained
	Fresh chives (optional)
	Chopped pimiento (optional)

1 In a large saucepan combine corn, onion, water, bouillon, and pepper. Bring to boiling; reduce heat. Simmer, covered, for 4 minutes or until corn is tender. Do not drain.

2 Stir together ½ cup of the milk and the flour; add to corn mixture along with the remaining milk. Cook and stir until slightly thickened and bubbly. Add cheese and the 1 tablespoon pimiento; heat and stir until cheese melts. If desired, garnish servings with chives and additional pimiento.

Per serving: 283 cal., 13 g total fat (8 g sat. fat), 42 mg chol., 462 mg sodium, 28 g carbo., 2 g fiber, 15 g pro.

Let this elegant, easy bisque star at your next special occasion dinner. Don't tell anyone that it starts with two cans of soup.

crab-tomato bisque

Start to Finish: 15 minutes Makes: 4 servings

1 19-ounce can ready-
   to-eat tomato-basil
   soup
1 10.75-ounce can
   condensed cream of
   shrimp soup
1 cup vegetable broth
1 cup half-and-half,
   light cream, or milk
1 tablespoon dried
   minced onion
1 tablespoon snipped
   fresh parsley or
   1 teaspoon dried
   parsley flakes
1 6.5-ounce can
   crabmeat, drained,
   flaked, and cartilage
   removed

1 In a large saucepan combine tomato-basil soup, cream of shrimp soup, broth, half-and-half, onion, and dried parsley (if using).

2 Cook over medium heat until bubbly, stirring occasionally. Stir in crabmeat and fresh parsley (if using); heat through.

Per serving: *242 cal., 12 g total fat (6 g sat. fat), 73 mg chol., 1,447 mg sodium, 20 g carbo., 1 g fiber, 15 g pro.*

Though olives may not be the first condiment most cooks would think of to season a stew, they give grand flavor to this Spanish-inspired chicken dish.

spanish chicken stew

Prep: 15 minutes Cook: 20 minutes Makes: 4 servings

1¼ pounds skinless, boneless chicken thighs, cut into 1½-inch pieces
¼ teaspoon salt
¼ teaspoon freshly ground black pepper
1 tablespoon olive oil
1 medium onion, thinly sliced (1 medium)
1 red sweet pepper, cut into ¼-inch strips
2 cloves garlic, minced
1 cup chicken broth
12 ounces red potatoes, cut into ½-inch wedges
½ teaspoon dried savory, crushed
¼ teaspoon dried thyme, crushed
1 14.5-ounce can diced tomatoes, undrained
⅓ cup small pimiento-stuffed olives, cut up
Purchased breadsticks (optional)

1 Season chicken with salt and black pepper. In a large Dutch oven cook chicken in hot oil over medium-high heat until light brown.

2 Add onion and sweet pepper to Dutch oven; cook for 3 minutes or until crisp-tender. Add garlic; cook for 30 seconds more. Add broth, potato wedges, savory, and thyme. Bring to boiling; reduce heat. Simmer, covered, for 15 minutes or until chicken and potato are tender. Stir in undrained tomatoes. Return to boiling; reduce heat. Simmer, covered, for 5 minutes. Remove from heat. Stir in olives. If desired, serve with breadsticks.

Per serving: 334 cal., 11 g total fat (2 g sat. fat), 113 mg chol., 918 mg sodium, 24 g carbo., 3 g fiber, 32 g pro.

Serrano chile peppers give this stew a real Tex-Mex kick. Serranos are classified as very hot, but a dollop of cool sour cream helps mellow the heat.

ranch chicken stew

Prep: 25 minutes Cook: 20 minutes Makes: 4 to 6 servings

1 pound skinless, boneless chicken breasts, cut into bite-size pieces
2 tablespoons butter or margarine
1 large sweet potato, peeled and sliced (about 8 ounces)
½ cup chopped onion (1 medium)
1 to 2 fresh serrano chile peppers, halved and seeded (see note, page 126)
½ teaspoon ground coriander
¼ teaspoon ground cumin
3 cups chicken broth
1 14.5-ounce can golden hominy, rinsed and drained
Chopped, seeded serrano chili pepper (see note, page 126) (optional)

1 In a large saucepan or Dutch oven cook chicken, half at a time, in hot butter until no longer pink. Remove chicken with a slotted spoon, reserving drippings in saucepan. Set chicken aside.

2 Add sweet potato, onion, serrano pepper halves, coriander, and cumin to saucepan; add 1½ cups of the chicken broth. Bring to boiling; reduce heat. Simmer, covered, for 20 minutes or until vegetables are very tender. Cool slightly.

3 Spoon sweet potato mixture into blender. Cover and blend until smooth. Return to saucepan. Stir in cooked chicken, remaining chicken broth, and hominy. Heat through. If desired, garnish with chopped serrano pepper.

Per serving: 307 cal., 8 g total fat (4 g sat. fat), 83 mg chol., 1,066 mg sodium, 26 g carbo., 4 g fiber, 29 g pro.

easy beef stew

Prep: 15 minutes Cook: 10 minutes Makes: 4 servings

1 17-ounce package refrigerated cooked beef roast au jus
2 10.75-ounce cans condensed beefy mushroom soup
1 16-ounce package frozen mixed vegetables (any combination)
4 teaspoons snipped fresh basil or 1½ teaspoons dried basil, crushed
1½ cups milk

1 Cut beef into bite-size pieces. In a 4-quart Dutch oven combine beef and the juices, soup, vegetables, and dried basil (if using).

2 Bring to boiling; reduce heat. Simmer, covered, for 10 minutes. Stir in milk and fresh basil (if using). Heat through.

Per serving: 386 cal., 15 g total fat (7 g sat. fat), 80 mg chol., 1,688 mg sodium, 33 g carbo., 5 g fiber, 33 g pro.

lamb curry stew

Prep: 20 minutes Cook: 1½ hours Makes: 8 servings

3 pounds lamb
shoulder
3 tablespoons olive oil
or cooking oil
½ cup chopped onion
(1 medium)
2 tablespoons all-
purpose flour
2 tablespoons curry
powder
2 cups chicken broth
2¼ cups coarsely
chopped tomato (3
medium)
2 cups peeled, diced
celery root
1 cup whipping cream
1⅓ cups coarsely
chopped, peeled
Golden Delicious or
other cooking apple
(2 medium)
¾ cup coarsely chopped
tomato (1 medium)
Hot cooked rice
(optional)
Desired condiments
(such as chutney,
toasted shredded
coconut, or chopped
apple or nuts)

1 Trim fat from lamb. Cut lamb into 1-inch cubes, discarding bone.

2 In a large saucepan or Dutch oven brown lamb, one-third at a time, in hot oil, cooking onion with last portion of lamb. Stir in flour; cook for 7 minutes, stirring frequently. Stir in curry powder; stir in broth. Add the 2¼ cups chopped tomato and the celery root. Bring to boiling; reduce heat. Simmer, covered, for 1½ hours or until lamb is tender.

3 Stir in whipping cream. Simmer, uncovered, for 2 minutes more. Stir in apple and the remaining ¾ cup chopped tomato. Heat through. If desired, serve with rice and desired condiments.

Per serving: 434 cal., 25 g total fat (10 g sat. fat), 99 mg chol., 298 mg sodium, 32 g carbo., 3 g fiber, 22 g pro.

Maybe the Irish invented stew, maybe not, but for generations lamb stew with potatoes, carrots, and onions has been associated with the land of the leprechauns.

luck o' the irish stew

Prep: 30 minutes Cook: 1¼ hours Makes: 6 servings

1 pound boneless lamb or boneless beef chuck roast, trimmed and cut into ¾-inch pieces

4 cups beef broth

2 medium onions, cut into wedges

¼ teaspoon ground black pepper

1 bay leaf

4 medium potatoes (about 1½ pounds), peeled and quartered

6 medium carrots, cut into ½-inch slices

½ teaspoon dried thyme, crushed

¼ teaspoon dried basil, crushed

½ cup water

¼ cup all-purpose flour

Salt

Ground black pepper

Fresh thyme sprigs (optional)

1 In a large saucepan combine lamb, broth, onion, ¼ teaspoon pepper, and the bay leaf. Bring to boiling; reduce heat. Simmer, covered, for 45 minutes. Skim off fat.

2 Add potato, carrot, dried thyme, and basil. Bring to boiling; reduce heat. Simmer, covered, for 30 to 35 minutes more or until vegetables are tender. Discard bay leaf.

3 In a small bowl stir together water and flour. Stir into the stew. Cook and stir until thickened and bubbly. Cook and stir for 1 minute more. Season to taste with salt and additional pepper. If desired, garnish with thyme sprigs.

Per serving: *230 cal., 3 g total fat (1 g sat. fat), 48 mg chol., 649 mg sodium, 30 g carbo., 4 g fiber, 20 g pro.*

turkey chili with hominy

Start to Finish: 20 minutes Makes: 4 or 5 servings

1 In a large saucepan cook the turkey sausage over medium heat until brown.

12 ounces uncooked Italian turkey sausage (remove casings, if present) or uncooked ground turkey

2 15-ounce cans chili beans with chili gravy, undrained

1 14.5-ounce can golden hominy, drained

1 cup bottled salsa with lime

⅔ cup water

⅓ cup sliced green onion (optional)

2 Stir in undrained chili beans, drained hominy, salsa, and water. Heat through. Ladle chili into bowls. If desired, sprinkle with green onion.

Per serving: 470 cal., 11 g total fat (3 g sat. fat), 45 mg chol., 1,897 mg sodium, 64 g carbo., 16 g fiber, 28 g pro.

white & green chili

Prep: 15 minutes Cook: 15 minutes Makes: 4 servings

1 pound unseasoned
   meat loaf mix
   (⅓ pound each
   ground beef, pork,
   and veal), lean
   ground beef, or
   ground pork
⅓ cup chopped onion
   (1 small)
2 15-ounce cans Great
   Northern beans or
   white beans, rinsed
   and drained
1 16-ounce jar green
   salsa
1 14-ounce can
   reduced-sodium
   chicken broth
1½ teaspoons ground
   cumin
1 tablespoon snipped
   fresh cilantro
¼ cup dairy sour cream
   (optional)
   Snipped fresh cilantro
   (optional)

1 In a 4-quart Dutch oven cook ground
meat and onion over medium heat about
5 minutes or until brown. Drain off fat. Add
beans, salsa, broth, and cumin. Bring to boiling;
reduce heat. Simmer, covered, for 15 minutes.

2 Stir the 1 tablespoon cilantro into the
chili. If desired, top servings with sour
cream and sprinkle with additional cilantro.

Per serving: 440 cal., 15 g total fat (5 g sat. fat), 81 mg chol.,
1,256 mg sodium, 41 g carbo., 13 g fiber, 32 g pro.

zesty black bean chili

Prep: 10 minutes Cook: 20 minutes Makes: 4 servings

1	16-ounce jar thick and chunky salsa
1	15- to 16-ounce can black beans, rinsed and drained
1½	cups vegetable juice or hot-style vegetable juice
8	ounces fully cooked turkey kielbasa (Polish sausage), halved lengthwise and sliced
¼	cup water
2	teaspoons chili powder
2	cloves garlic, minced or ¼ teaspoon garlic powder
	Dairy sour cream, sliced green onion, and/or chopped, peeled avocado (optional)

1 In a large saucepan stir together salsa, beans, vegetable juice, turkey kielbasa, water, chili powder, and garlic. Bring to boiling; reduce heat. Simmer, covered, for 20 minutes, stirring occasionally.

2 Ladle chili into bowls. If desired, top with sour cream, green onion, and/or avocado.

Per serving: 210 cal., 5 g total fat (2 g sat. fat), 35 mg chol., 1,878 mg sodium, 28 g carbo., 6 g fiber, 16 g pro.

You'd swear there was meat in this chili, but it's the mushrooms. As brown mushrooms grow to become portobellos, they also gain meaty texture.

chili con portobello

Prep: 30 minutes Cook: 1 hour Makes: 4 servings

1 cup chopped onion
      (1 large)
2 cloves garlic, minced
2 tablespoons olive oil
8 ounces portobello
      mushroom caps,
      coarsely chopped
      (about 4 cups)
1 28-ounce can
      whole tomatoes,
      undrained and
      chopped
1 15- to 16-ounce can
      red kidney beans,
      rinsed and drained
1 tablespoon ground
      cumin
1 tablespoon medium
      or hot chili powder
   Dairy sour cream
      (optional)

1 In a large saucepan cook onion and garlic in hot oil until onion is tender. Stir in mushrooms. Cook and stir for 3 minutes more. Stir in undrained tomatoes, drained kidney beans, cumin, and chili powder.

2 Bring chili to boiling; reduce heat. Cover and simmer for 1 hour. If desired, top servings with sour cream.

Per serving: *157 cal., 5 g total fat (1 g sat. fat), 0 mg chol., 377 mg sodium, 23 g carbo., 8 g fiber, 6 g pro.*

comfort food

Casseroles are the ultimate one-dish meal—as well as the ultimate comfort food. And could they be any easier? Just put all the ingredients in the dish and pop it in the oven!

cass

5

eroles

chicken-biscuit pie

Prep: 15 minutes Bake: 10 minutes Oven: 450°F Makes: 4 servings

1   10.75-ounce can
    condensed cream of
    chicken soup
½   cup milk
¼   cup dairy sour cream
1   cup cubed cooked
    chicken or turkey
    (5 ounces)
1½ cups frozen mixed
    vegetables
½   teaspoon dried basil,
    crushed
⅛   teaspoon ground
    black pepper
1   package (5 or 6)
    refrigerated
    biscuits, quartered

1 Preheat oven to 450°F. Lightly grease a 1½-quart casserole; set aside. In a medium saucepan stir together soup, milk, and sour cream. Stir in chicken, mixed vegetables, basil, and pepper. Cook and stir over medium heat until boiling.

2 Spoon chicken mixture into the prepared casserole. Top with quartered biscuits.

3 Bake, uncovered, in the preheated oven for 10 to 12 minutes or until biscuits are light brown.

Per serving: 335 cal., 14 g total fat (5 g sat. fat), 49 mg chol., 1,049 mg sodium, 33 g carbo., 3 g fiber, 20 g pro.

This old-fashioned, family-friendly dish is quintessential "Sunday afternoon with the folks" fare. Why not rekindle the tradition and ask some relatives over for lunch this weekend?

chicken supreme casserole

Prep: 25 minutes Bake: 30 minutes Stand: 10 minutes Oven: 350°F Makes: 6 to 8 servings

8   ounces dried rotini
      pasta
1   16-ounce package
      frozen stir-fry
      vegetables
      (broccoli, carrots,
      onions, red peppers,
      celery, water
      chestnuts, and
      mushrooms)
2   10.75-ounce cans
      condensed cream of
      chicken soup
2   cups milk
¼   cup mayonnaise or
      salad dressing
¼   teaspoon ground
      black pepper
2   cups chopped cooked
      chicken (about
      10 ounces)
2   cups cubed French
      bread
2   tablespoons butter or
      margarine, melted
¼   teaspoon garlic
      powder

1 Preheat oven to 350°F. Cook rotini according to package directions, except add the stir-fry vegetables for the last 5 minutes of cooking; drain well.

2 Meanwhile, in a large bowl stir together soup, milk, mayonnaise, and pepper. Stir in cooked pasta mixture and chicken.

3 Transfer to an ungreased 3-quart rectangular baking dish. In a medium bowl toss bread cubes with melted butter and garlic powder; sprinkle over pasta mixture.

4 Bake, uncovered, in the preheated oven for 30 to 35 minutes or until heated through and bread cubes are golden brown. Let stand for 10 minutes before serving.

Per serving: *584 cal., 25 g total fat (8 g sat. fat), 71 mg chol., 1,123 mg sodium, 60 g carbo., 4 g fiber, 28 g pro.*

If desired, substitute another frozen vegetable or mixed vegetables for the broccoli.

parmesan
chicken & broccoli

Prep: 30 minutes Bake: 30 minutes Oven: 350°F Makes: 4 servings

1	cup converted rice
½	cup sliced green onions (4)
12	ounces skinless, boneless chicken breast halves, cut into strips
¾	teaspoon dried Italian seasoning, crushed
1	clove garlic, minced
1	tablespoon cooking oil
1	16-ounce jar reduced-fat Alfredo pasta sauce
3	cups frozen cut broccoli
⅓	cup grated Parmesan cheese
¼	cup diced cooked ham
1	2-ounce jar diced pimiento, drained Ground black pepper

1 Preheat oven to 350°F. Cook rice according to package directions; remove from heat and stir in half of the green onions. Divide the rice mixture among four 12- to 16-ounce individual au gratin dishes or casseroles; set aside.

2 In a large skillet cook the chicken strips, Italian seasoning, and garlic in hot oil over medium heat for 4 to 6 minutes or until chicken is no longer pink. Remove from heat. Stir in Alfredo sauce, broccoli, cheese, ham, and pimiento. Season to taste with pepper.

3 Spoon chicken mixture over rice in dishes. Cover and bake in the preheated oven for 15 minutes. Uncover and bake for 15 minutes more or until heated through.

Make-Ahead Directions: After preparing casseroles, cover with freezer wrap, label, and freeze for up to 3 months. To serve, thaw frozen dishes overnight in the refrigerator (they may still be icy). Preheat oven to 350°F. Remove freezer wrap; cover each dish with foil. Bake in the preheated oven for 20 minutes. Uncover and bake for 20 minutes more or until heated through.

Per serving: 660 cal., 25 g total fat (12 g sat. fat), 109 mg chol., 1,277 mg sodium, 71 g carbo., 5 g fiber, 39 g pro.

Chipotle chiles are actually smoked jalapeño peppers. Here they add a smoky-hot appeal to this family-style dish. Look for canned chipotles in adobo sauce in the international food aisle of your supermarket or at Hispanic food markets.

chipotle-chicken
casserole

Prep: 20 minutes Bake: 20 minutes Oven: 375°F Makes: 4 servings

2 cups frozen or fresh whole kernel corn
3 cups frozen diced hash brown potatoes
1 14.5-ounce can diced tomatoes with basil, garlic, and oregano, undrained
2 chipotle peppers in adobo sauce, chopped
½ teaspoon chili powder
½ teaspoon ground cumin
½ teaspoon dried oregano, crushed
1 tablespoon olive oil
4 skinless, boneless chicken breast halves (1 pound)
¼ teaspoon salt
¼ teaspoon chili powder
¼ teaspoon ground cumin
¾ cup shredded Colby and Monterey Jack cheese (3 ounces)

1 Preheat oven to 375°F. Coat a 2-quart round casserole with *nonstick cooking spray*; set aside. Coat an unheated large nonstick skillet with cooking spray. Heat skillet over medium-high heat. Add corn; cook for 5 minutes or until corn begins to lightly brown. Add potatoes; cook and stir 5 to 8 minutes more or until potatoes begin to brown. Stir in undrained tomatoes, chipotle peppers, the ½ teaspoon chili powder, the ½ teaspoon cumin, and the oregano. Remove from heat; transfer vegetable mixture to the prepared casserole.

2 Wipe skillet clean. Add oil to skillet and heat over medium-high heat. Sprinkle chicken evenly with salt, the ¼ teaspoon chili powder, and the ¼ teaspoon cumin. Brown chicken in hot oil about 6 minutes, turning once to brown both sides. Place chicken on top of potato mixture in casserole.

3 Bake, uncovered, in the preheated oven for 20 minutes or until bubbly and chicken is no longer pink. Sprinkle with cheese.

Per serving: 460 cal., 15 g total fat (6 g sat. fat), 79 mg chol., 939 mg sodium, 50 g carbo., 4 g fiber, 33 g pro.

It's amazing the gourmet touch that prosciutto and capers can bring to a dish that's based on two super-simple refrigerated pasta sauces.

chicken & prosciutto pasta

Prep: 30 minutes Bake: 25 minutes Oven: 350°F Makes: 6 servings

Nonstick cooking spray
6 ounces dried penne pasta (about 2 cups)
1 tablespoon olive oil
12 ounces skinless, boneless chicken breast halves, cut into ½-inch wide strips
2 cloves garlic, minced
4 ounces sliced prosciutto or ham, coarsely chopped
½ of a medium green sweet pepper, cut into bite-size strips
½ of a medium yellow sweet pepper, cut into bite-size strips
1 teaspoon dried basil, crushed
1 tablespoon drained capers (optional)
1 15-ounce container refrigerated marinara sauce
1 10-ounce container refrigerated Alfredo sauce
⅓ cup finely shredded Parmesan cheese
Fresh basil (optional)

1 Preheat oven to 350°F. Coat a 2-quart casserole with cooking spray; set aside. Cook pasta according to package directions. Drain and return pasta to saucepan; set aside.

2 Meanwhile, in a large skillet heat oil over medium-high heat. Add chicken and garlic; cook and stir for 2 minutes. Add prosciutto, pepper strips, basil, and, if desired, capers. Cook and stir for 2 to 3 minutes more or until chicken is no longer pink and pepper is crisp-tender. Add to pasta in saucepan; mix well.

3 Layer half of the pasta mixture in the prepared casserole. Top with 1 cup of the marinara sauce. Top with the remaining pasta mixture; then add the Alfredo sauce. Drizzle with remaining marinara sauce. Sprinkle with Parmesan cheese.

4 Bake, uncovered, in the preheated oven for 25 to 35 minutes or until heated through. If desired, garnish with fresh basil.

Per serving: 465 cal., 26 g total fat (2 g sat. fat), 62 mg chol., 839 mg sodium, 30 g carbo., 1 g fiber, 28 g pro.

To add extra heat, choose serrano peppers, which provide more kick than jalapeño peppers.

chicken-orzo casserole

Prep: 15 minutes Bake: 20 minutes Stand: 10 minutes Oven: 350°F
Makes: 4 to 6 servings

2 teaspoons cumin
   seeds
1 14.5-ounce can
   Mexican-style
   stewed tomatoes,
   undrained, or one
   10-ounce can diced
   tomatoes and green
   chile peppers,
   undrained
1 14-ounce can chicken
   broth
1 cup dried orzo pasta
¼ cup oil-packed dried
   tomatoes, cut up
2 9-ounce packages
   frozen cooked
   southwestern
   chicken breast
   strips, thawed
   Fresh jalapeño
   or serrano chile
   peppers, seeded
   and chopped
   (optional) (see note,
   page 126)
   Smoked paprika
   (optional)

1 Preheat oven to 350°F. In a large saucepan cook cumin seeds over medium heat for 3 to 4 minutes or until seeds are toasted and aromatic, shaking pan occasionally.

2 Carefully stir in undrained canned tomatoes, broth, uncooked pasta, and dried tomato. Bring to boiling. Transfer pasta mixture to an ungreased 2-quart oval or rectangular baking dish. Top with chicken breast strips.

3 Bake, covered, in the preheated oven for 20 minutes or until pasta is tender. Let stand, covered, for 10 minutes before serving. If desired, sprinkle with chile peppers and smoked paprika.

Per serving: 388 cal., 7 g total fat (2 g sat. fat), 60 mg chol., 1,227 mg sodium, 44 g carbo., 3 g fiber, 35 g pro.

chicken-wild rice
casserole

Prep: 30 minutes Bake: 50 minutes Oven: 350°F Makes: 8 to 10 servings

1   6-ounce package long
    grain and wild rice
    mix
3   cups cubed cooked
    chicken (about
    1 pound)
1   14.5-ounce can
    French-cut green
    beans, drained
1   10.75-ounce can
    condensed cream of
    celery soup
1   8-ounce can sliced
    water chestnuts,
    drained
½   cup mayonnaise or
    salad dressing
½   cup chopped onion
    (1 medium)
3   tablespoons sliced
    almonds
1   2-ounce jar sliced
    pimientos, drained
1   teaspoon lemon juice
1   cup shredded
    cheddar cheese
    (4 ounces)

1 Preheat oven to 350°F. Cook rice mix according to package directions. Meanwhile, in a very large bowl combine chicken, green beans, soup, drained water chestnuts, mayonnaise, onion, almonds, pimientos, and lemon juice. Stir in cooked rice mix. Transfer to an ungreased 3-quart rectangular baking dish.

2 Bake, covered, in the preheated oven for 45 minutes. Sprinkle with cheese. Bake, uncovered, for 5 minutes more or until heated through and cheese is melted.

Per serving: 434 cal., 25 g total fat (6 g sat. fat), 75 mg chol., 971 mg sodium, 30 g carbo., 2 g fiber, 24 g pro.

To add a little American ease to this French country supper, we called on canned beans—no soaking required. The results are equally as "ooh-la-la" as the classic.

two-bean cassoulet

Prep: 25 minutes Bake: 25 minutes Oven: 350°F Makes: 6 servings

6	skinless, boneless chicken thighs (about 1¼ pounds)
1	tablespoon olive oil or cooking oil
1½	cups thinly sliced carrot (3 medium)
½	cup chopped onion (1 medium)
2	cloves garlic, minced
1	15-ounce can butter beans, rinsed and drained
1	15-ounce can black beans, rinsed and drained
1	8-ounce can tomato sauce
¼	cup dry red wine
1	teaspoon dried thyme, crushed
¼	teaspoon ground allspice
8	ounces smoked turkey sausage, cut into ½-inch slices

1 Preheat oven to 350°F. In a large skillet brown chicken slowly in hot oil over medium-low heat about 10 minutes, turning occasionally. Remove chicken from skillet, reserving drippings. Add carrot, onion, and garlic to drippings in skillet. Cook, covered, for 10 minutes or just until carrot is tender, stirring occasionally.

2 Stir in the beans, tomato sauce, wine, thyme, and allspice. Stir in sausage. Transfer the sausage mixture to an ungreased 2-quart casserole. Arrange chicken thighs on top.

3 Bake, uncovered, in the preheated oven for 25 to 30 minutes or until chicken is no longer pink.

Per serving: 332 cal., 9 g total fat (2 g sat. fat), 101 mg chol., 1,022 mg sodium, 27 g carbo., 7 g fiber, 34 g pro.

Italian-flavored chicken meets Mexican tortillas and toppings for a dream-team match.

italian-style enchiladas

Prep: 20 minutes Bake: 25 minutes Oven: 350°F Makes: 6 servings

3 cups shredded cooked chicken
6 oil-pack dried tomato halves, drained and finely chopped
2 cups shredded mozzarella or Monterey Jack cheese (8 ounces)
½ cup sliced green onion (4)
   Nonstick cooking spray
2 15-ounce containers refrigerated tomato-basil or marinara sauce
12 6-inch flour tortillas
   Dairy sour cream and sliced green onion (optional)

1 Preheat oven to 350°F. Toss together the chicken, tomatoes, 1 cup of the cheese, and the ½ cup green onion. Coat a 3-quart rectangular baking dish with cooking spray. Spread 3 tablespoons of the sauce over the bottom of the dish.

2 To assemble enchiladas, spoon about ¼ cup of the chicken mixture just below the center of each tortilla. Roll up and place seam-side down in dish. Pour remaining sauce over enchiladas. Sprinkle with remaining cheese.

3 Bake, covered, in the preheated oven for 25 to 30 minutes or until heated through and cheese melts. If desired, garnish with sour cream and additional green onion.

Make-Ahead Directions: Prepare as directed through Step 2. Cover with plastic wrap and chill for up to 24 hours. Preheat oven to 350°F. Remove plastic wrap and cover dish with foil. Bake in the preheated oven for 35 to 40 minutes or until heated through and cheese melts.

Per serving: 537 cal., 22 g total fat (8 g sat. fat), 82 mg chol., 1,090 mg sodium, 47 g carbo., 6 g fiber, 37 g pro.

This Mexicali casserole includes black beans and corn. Adjust the cayenne pepper, adding more or less to get the hotness you like.

spicy chicken & rice bake

Prep: 25 minutes Bake: 55 minutes Oven: 375°F Makes: 6 servings

1 tablespoon cooking oil

½ cup chopped onion (1 medium)

½ cup chopped green sweet pepper (1 small)

2 cloves garlic, minced

1 15-ounce can black beans, rinsed and drained

1 14.5-ounce can diced tomatoes, undrained

1 cup tomato juice

1 cup frozen whole kernel corn

⅔ cup long grain rice

1 teaspoon chili powder

½ teaspoon salt

⅛ to ¼ teaspoon cayenne pepper

3 pounds meaty chicken pieces (small breast halves, thighs, and drumsticks), skinned

Salt

Ground black pepper

Paprika

1 Preheat oven to 375°F. In a large saucepan heat oil over medium heat. Add onion, sweet pepper, and garlic. Cook and stir until vegetables are tender. Stir in black beans, undrained tomatoes, tomato juice, corn, uncooked rice, chili powder, salt, and cayenne pepper. Bring to boiling. Transfer rice mixture to an ungreased 3-quart rectangular baking dish.

2 Arrange chicken pieces on top of the rice mixture. Sprinkle chicken lightly with salt, black pepper, and paprika.

3 Cover tightly with foil. Bake in preheated oven for 55 to 60 minutes or until chicken is no longer pink (170°F for breasts; 180°F for thighs and drumsticks) and rice is tender.

Per serving: 446 cal., 15 g total fat (4 g sat. fat), 104 mg chol., 854 mg sodium, 39 g carbo., 6 g fiber, 40 g pro.

creamy turkey pie

Prep: 25 minutes Bake: 25 minutes Stand: 10 minutes Oven: 350°F Makes: 6 servings

1 pound ground turkey
   sausage or ground
   raw turkey*
½ of an 8-ounce tub
   cream cheese with
   chive and onion
1 4½-ounce jar
   (drained weight)
   sliced mushrooms,
   drained
1 package (10)
   refrigerated biscuits
1 egg
1 cup cream-style
   cottage cheese
1 tablespoon all-
   purpose flour
   Chopped fresh
   tomato (optional)
   Fresh chives
   (optional)

1 Preheat oven to 350°F. In a large skillet cook turkey sausage until meat is brown, stirring to break up meat. Drain off any fat. Stir in cream cheese until combined. Stir in drained mushrooms; set aside.

2 For the crust, lightly grease a 9-inch pie plate. Unwrap and separate biscuits. Arrange biscuits in pie plate; press onto bottom and up sides of the plate, extending about ½ inch above the plate. If desired, use kitchen scissors to cut edges of biscuits at half-inch intervals. Spoon turkey mixture into the shell, spreading evenly.

3 In a blender or food processor combine egg, cottage cheese, and flour. Cover and blend or process until smooth. Spoon over turkey mixture. Bake, uncovered, in the preheated oven for 25 to 30 minutes or until edges are brown and filling is set. Let stand for 10 minutes. If desired, garnish with chopped tomato and chives.

*Note: If using ground turkey, add ¼ teaspoon each of salt and pepper to the meat mixture.

Per serving: 382 cal., 22 g total fat (9 g sat. fat), 111 mg chol., 1,164 mg sodium, 26 g carbo., 0 g fiber, 22 g pro.

monterey turkey casserole

Prep: 15 minutes Bake: 30 minutes Oven: 350°F Makes: 8 servings

5 cups slightly crushed tortilla chips
4 cups cubed cooked turkey or chicken (about 1¼ pounds)
2 16-ounce jars salsa
1 10-ounce package frozen whole kernel corn
½ cup dairy sour cream
2 tablespoons all-purpose flour
1 cup shredded Monterey Jack cheese with jalapeño peppers or mozzarella cheese (4 ounces)
Dairy sour cream and/or guacamole (optional)

1 Preheat oven to 350°F. Lightly grease a 3-quart rectangular baking dish. Place 3 cups of the tortilla chips in the bottom of the prepared baking dish. In a large bowl combine turkey, salsa, corn, the ½ cup sour cream, and flour; spoon over tortilla chips.

2 Bake, uncovered, in the preheated oven for 25 minutes. Sprinkle with the remaining 2 cups tortilla chips and the cheese. Bake for 5 to 10 minutes more or until heated through. If desired, serve with additional sour cream and/or guacamole.

Per serving: 444 cal., 17 g total fat (7 g sat. fat), 74 mg chol., 1,127 mg sodium, 46 g carbo., 4 g fiber, 29 g pro.

For this robust lasagna-style entrée, roll the noodles around a cheesy filling, then top the rolls with a ground turkey and tomato sauce.

turkey lasagna rolls

Prep: 30 minutes Bake: 40 minutes Stand: 5 minutes Oven: 375°F
Makes: 8 servings

8   dried lasagna noodles
8   ounces uncooked ground turkey
2   cups meatless pasta sauce
1   4½-ounce jar (drained weight) sliced mushrooms, drained (optional)
1   egg, slightly beaten
1   15-ounce carton ricotta cheese
1   10-ounce package frozen chopped spinach, thawed and well drained
1¼ cups shredded mozzarella cheese (5 ounces)
¾   cup grated Parmesan cheese

1 Preheat oven to 375°F. Cook pasta according to package directions; drain. Rinse with cold water; drain again. Set aside.

2 For sauce, in a large skillet cook ground turkey until brown; drain. Stir in pasta sauce and, if desired, drained mushrooms; set aside. In a large bowl combine egg, ricotta cheese, spinach, 1 cup of the mozzarella cheese, and the Parmesan cheese.

3 To assemble rolls, spread about ½ cup of the filling over each lasagna noodle. Roll up noodles, starting from short ends. Spread about ¾ cup of the sauce in the bottom of an ungreased 2-quart rectangular baking dish. Place lasagna rolls, seam sides down, on top of sauce. Pour remaining sauce over lasagna rolls.

4 Bake, covered, in the preheated oven for 40 minutes or until rolls are heated through. Sprinkle with remaining mozzarella cheese. Let stand for 5 minutes before serving.

Per serving: 374 cal., 17 g total fat (9 g sat. fat), 95 mg chol., 655 mg sodium, 31 g carbo., 3 g fiber, 24 g pro.

*Serve this hearty dish with
something light, such as crisp, fresh
apples or pears.*

beef-corn casserole

Prep: 30 minutes Bake: 20 minutes Oven: 350°F Makes: 6 servings

1 8-ounce package
   extra-wide egg
   noodles
1 pound lean ground
   beef or ground raw
   turkey
¾ cup coarsely chopped
   green sweet pepper
   (1 medium)
½ cup chopped onion
   (1 medium)
1 10-ounce package
   frozen whole kernel
   corn
1 10.75-ounce can
   condensed golden
   mushroom soup
1 cup chopped fresh
   mushrooms
1 3-ounce package
   cream cheese, cut
   up
⅓ cup milk
1 2-ounce jar diced
   pimientos

1 Cook noodles according to package
directions; drain and rinse.

2 Preheat oven to 350°F. In a 4-quart Dutch
oven cook ground beef until brown. Drain
off fat. Add sweet pepper and onion. Cook and
stir for 2 minutes. Add corn, soup, mushrooms,
cream cheese, milk, and pimientos. Heat and
stir until cheese melts. Gently stir in noodles.
Spread beef mixture in an ungreased 2-quart
rectangular baking dish.

3 Bake, covered, in the preheated oven for
20 to 25 minutes or until heated through.

Make-Ahead Directions: Place drained
noodles in a self-sealing plastic bag. Seal; chill
for up to 24 hours. Cook beef, adding sweet
pepper, onion, corn, soup, mushrooms, cream
cheese, milk, and pimientos as directed. Cool;
transfer to a large bowl. Cover; chill for up to
24 hours. To serve, combine beef mixture and
noodles; spread in a 2-quart baking dish. Bake,
covered, in a preheated 350°F oven for 75 to
80 minutes or until heated through.

Per serving: *411 cal., 16 g total fat (7 g sat. fat), 102 mg chol.,
478 mg sodium, 45 g carbo., 3 g fiber, 23 g pro.*

Traditionally, enchiladas are made with corn tortillas. This layered version uses flour tortillas.

enchilada grande casserole

Prep: 30 minutes **Bake:** 30 minutes **Stand:** 10 minutes **Oven:** 350°F
Makes: 8 to 10 servings

1 pound lean ground
   beef
1 16-ounce can refried
   beans
1 15-ounce can no-salt-
   added tomato sauce
½ cup water
1 1⅜-ounce package
   enchilada sauce mix
8 7- to 8-inch flour
   tortillas
2 cups shredded
   cheddar cheese
   (8 ounces)
   Dairy sour cream
   (optional)
   Sliced green onion
   (optional)

1 Preheat oven to 350°F. In a large skillet cook ground beef over medium-high heat until brown. Drain off fat. Stir in refried beans, tomato sauce, water, and enchilada sauce mix. Bring to boiling; reduce heat. Simmer, uncovered, for 15 minutes, stirring occasionally.

2 Arrange half of the tortillas in the bottom of a greased 3-quart rectangular baking dish, trimming and overlapping as necessary to fit. Top with half of the beef mixture and half of the cheddar cheese. Repeat with remaining tortillas and remaining beef mixture.

3 Bake, uncovered, in the preheated oven for 20 minutes. Sprinkle with remaining cheese. Bake about 10 minutes more or until heated through. Let stand for 10 minutes before serving. If desired, top with sour cream and green onion.

Make-Ahead Directions: Assemble casserole as directed (do not bake). Cover and chill for up to 24 hours. Seal remaining cheese in plastic bag and chill. To serve, preheat oven to 350°F. Uncover and bake in preheated oven for 35 minutes or until heated through. Sprinkle with remaining cheese. Let stand for 10 minutes. Serve as directed.

Per serving: 442 cal., 20 g total fat (10 g sat. fat), 60 mg chol., 1,227 mg sodium, 41 g carbo., 8 g fiber, 24 g pro.

Think of this hearty casserole as comfort food with a south-of-the-border twist. It is a great choice for a potluck meal.

bean & beef enchilada casserole

Prep: 35 minutes Bake: 40 minutes Oven: 350°F Makes: 12 servings

12	ounces lean ground beef
¾	cup chopped onion
1½	teaspoons chili powder
¾	teaspoon ground cumin
2	15-ounce cans pinto beans, rinsed and drained
2	4-ounce cans diced green chile peppers, undrained
1½	cups dairy sour cream
3	tablespoons all-purpose flour
½	teaspoon garlic powder
12	6 inch corn tortillas
2	10-ounce cans enchilada sauce
1	cup shredded cheddar cheese (4 ounces)

1 Preheat oven to 350°F. Lightly grease a 3-quart rectangular baking dish; set aside. In a large skillet cook the ground beef and onion until beef is cooked through, using a wooden spoon to break up beef as it cooks; drain off fat. Stir chili powder and cumin into beef mixture; cook and stir for 1 minute more. Stir pinto beans and undrained chile peppers into beef mixture; set aside. In a small bowl stir together sour cream, flour, and garlic powder; set aside.

2 Place half of the tortillas in the prepared dish, cutting to fit and overlapping as necessary. Top with half of the beef mixture, half of the sour cream mixture, and half of the enchilada sauce. Repeat layers.

3 Bake, covered, in the preheated oven for 35 to 40 minutes or until heated through. Uncover and sprinkle with cheese. Bake for 5 minutes more or until cheese is melted.

Per serving: *304 cal., 14 g total fat (7 g sat. fat), 38 mg chol., 682 mg sodium, 32 g carbo., 6 g fiber, 15 g pro.*

*Refrigerated biscuits top the ground
beef mixture in this "pizza."*

upside-down pizza casserole

Prep: 20 minutes Bake: 15 minutes Oven: 400°F Makes: 10 small or 5 large servings

1½	pounds lean ground beef
1	15-ounce can Italian-style tomato sauce
1½	cups shredded mozzarella cheese (6 ounces)
1	10-ounce package refrigerated biscuits (10 biscuits)

1 Preheat oven to 400°F. In a large skillet cook ground beef over medium heat until brown. Drain off fat. Stir in tomato sauce; heat through. Transfer beef mixture to an ungreased 2-quart rectangular baking dish or 10-inch deep-dish pie plate. Sprinkle with cheese. Flatten each biscuit with your hands; arrange the biscuits on top of cheese.

2 Bake, uncovered, in the preheated oven for 15 minutes or until biscuits are golden brown.

Per small serving: 321 cal., 20 g total fat (8 g sat. fat), 58 mg chol., 551 mg sodium, 15 g carbo., 1 g fiber, 17 g pro.

hamburger-mash
surprise

Prep: 25 minutes Bake: 30 minutes Stand: 5 minutes Oven: 375°F
Makes: 6 servings

¾ cup shredded
   cheddar cheese
   (3 ounces)
2 cups refrigerated
   mashed potatoes
12 ounces lean ground
   beef
½ cup chopped onion
2 cups sliced zucchini
   or yellow summer
   squash
1 14.5-ounce can diced
   tomatoes with basil,
   oregano, and garlic,
   undrained
½ of a 6-ounce can
   (⅓ cup) no-salt-
   added tomato paste
¼ teaspoon ground
   black pepper
   Paprika (optional)

1 Preheat oven to 375°F. Stir ½ cup of the cheese into the potatoes; set aside. In a large oven-safe skillet cook ground beef and onion over medium heat until beef is brown and onion is tender. Drain off fat. Stir in squash, undrained tomatoes, tomato paste, and pepper. Bring to boiling. Remove from heat.

2 Spoon mashed potato mixture into a large heavy-duty resealable plastic bag. Seal bag and snip off a corner of the plastic bag. Pipe the potato mixture in rows over beef mixture. (Or spoon mashed potato mixture in mounds on top of hot mixture.) Sprinkle with remaining cheese. If desired, sprinkle with paprika.

3 Bake, uncovered, in the preheated oven for 30 minutes or until mashed potato top is golden brown. Let stand for 5 minutes before serving.

*Tip: If you do not have an oven-safe skillet, you can transfer the beef mixture to a 2-quart baking dish or casserole, then top with the mashed potatoes.

Per serving: 254 cal., 12 g total fat (3 g sat. fat), 39 mg chol., 644 mg sodium, 21 g carbo., 3 g fiber, 16 g pro.

luscious lasagna

Prep: 20 minutes Bake: 30 minutes Stand: 10 minutes Oven: 375°F
Makes: 8 servings

12 ounces lean ground
beef and/or bulk
Italian sausage
1 cup chopped onion
(1 large)
2 cloves garlic, minced
1 26-ounce jar pasta
sauce
2 tablespoons snipped
fresh basil or
1 teaspoon dried
basil, crushed
1 egg, slightly beaten
2 cups cream-style
cottage cheese,
drained
¼ cup grated Parmesan
cheese
6 no-boil lasagna
noodles
1½ cups shredded
mozzarella cheese
(6 ounces)
Grated Parmesan
cheese (optional)
Fresh basil (optional)

1 Preheat oven to 375°F. For meat sauce, in a large saucepan cook ground beef, onion, and garlic until beef is brown. Drain off fat. Stir in pasta sauce and basil.

2 For filling, in a medium bowl combine egg, cottage cheese, and the ¼ cup Parmesan cheese.

3 To assemble, spread about ½ cup of the meat sauce over the bottom of a 2-quart rectangular baking dish. Layer half of the noodles in the bottom of the dish. Spread with half of the filling. Top with half of the mozzarella cheese and half of the remaining sauce. Repeat layers.

4 Cover baking dish loosely with foil. Bake in the preheated oven for 30 to 35 minutes or until heated through. Let stand for 10 minutes before serving. If desired, sprinkle with Parmesan cheese and garnish with fresh basil leaves.

Make-Ahead Directions: Prepare as directed through Step 3. Cover with plastic wrap, then foil; chill for 2 to 24 hours. To serve, remove plastic wrap; cover loosely with foil. Bake in a preheated 375°F oven about 1 hour or until heated through. Let stand for 10 minutes before serving.

Per serving: 374 cal., 22 g total fat (9 g sat. fat), 83 mg chol., 978 mg sodium, 20 g carbo., 2 g fiber, 23 g pro.

baked penne with meat sauce

Prep: 30 minutes Bake: 25 minutes Oven: 350°F Makes: 6 servings

8 ounces dried penne pasta
1 pound lean ground beef
½ cup chopped onion (1 medium)
1 14.5-ounce can diced tomatoes, undrained
½ of a 6-ounce can (⅓ cup) Italian-style tomato paste
⅓ cup dry red wine or tomato juice
⅓ cup water
½ teaspoon sugar
½ teaspoon dried oregano, crushed
¼ teaspoon salt
¼ teaspoon ground black pepper
¼ cup sliced pitted ripe olives
1 cup shredded reduced-fat mozzarella cheese (4 ounces)

1 Preheat oven to 350°F. Cook pasta according to package directions; drain well.

2 Meanwhile, in a large skillet cook ground beef and onion over medium heat until beef is brown. Drain off fat. Stir in undrained tomatoes, tomato paste, wine, water, sugar, dried oregano (if using), salt, and pepper. Bring to boiling; reduce heat. Simmer, covered, for 10 minutes. Stir in pasta, fresh oregano (if using), and olives. Transfer to a 3-quart rectangular baking dish; cover with foil.

3 Bake in the preheated oven for 20 minutes or until heated through. Sprinkle with mozzarella cheese. Bake, uncovered, for 5 minutes more or until cheese melts.

Make-Ahead Directions: Cover dish with plastic wrap, then foil. Chill for up to 24 hours. To heat, remove plastic wrap. Bake, covered with foil, in a preheated 350°F oven for 45 minutes or until heated through. Sprinkle with cheese; bake, uncovered, for 5 minutes more or until melted.

Per serving: 342 cal., 10 g total fat (4 g sat. fat), 51 mg chol., 465 mg sodium, 37 g carbo., 2 g fiber, 22 g pro.

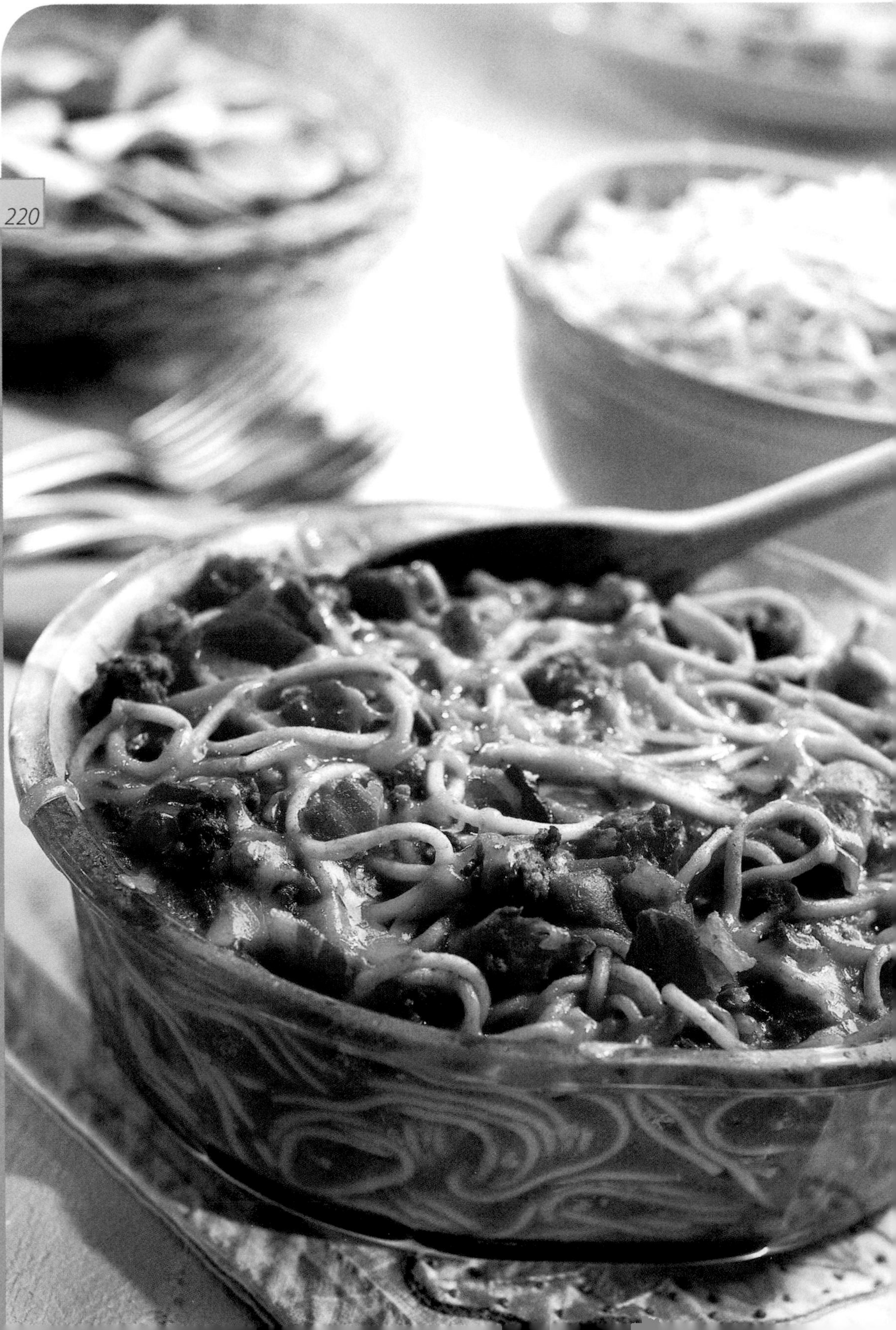

hearty spaghetti casserole

Prep: 30 minutes Bake: 45 minutes Oven: 350°F Makes: 4 to 6 servings

8 ounces dried spaghetti

8 ounces lean ground beef

½ cup chopped onion (1 medium)

½ cup chopped green sweet pepper (1 small)

1 14.5-ounce can diced tomatoes, undrained

1 10.75-ounce can condensed tomato soup

½ teaspoon ground black pepper

2 cups shredded cheddar cheese (8 ounces)

4 slices bacon, crisp-cooked, drained, and crumbled

1 Preheat oven to 350°F. Cook spaghetti according to package directions; drain. Set aside.

2 In a large skillet cook ground beef, onion, and sweet pepper until beef is brown. Drain off fat. Stir in undrained tomatoes, soup, and black pepper. Bring just to boiling. Add 1 cup of the cheddar cheese, stirring until melted.

3 Add bacon and cooked spaghetti to tomato mixture; toss gently to combine. Transfer tomato-spaghetti mixture to greased 2-quart casserole.

4 Bake, covered, in the preheated oven for 30 minutes. Sprinkle with remaining cheese. Bake, uncovered, for 15 minutes more or until heated through and bubbly.

Per serving: 675 cal., 31 g total fat (16 g sat. fat), 100 mg chol., 1,007 mg sodium, 61 g carbo., 3 g fiber, 35 g pro.

cheeseburger pasta

Prep: 20 minutes Bake: 30 minutes Oven: 350°F Makes: 6 to 8 servings

1   pound lean ground
     beef
½   cup chopped onion
     (1 medium)
8   ounces dried bow tie
     or campanelle pasta
1   10.75-ounce can
     condensed cheddar
     cheese soup
1   8-ounce can tomato
     sauce
1   tablespoon yellow
     mustard
1   cup shredded
     cheddar cheese
     (4 ounces)
½   cup chopped tomato
     (1 medium)
     Chopped sweet
     pickles (optional)

1 Preheat oven to 350°F. In a large skillet cook ground beef and onion until beef is brown and onion is tender. Drain off fat. Meanwhile, cook pasta according to package directions; drain. Rinse pasta with cold water; drain again.

2 In a large bowl combine soup, tomato sauce, and mustard. Add beef mixture and pasta; stir to combine. Spoon into a 2-quart rectangular baking dish.

3 Bake, covered, in the preheated oven for 25 minutes or until heated through. Uncover and sprinkle with cheese. Bake for 5 minutes more or until cheese melts. Sprinkle with chopped tomato and, if desired, pickles.

Per serving: 399 cal., 16 g total fat (8 g sat. fat), 72 mg chol., 738 mg sodium, 37 g carbo., 2 g fiber, 25 g pro.

Just six ingredients make up these shells. Not only is this recipe convenient, it will appeal to the entire family.

tacos in pasta shells

Prep: 40 minutes Bake: 30 minutes Oven: 350°F Makes: 6 servings

½   of a 12-ounce
     package (about 18)
     dried jumbo shell
     macaroni
1¼ pounds ground beef
1   3-ounce package
     cream cheese, cut
     up
1   teaspoon chili
     powder
1   16-ounce jar salsa
¾   cup shredded
     cheddar cheese
     (3 ounces)
     Chopped tomato
     (optional)
     Sliced pitted ripe
     olives (optional)

1 Preheat oven to 350°F. Cook shells according to package directions. Drain shells; rinse with cold water. Drain well.

2 Meanwhile, in a large skillet cook ground beef until brown; drain off fat. Stir in cream cheese and chili powder. Remove from heat; cool slightly. Divide beef mixture evenly among the cooked shells.

3 Spread about ½ cup salsa in a 2-quart rectangular baking dish. Arrange filled shells in dish; top with remaining salsa.

4 Bake, covered, in the preheated oven for 15 minutes. Remove from oven and sprinkle with cheddar cheese. Bake, uncovered, for 15 minutes more or until heated through. If desired, sprinkle with tomato and olives.

Per serving: 416 cal., 22 g total fat (11 g sat. fat), 90 mg chol., 513 mg sodium, 27 g carbo., 2 g fiber, 27 g pro.

comfort food **casseroles**

zucchini pork chop supper

Prep: 25 minutes Bake: 50 minutes Oven: 350°F Makes: 6 servings

1 14-ounce package herb-seasoned stuffing croutons (about 9½ cups)
¼ cup butter or margarine, melted
4 cups coarsely chopped zucchini
1 10.75-ounce can condensed cream of celery soup
1 8-ounce carton light dairy sour cream
¾ cup milk
½ cup shredded carrot
1 tablespoon snipped fresh parsley or 1 teaspoon dried parsley
¼ to ½ teaspoon ground black pepper
6 pork loin chops, cut ¾ inch thick (about 2¼ pounds)

1 Preheat oven to 350°F. In a large bowl stir together 7½ cups of the stuffing croutons and the melted butter; toss to combine. Place half of the buttered croutons in a greased 3-quart rectangular baking dish.

2 In another large bowl stir together zucchini, soup, sour cream, ½ cup of the milk, carrot, parsley, and pepper. Spoon over croutons in the baking dish. Sprinkle the remaining buttered croutons on top of the zucchini mixture.

3 Coarsely crush remaining stuffing croutons and place in a shallow dish. Place remaining milk in another shallow dish. Dip the pork chops in milk and then in crushed stuffing to coat.

4 Place pork chops on top of stuffing in baking dish. Sprinkle with any remaining crushed stuffing.

5 Bake, uncovered, in the preheated oven for 50 to 60 minutes or until the chops are slightly pink in the center and the juices run clear (160°F).

Per serving: *639 cal., 24 g total fat (10 g sat. fat), 130 mg chol., 1,417 mg sodium, 57 g carbo., 4 g fiber, 46 g pro.*

Diced green chile peppers and a little salsa add spunk to this hearty rice, bean, and pork dish. For a mild version use cheddar cheese instead of the pepper cheese.

pork & green chiles casserole

Prep: 15 minutes Bake: 30 minutes Stand: 5 minutes Oven: 350°F
Makes: 6 servings

1   pound ground pork
1   15-ounce can pinto beans or black beans, rinsed and drained
1   10.75-ounce can condensed cream of chicken soup
1½   cups bottled salsa
1   4.5-ounce can diced green chile peppers, drained
1   cup quick-cooking brown rice
¼   cup water
1   teaspoon ground cumin
½   cup shredded cheddar cheese or Monterey Jack with jalapeño peppers (2 ounces)

1 Preheat oven to 350°F. In a large skillet cook pork until no pink remains; drain off fat. Stir in beans, soup, salsa, chile peppers, brown rice, water, and cumin. Heat and stir just until bubbly. Pour into a 2-quart casserole.

2 Bake, uncovered, in the preheated oven for 30 to 35 minutes or until edges are bubbly. Remove from oven. Sprinkle with cheese; let stand for 5 minutes to melt cheese.

Per serving: 314 cal., 13 g total fat (6 g sat. fat), 49 mg chol., 820 mg sodium, 31 g carbo., 5 g fiber, 19 g pro.

This creamy, colorful dish is a real kid-pleaser.

baked rotini with ham

Prep: 25 minutes Bake: 20 minutes Stand: 10 minutes Oven: 350°F
Makes: 4 servings

8 ounces dried
  tricolored rotini
  (3 cups)
1 16- to 17-ounce jar
  Alfredo pasta sauce
½ cup milk
½ cup shredded
  mozzarella cheese
  (2 ounces)
2 ounces cooked ham,
  chopped (½ cup)
1 teaspoon dried Italian
  seasoning, crushed
⅛ teaspoon ground
  black pepper
¼ cup grated Parmesan
  cheese

1 Preheat oven to 350°F. Cook rotini according to package directions; drain and return to pan. Stir in Alfredo sauce, milk, mozzarella cheese, ham, Italian seasoning, and pepper.

2 Transfer rotini mixture to four 7- to 8-ounce individual au gratin dishes or ramekins or a 1½-quart au gratin dish. Sprinkle with Parmesan cheese.

3 Cover with foil. Bake in the preheated oven for 20 minutes for the individual dishes or until mixture is heated through. (For the large dish, bake for 35 minutes.) Let stand for 10 minutes.

Make-Ahead Directions: Prepare recipe through Step 2. Cover and chill for up to 24 hours. To serve, preheat oven to 350°F. Cover with foil and bake in the preheated oven for 25 to 30 minutes for the individual dishes or until mixture is heated through. (For the large dish, bake for 45 minutes). Let stand for 10 minutes before serving.

Per serving: 503 cal., 28 g total fat (13 g sat. fat), 121 mg chol., 1,084 mg sodium, 51 g carbo., 2 g fiber, 20 g pro.

denver potato casserole

Prep: 20 minutes **Bake:** 1 hour 5 minutes **Oven:** 350°F **Makes:** 4 servings

4 medium Yukon gold
potatoes, thinly
sliced (1⅓ pounds
total)

8 ounces cooked ham,
cubed

¾ cup chopped green
sweet pepper
(1 medium)

⅓ cup chopped sweet
yellow onion
(1 small)

1 cup shredded Colby
and Monterey Jack
cheese (4 ounces)

1 Preheat oven to 350°F. Grease a 2-quart
square baking dish; layer half of the
potatoes, half of the ham, half of the sweet
pepper, half of the onion, and half of the
cheese in prepared baking dish. Repeat with
the remaining ham, sweet pepper, and onion.
Top with the remaining potatoes.

2 Bake, covered, in the preheated oven
for 45 minutes. Uncover and bake
for 15 minutes more or until potatoes are
tender. Sprinkle with remaining cheese. Bake,
uncovered, for 5 minutes more or until cheese
is melted.

*Per serving: 315 cal., 12 g total fat (6 g sat. fat), 56 mg chol.,
1,010 mg sodium, 27 g carbo., 3 g fiber, 24 g pro.*

Busy day tomorrow? Assemble this casserole tonight, then store it in the refrigerator. The next evening when you get home, all you have to do is pop it in the oven to heat through.

white bean & sausage rigatoni

Prep: 25 minutes Bake: 30 minutes Oven: 375°F Makes: 6 servings

8 ounces dried rigatoni (5 cups)
8 ounces cooked kielbasa
½ of a 6-ounce can Italian-style tomato paste (⅓ cup)
¼ cup dry red wine*
1 10-ounce package frozen chopped spinach, thawed and well drained
2 14.5-ounce cans diced tomatoes with basil, oregano, and garlic, undrained
1 15-ounce can Great Northern beans, rinsed and drained
⅓ cup shredded Parmesan cheese

1 Preheat oven to 375°F. Cook pasta according to package directions; drain. Return to saucepan. Cut kielbasa in half lengthwise and then into bias slices. In a small bowl combine tomato paste and wine.

2 Add kielbasa, spinach, undrained tomatoes, beans, and tomato paste mixture to the cooked pasta; mix well. Transfer to an ungreased 3-quart rectangular baking dish.

3 Bake, covered, in the preheated oven for 25 minutes or until heated through. Sprinkle with cheese. Bake, uncovered, for 5 minutes more or until cheese is melted.

*Tip: You can substitute ¼ cup reduced-sodium chicken broth for the dry red wine.

Per serving: 564 cal., 20 g total fat (11 g sat. fat), 48 mg chol., 1,706 mg sodium, 62 g carbo., 7 g fiber, 30 g pro.

spicy sausage potpie

Prep: 40 minutes Bake: 40 minutes Oven: 375°F Makes: 4 servings

¾ cup all-purpose flour
½ cup yellow cornmeal
¼ teaspoon salt
⅓ cup shortening
2 tablespoons snipped fresh cilantro or Italian (flat-leaf) parsley
3 to 5 tablespoons cold water
6 ounces hot Italian sausage (casings removed, if present), crumbled
1½ cups coarsely chopped, peeled rutabaga or turnip (about 8 ounces)
1 cup mild or medium salsa
¾ cup cooked ham, cut into ½-inch cubes (4 ounces)
½ cup reduced-sodium chicken broth
1 14.5- or 15-ounce can golden hominy, rinsed and drained
Fresh cilantro sprigs (optional)

1 For pastry, in a medium bowl combine flour, cornmeal, and salt. Using a pastry blender, cut in shortening until pieces are pea-size. Stir in the snipped cilantro. Sprinkle 1 tablespoon cold water over flour mixture, tossing with a fork until moistened. Push moistened pastry to the side of the bowl. Repeat moistening flour mixture, using 1 tablespoon water at a time, until all of the flour mixture has been moistened. Form dough into a ball. Set aside.

2 In a large skillet cook sausage for 8 to 10 minutes or until brown. Drain off fat. Stir in rutabaga, salsa, ham, and broth. Bring to boiling; reduce heat. Simmer, covered, for 8 to 10 minutes or until rutabaga is crisp-tender. Stir in hominy. Spoon sausage mixture into an ungreased round 1½-quart casserole dish.

3 Preheat oven to 375°F. Measure diameter of top of casserole. On a lightly floured surface roll pastry about 1 inch larger than top of casserole. Place pastry on top of casserole. Turn pastry edges under and flute; cut slits in top for steam to escape.

4 Bake, uncovered, in the preheated oven for 40 to 45 minutes or until pastry is golden brown. If desired, garnish with cilantro sprigs.

Per serving: 422 cal., 38 g total fat (11 g sat. fat), 14 mg chol., 909 mg sodium, 48 g carbo., 3 g fiber, 22 g pro.

italian sausage & spinach pie

Prep: 30 minutes Bake: 50 minutes Stand: 10 minutes Oven: 375°F
Makes: 10 servings

1   15-ounce package
    rolled refrigerated
    unbaked piecrust
    (2 crusts)
1   pound bulk Italian
    sausage
½   cup chopped onion
    (1 medium)
5   eggs
1   egg white
1   10-ounce package
    frozen chopped
    spinach, thawed
    and well drained
2   cups shredded
    mozzarella cheese
    (8 ounces)
½   of a 15-ounce
    carton part-skim
    ricotta cheese
    (about 1 cup)
½   teaspoon garlic
    powder
1   beaten egg yolk
1   tablespoon water

1 Preheat oven to 375°F. Let piecrusts stand at room temperature according to package directions. Meanwhile, in a large skillet cook sausage and onion for 10 to 15 minutes or until sausage is no longer pink and onion is tender. Drain off fat.

2 In a large bowl beat together whole eggs and egg white. Stir in drained spinach, mozzarella cheese, ricotta cheese, garlic powder, and the sausage mixture.

3 Unroll piecrusts. Line a 9- or 10-inch pie plate with one crust. Spread filling evenly in pastry-lined plate. Trim pastry to edge of pie plate. Top with remaining crust. Seal and crimp edge as desired. Brush top of crust with a mixture of egg yolk and the water. Cut slits in crust to allow steam to escape.

4 Bake pie in the preheated oven for 50 to 55 minutes or until top is golden brown. Cover edge with foil, if necessary, to prevent overbrowning. Let stand for 10 minutes before serving. Cut into wedges to serve.

Per serving: *459 cal., 32 g total fat (11 g sat. fat), 178 mg chol., 578 mg sodium, 22 g carbo., 1 g fiber, 20 g pro.*

Polenta is a northern Italian staple made of cornmeal that can be served soft, like mashed potatoes, or chilled and shaped, as it is here.

layered polenta casserole

Prep: 35 minutes Bake: 30 minutes Stand: 10 minutes Chill: 2 hours Oven: 400°F
Makes: 6 servings

Nonstick cooking
spray
2¾ cups cold water
1 cup yellow cornmeal
1 cup water
1 tablespoon snipped
fresh basil or
¾ teaspoon dried
basil, crushed
½ teaspoon salt
¼ cup finely shredded
Parmesan cheese
8 ounces Italian
sausage, casings
removed, or
uncooked turkey
Italian sausage
½ cup chopped carrot
(1 medium)
1⅓ cups tomato and herb
pasta sauce
1 cup shredded
provolone or
mozzarella cheese
(4 ounces)
¼ cup finely shredded
Parmesan cheese

1 Coat a 2-quart rectangular baking dish with cooking spray. In a saucepan bring 2¾ cups water to boiling. Meanwhile, combine cornmeal, 1 cup cold water, basil, and salt. Slowly add the cornmeal mixture to the boiling water, stirring constantly. Cook and stir until the cornmeal mixture returns to boiling. Reduce heat to low. Cook, uncovered, for 10 to 15 minutes or until cornmeal mixture is thick, stirring constantly. Stir in ¼ cup Parmesan cheese until melted. Spread polenta in prepared dish. Cover and chill for 2 hours. In a medium saucepan cook sausage and carrot until sausage is no longer pink. Drain fat. Reserve ¾ cup of the pasta sauce; cover. Stir remaining sauce into sausage mixture. Cool slightly; cover and chill for 2 hours.

2 Preheat oven to 400°F. Remove polenta from dish; cut into 24 triangles. Spread the reserved ¾ cup sauce in bottom of the same dish. Arrange polenta on sauce. Spoon sausage mixture over polenta. Sprinkle with provolone cheese. Cover with foil. Bake in the preheated oven for 25 minutes. Remove foil. Sprinkle ¼ cup Parmesan cheese over top. Bake, uncovered, for 5 to 10 minutes more or until cheese is bubbly. Let stand for 10 minutes.

Per serving: 340 cal., 16 g total fat (6 g sat. fat), 42 mg chol., 932 mg sodium, 31 g carbo., 2 g fiber, 17 g pro.

tuna alfredo casserole

Prep: 20 minutes Bake: 10 minutes Oven: 425°F Makes: 6 servings

3   cups dried rigatoni or
    penne pasta
1   cup fresh or frozen
    pea pods (optional)
1   10-ounce container
    refrigerated Alfredo
    pasta sauce or four-
    cheese pasta sauce
3   tablespoons milk
2   tablespoons
    purchased dried
    tomato pesto
1   12-ounce can solid
    white tuna (water
    pack), drained and
    broken into chunks
¼   cup finely shredded
    Parmesan cheese
    (1 ounce)

1 Preheat oven to 425°F. In a Dutch oven cook pasta according to package directions. If desired, add the pea pods during the last minute of cooking. Drain well; return to Dutch oven.

2 Meanwhile, in a medium bowl combine Alfredo sauce, milk, and pesto. Add to pasta, stirring gently to coat. Gently fold in tuna. Transfer pasta mixture to a 2-quart oval or rectangular baking dish. Sprinkle with Parmesan cheese.

3 Bake, uncovered, in the preheated oven for 10 to 15 minutes or until heated through and cheese is just melted.

Per serving: 414 cal., 20 g total fat (2 g sat. fat), 51 mg chol., 516 mg sodium, 33 g carbo., 1 g fiber, 23 g pro.

Italian canned tuna is delicious in this recipe. You'll find the tuna, called Genova tonno, in Italian specialty-food stores.

tuna, fennel & rotini bake

Prep: 20 minutes Bake: 20 minutes Oven: 375°F Makes: 6 servings

1½ cups dried rotini pasta
¾ cup seasoned croutons, slightly crushed
2 tablespoons butter
2 cups sliced fennel (2 small bulbs)
1 10-ounce container refrigerated light Alfredo pasta sauce
2 tablespoons drained capers (optional)
2 6-ounce cans tuna (packed in oil), drained and broken into chunks

1 Preheat oven to 375°F. Cook pasta according to package directions; drain.

2 Meanwhile, place croutons in a small bowl. In a medium saucepan melt butter. Remove 1 tablespoon of the melted butter; toss with croutons. Set aside.

3 Add fennel to remaining butter in saucepan. Cover and cook for 6 to 8 minutes or just until fennel is tender, stirring occasionally. Stir in Alfredo sauce, capers (if desired), and cooked pasta. Gently fold in tuna. Transfer tuna mixture to an ungreased 1½-quart casserole. Top with croutons.

4 Bake, uncovered, in the preheated oven for 20 minutes or until heated through.

Per serving: *306 cal., 11 g total fat (6 g sat. fat), 44 mg chol., 527 mg sodium, 29 g carbo., 9 g fiber, 20 g pro.*

No need to make pastry for this pot pie. Shards of phyllo dough sprinkled on top of the creamy crab mixture provide a crispy contrast in texture.

crab potpie

Prep: 40 minutes Bake: 25 minutes Chill: 4 hours Oven: 375°F Makes: 6 servings

3 sheets frozen phyllo dough (14×9-inch rectangles), thawed
3 tablespoons butter, melted
   Paprika
3 tablespoons butter
1 cup chopped onion (1 large)
½ cup sliced celery (1 stalk)
¼ cup all-purpose flour
2 cups milk
3 6.5-ounce cans lump crabmeat, drained, or three 6- to 8-ounce packages chunk- or flake-style imitation crabmeat
½ cup frozen peas
2 tablespoons dry sherry (optional)
¼ teaspoon dried tarragon, crushed
¼ teaspoon salt
¼ teaspoon ground black pepper

1 Preheat oven to 375°F. Unfold phyllo dough; remove 1 sheet. (Cover the remaining phyllo dough.) Lightly brush dough with some of the 3 tablespoons melted butter; fold in half crosswise. Brush again with butter. Repeat with remaining sheets, brushing each sheet with some of the melted butter. Stack the sheets on a baking sheet to make 6 layers. Brush top of stack with any remaining melted butter. Sprinkle with paprika. Bake in the preheated oven for 8 to 10 minutes or until brown and crisp. Cool on baking sheet on a wire rack. Break into large shards; store in an airtight container until ready to serve.

2 In a large skillet, melt 3 tablespoons butter over medium heat. Add onion and celery; cook and stir for 2 to 3 minutes or just until tender. Add flour to the skillet; cook and stir for 1 minute. Stir in milk; cook and stir until mixture is slightly thickened. Remove from heat; stir in crabmeat, peas, dry sherry (if desired), tarragon, salt, and pepper. Spoon crab mixture into a 2-quart baking dish. Cover; chill for 4 hours. Preheat oven to 375°F. Bake, covered, for 25 to 30 minutes or until heated through. Serve with phyllo.

Per serving: 295 cal., 15 g total fat (9 g sat. fat), 121 mg chol., 619 mg sodium, 15 g carbo., 1 g fiber, 24 g pro.

Tangy goat cheese, roasted red peppers, and a splash of red wine take this dish from simple to special!

roasted red pepper lasagna

Prep: 20 minutes Bake: 50 minutes Stand: 20 minutes Oven: 350°F
Makes: 4 to 6 servings

Nonstick cooking
  spray
1 26-ounce jar red
  pasta sauce, such
  as portobello
  mushroom or
  garden vegetable
6 no-boil lasagna
  noodles
½ of a 15-ounce
  container ricotta
  cheese
6 ounces goat
  cheese or
  1½ cups shredded
  mozzarella cheese
  (6 ounces)
1 tablespoon Chianti or
  other dry red wine
  (optional)
¼ cup finely shredded
  Parmesan cheese
1 cup roasted red
  sweet peppers,
  drained well and
  cut into strips

1 Preheat oven to 350°F. Lightly coat a 2-quart square baking dish with cooking spray. Spoon ⅓ cup of the pasta sauce in the dish. Top with 2 lasagna noodles. In a small bowl stir together the ricotta cheese, ⅔ of the goat cheese, and, if desired, the Chianti. Spoon half of the ricotta mixture over the noodles in the dish. Sprinkle with 2 tablespoons Parmesan cheese. Top with half of the roasted pepper strips. Spoon half of the remaining sauce over the pepper layer.

2 Top with 2 more noodles, the remaining ricotta mixture, and the remaining roasted pepper strips. Add 2 more noodles and the remaining sauce. Dot top with the remaining goat cheese and sprinkle with remaining Parmesan cheese.

3 Bake, covered, in the preheated oven for 50 minutes or until heated through. Let stand, covered, on a wire rack for 20 minutes before serving.

Make-Ahead Directions: Prepare through Step 2. Cover with plastic wrap. Chill 2 to 24 hours. Remove plastic wrap. Cover with foil. Bake in a preheated 350°F oven for 1 hour or until heated through. Let stand as above.

Per serving: 459 cal., 24 g total fat (14 g sat. fat), 64 mg chol., 975 mg sodium, 37 g carbo., 4 g fiber, 23 g pro.

The challenge of meatless lasagna is to make it as satisfying as the beef- or sausage-layered classic. Crunchy walnuts stand in for the meat, adding heartiness and texture.

lasagna with zucchini & walnuts

Prep: 35 minutes Bake: 40 minutes Stand: 15 minutes Oven: 375°F
Makes: 6 servings

2	medium zucchini, thinly sliced lengthwise (9 long slices total)
4	teaspoons olive oil
1½	cups finely chopped carrot (2 large)
2	cups finely chopped onion (2 large)
4	cloves garlic, minced
2	cups purchased marinara sauce
1	tablespoon snipped fresh basil or 1 teaspoon dried basil, crushed
⅛	teaspoon ground black pepper
1½	cups shredded mozzarella cheese (6 ounces)
½	cup grated Parmesan cheese
6	no-boil lasagna noodles
½	cup chopped toasted walnuts

1 Preheat broiler. Place zucchini in a single layer on a greased baking sheet; brush with 1 teaspoon of the oil. Broil 3 to 4 inches from heat about 5 minutes or until crisp-tender, turning once. Cool; set aside. Turn oven to 375°F. In a large saucepan heat the remaining oil over medium-high heat. Add carrot, onion, and garlic; cook and stir for 5 minutes or until tender. Add marinara sauce, basil, and pepper. Bring to boiling; reduce heat. Simmer, covered, for 10 minutes, stirring occasionally. In a bowl combine the mozzarella cheese and Parmesan cheese; set aside.

2 Grease a 2-quart square baking dish; arrange two noodles in the dish. Spread with a third of the sauce. Sprinkle with a third of the nuts. Top with a third of the zucchini; sprinkle with a third of the cheese mixture. Repeat layering, alternating direction of the zucchini in each layer and finishing with the zucchini; set remaining cheese aside. Bake, covered, in the preheated 375°F oven for 20 minutes. Uncover and sprinkle with remaining cheese mixture. Bake, uncovered, for 20 minutes more or until heated through. Let stand for 15 minutes before serving.

Per serving: 358 cal., 19 g total fat (6 g sat. fat), 23 mg chol., 839 mg sodium, 33 g carbo., 3 g fiber, 17 g pro.

rotini-bean bake

Prep: 40 minutes Bake: 35 minutes Stand: 10 minutes Oven: 375°F
Makes: 8 servings

12 ounces packaged
dried rotini pasta
½ cup bottled balsamic
vinaigrette
1 15-ounce can
cannellini (white
kidney) beans or
garbanzo beans,
rinsed and drained
8 ounces feta cheese,
crumbled
1 cup coarsely chopped
pitted Greek black
olives
1 pound plum tomatoes,
coarsely chopped
½ cup seasoned fine dry
bread crumbs
1 8-ounce carton plain
low-fat yogurt
¾ cup milk
⅓ cup grated Parmesan
cheese
1 tablespoon all-
purpose flour

1 Preheat oven to 375°F. Lightly grease a
3-quart rectangular baking dish; set aside.
Cook pasta according to package directions.
Drain. In a very large bowl combine vinaigrette
and pasta; toss to coat. Stir in beans, feta
cheese, olives, and tomato.

2 Sprinkle ¼ cup of the bread crumbs in
prepared dish. Spoon pasta mixture into
dish. In a medium bowl stir together yogurt,
milk, Parmesan cheese, and flour until smooth.
Pour evenly over pasta mixture. Sprinkle top
with remaining ¼ cup bread crumbs.

3 Bake, covered, in the preheated oven for
25 minutes. Uncover and bake for 10 to
15 minutes more until heated through and
top is light brown. Let stand for 10 minutes
before serving.

Per serving: *425 cal., 15 g total fat (6 g sat. fat), 31 mg chol.,
1,045 mg sodium, 57 g carbo., 6 g fiber, 19 g pro.*

Light sour cream, salsa, and sliced green onion are tasty toppers, too.

tortilla & black bean bake

Prep: 25 minutes Bake: 30 minutes Stand: 10 minutes Oven: 350°F
Makes: 8 servings

2 cups chopped onion (2 large)
1 14.5-ounce can diced tomatoes, undrained
1½ cups chopped green sweet pepper (2 medium)
¾ cup picante sauce
2 teaspoons ground cumin
2 cloves garlic, minced
2 15-ounce cans black beans and/or red kidney beans, rinsed and drained
12 6-inch corn tortillas
2 cups shredded reduced-fat Monterey Jack cheese (8 ounces)
Shredded lettuce (optional)
Sliced hot red peppers (optional)

1 Preheat oven to 350°F. In a large skillet, combine onion, undrained tomatoes, sweet pepper, picante sauce, cumin, and garlic. Bring to boiling; reduce heat. Simmer, uncovered, for 10 minutes. Stir in black beans.

2 To assemble, spread one-third of the bean mixture over the bottom of a 3-quart rectangular baking dish. Top with half of the tortillas, overlapping as necessary, and half of the Monterey Jack cheese. Add another one-third of the bean mixture; top with remaining tortillas and remaining bean mixture.

3 Cover dish with foil. Bake in the preheated oven for 30 to 35 minutes or until heated through. Sprinkle with remaining cheese. Let stand for 10 minutes before serving.

4 If desired, arrange shredded lettuce on dinner plates. Cut casserole into squares and place on top of the lettuce. If desired, garnish with hot peppers.

Per serving: *266 cal., 7 g total fat (4 g sat. fat), 20 mg chol., 971 mg sodium, 43 g carbo., 10 g fiber, 15 g pro.*

Some like it hot—but remember, others don't! No problem—you can adjust the heat in this layered, low-fat casserole by choosing mild, medium, or hot salsa.

tortilla bean-rice bake

Prep: 30 minutes Bake: 25 minutes Oven: 350°F Makes: 6 servings

1½   cups water
⅔   cup uncooked long
      grain rice
6   6-inch corn tortillas
¾   cup fat-free dairy
      sour cream
1   tablespoon all-
      purpose flour
1   tablespoon skim milk
1   14.5-ounce can
      Mexican-style
      stewed tomatoes,
      undrained
1   8-ounce jar salsa
1   15-ounce can kidney
      beans or small red
      beans, rinsed and
      drained
    Nonstick cooking
      spray
    Shredded reduced-
      fat Monterey Jack
      cheese (optional)
    Sliced jalapeño chile
      peppers (see note,
      page 126) (optional)

1 Preheat oven to 350°F. In a medium saucepan bring water to boiling. Add rice and return to boiling; reduce heat. Simmer, covered, for 20 minutes or until rice is tender. Meanwhile, stack tortillas; wrap in foil. Heat in the preheated oven for 10 minutes to soften.

2 In a small bowl stir together sour cream, flour, and milk; set aside. In a medium bowl combine the undrained tomatoes and salsa. Stir beans into cooked rice. Coat a 2-quart casserole or baking dish with cooking spray. Cut softened tortillas into quarters. Arrange half of the tortillas in the bottom of the casserole. Layer half of the rice-bean mixture over tortillas, then half of the tomato mixture, and half of the sour cream mixture. Repeat layers.

3 Bake, covered, in the 350°F oven for 25 to 30 minutes or until heated through. If desired, garnish with Monterey Jack cheese and jalapeño peppers.

Per serving: *269 cal., 1 g total fat (0 g sat. fat), 0 mg chol., 540 mg sodium, 56 g carbo., 6 g fiber, 11 g pro.*

three-cheese spinach pie

Prep: 25 minutes Bake: 45 minutes Cool: 15 minutes Oven: 375°F
Makes: 12 servings

1   15-ounce package
    rolled refrigerated
    unbaked piecrust
    (2 crusts)
4   eggs
1   15-ounce carton
    ricotta cheese
1   cup finely shredded
    Asiago cheese
    (4 ounces)
¼   cup grated Parmesan
    cheese
1   teaspoon dried basil,
    crushed
¾   teaspoon coarsely
    ground black
    pepper
1   10-ounce package
    frozen chopped
    spinach, thawed
    and well drained
¼   cup seasoned fine dry
    bread crumbs
¼   cup oil-packed dried
    tomatoes, drained
    and coarsely
    chopped

1 Preheat oven to 375°F. Let piecrusts stand at room temperature according to package directions. Meanwhile, lightly beat one of the eggs; set aside. In a large bowl lightly beat remaining eggs with a fork. Add ricotta cheese, Asiago cheese, Parmesan cheese, basil, and pepper; stir well. Stir in spinach, bread crumbs, and tomatoes.

2 Line a 9-inch pie plate with one crust; brush generously with some of the reserved egg. Spread cheese mixture evenly in crust. Top with second crust. Fold edges under to seal. Flute as desired. Brush with remaining reserved egg. Cut slits in top crust.

3 Bake in the preheated oven for 45 minutes or until crust is golden brown and filling is set. If necessary to prevent overbrowning, cover edges with foil the last 20 minutes of baking. Cool on wire rack for 15 minutes before serving.

Per potluck serving: 320 cal., 20 g total fat (9 g sat. fat), 107 mg chol., 431 mg sodium, 21 g carbo., 1 g fiber, 11 g pro.

Crescent rolls make a scrumptious no-fuss crust for this cheese-and-egg main-dish pie.

italian zucchini crescent pie

Prep: 25 minutes **Bake:** 25 minutes **Stand:** 10 minutes **Oven:** 375°F
Makes: 6 to 8 servings

4   cups sliced zucchini (about 3)
1   cup chopped onion (1 large)
3   tablespoons butter or margarine
½   cup snipped fresh parsley
½   teaspoon salt
½   teaspoon ground black pepper
½   teaspoon dried oregano, crushed
½   teaspoon dried basil, crushed
¼   teaspoon garlic powder
2   eggs, slightly beaten
1   8-ounce package shredded mozzarella cheese (2 cups)
1   8-ounce can refrigerated crescent rolls (8)

1 Preheat oven to 375°F. In a large skillet cook zucchini and onion in hot butter for 8 minutes or just until tender, stirring occasionally. Remove from heat. Stir in parsley, salt, pepper, oregano, basil, and garlic powder. In a large bowl combine eggs and cheese. Stir in zucchini mixture; set aside.

2 For crust, separate crescent roll dough into triangles; press into bottom and up the side of a 10½- or 11-inch quiche dish or a 10-inch pie plate. Spoon zucchini mixture into crust, spreading evenly.

3 Bake in the preheated oven for 25 to 30 minutes or until knife inserted in center comes out clean. Let stand for 10 minutes; cut into wedges to serve.

Per serving: 360 cal., 24 g total fat (11 g sat. fat), 108 mg chol., 801 mg sodium, 22 g carbo., 2 g fiber, 16 g pro.

This homemade polenta, layered between a creamy white sauce and a fresh tomato sauce, is sprinkled with Asiago cheese and baked until bubbly.

polenta with two sauces

Prep: 45 minutes Bake: 12 minutes Chill: 2 hours Oven: 450°F
Makes: 4 servings

3 cups water
1 cup yellow cornmeal
1 cup cold water
½ teaspoon salt
¾ cup shredded Asiago
     cheese or Parmesan
     cheese (3 ounces)
1 15-ounce can Italian-
     style tomato sauce
2 tablespoons all-
     purpose flour
½ teaspoon dried basil,
     crushed
¼ teaspoon salt
⅛ teaspoon ground
     black pepper
     Dash ground nutmeg
1¼ cups milk

1 For polenta, in a medium saucepan bring the 3 cups water to boiling. In a small bowl combine cornmeal, the 1 cup cold water, and ½ teaspoon salt. Slowly add the cornmeal mixture to the boiling water, stirring constantly. Cook and stir until the cornmeal mixture returns to boiling. Reduce heat to low. Cook, uncovered, for 10 to 15 minutes or until thick, stirring frequently. Stir in ¼ cup of the cheese until melted. Spread hot polenta evenly in a lightly greased 2-quart square baking dish; cool slightly. Cover; chill for 2 hours or overnight. Cut polenta into 1-inch squares; set aside.

2 Preheat oven to 450°F. For red sauce, in a medium saucepan bring tomato sauce to boiling; reduce heat. Simmer, uncovered, for 10 minutes or until slightly thickened and reduced to 1⅓ cups. For white sauce, in another medium saucepan combine flour, basil, ¼ teaspoon salt, pepper, and nutmeg. Gradually stir in milk. Cook and stir over medium heat until thickened and bubbly. Cook and stir for 1 minute more. Remove from heat; stir in ¼ cup of the cheese until melted.

3 To assemble, divide red sauce among four shallow casseroles or au gratin dishes (about ⅓ cup sauce in each). Divide polenta cubes among casseroles. Spoon white sauce over cubes; sprinkle each serving with 1 tablespoon of the remaining ¼ cup cheese. Bake, uncovered, in the preheated oven for 12 to 15 minutes or until sauce is bubbly at edges and the cheese begins to brown.

Per serving: 318 cal., 11 g total fat (6 g sat. fat), 29 mg chol., 1,133 mg sodium, 42 g carbo., 5 g fiber, 13 g pro.

6

simmering

slow

Let your personal chef—the slow cooker—take care of dinner tonight! Just add the ingredients, turn the dial, and a home-cooked meal will be ready when you walk in the door.

cooker

If you're not feeding a crowd, refrigerate or freeze the leftover turkey to reheat for another meal.

sesame-ginger turkey wraps

Prep: 20 minutes Cook: 6 to 7 hours (low) or 3 to 3½ hours (high)
Stand: 5 minutes Makes: 12 servings

Nonstick cooking
spray
3 turkey thighs,
skinned (3½ to
4 pounds)
1 cup bottled sesame-
ginger stir-fry sauce
¼ cup water
1 16-ounce package
shredded broccoli
(broccoli slaw mix)
12 8-inch flour tortillas,
warmed*
¾ cup sliced green
onions (6)

1 Lightly coat the inside of a 3½- or 4-quart slow cooker with cooking spray. Place turkey thighs in cooker. In a small bowl stir together stir-fry sauce and the water. Pour over turkey in cooker.

2 Cover and cook on low-heat setting for 6 to 7 hours or on high-heat setting for 3 to 3½ hours.

3 Remove turkey from slow cooker; cool slightly. Remove turkey meat from bones; discard bones. Using two forks, shred turkey into bite-size pieces. Return to sauce mixture in slow cooker. Place broccoli slaw mix in sauce mixture in slow cooker. Stir to coat; cover and let stand for 5 minutes. Using a slotted spoon, remove turkey and broccoli from slow cooker.

4 To assemble, place some of the turkey mixture on each warmed tortilla. Top turkey mixture with green onions. If desired, spoon some of the sauce from slow cooker on top of green onion. Roll up tortilla and serve immediately.

*Tip: To warm tortillas, preheat oven to 350°F. Stack tortillas and wrap tightly in foil. Heat in the oven for about 10 minutes or until heated through.

Per serving: 207 cal., 5 g total fat (1 g sat. fat), 67 mg chol., 422 mg sodium, 20 g carbo., 2 g fiber, 20 g pro.

Cooking the noodles right in the slow cooker with the goulash (instead of on the stovetop) saves time and dishwashing.

turkey-vegetable
goulash

Prep: 20 minutes Cook: 6 to 8 hours (low) or 3 to 4 hours (high) plus 20 minutes (high) Makes: 6 servings

1 pound uncooked ground turkey
1 14.5-ounce can diced tomatoes with basil, garlic, and oregano, undrained
1 10-ounce package frozen mixed vegetables
1½ cups water
1 8-ounce can tomato sauce
1 cup sliced celery (2 stalks)
⅓ cup chopped onion (1 small)
1 0.9-ounce envelope turkey gravy mix
1 cup dried fine egg noodles
⅓ cup shredded sharp cheddar, Monterey Jack, or Parmesan cheese

1 In a large skillet cook ground turkey until brown. Drain off fat. Transfer turkey to a 3½- or 4-quart slow cooker. Stir in undrained tomatoes, frozen vegetables, water, tomato sauce, celery, onion, and dry gravy mix.

2 Cover and cook on low-heat setting for 6 to 8 hours or on high-heat setting for 3 to 4 hours.

3 If using low-heat setting, turn the slow cooker to high-heat setting. Stir in uncooked noodles. Cover and cook for 20 to 30 minutes more or until noodles are tender. Sprinkle with cheese.

Per serving: 251 cal., 9 g total fat (3 g sat. fat), 73 mg chol., 918 mg sodium, 22 g carbo., 3 g fiber, 19 g pro.

You can choose from numerous varieties of cooked smoked turkey at your supermarket deli. Also check out the selection of turkey sausage at the meat counter.

split pea & smoked turkey soup

Prep: 15 minutes Cook: 10 to 12 hours (low) or 5 to 6 hours (high) Makes: 4 servings

2½ cups dry green split peas (1 pound)
2 cups chopped cooked smoked turkey or sliced cooked smoked turkey sausage (8 to 10 ounces)
1½ cups coarsely chopped carrot (3 medium)
1 cup coarsely chopped yellow or green sweet pepper (1 large)
½ cup chopped onion (1 medium)
2 cloves garlic, minced
1 teaspoon dried basil, crushed
1 teaspoon dried oregano, crushed
3 14-ounce cans chicken broth

1 Rinse split peas; drain. In a 3½- or 4-quart slow cooker combine the split peas, turkey, carrot, sweet pepper, onion, garlic, basil, and oregano. Pour broth over all.

2 Cover and cook on low-heat setting for 10 to 12 hours or on high-heat setting for 5 to 6 hours. Stir before serving.

Per serving: 551 cal., 5 g total fat (1 g sat. fat), 22 mg chol., 2,258 mg sodium, 86 g carbo., 33 g fiber, 45 g pro.

spinach, chicken
& wild rice soup

Prep: 15 minutes Cook: 7 to 8 hours (low) or 3½ to 4 hours (high) Makes: 6 servings

3   cups water
1   14-ounce can
    reduced-sodium
    chicken broth
1   10.75-ounce can
    reduced-fat and
    reduced-sodium
    condensed cream of
    chicken soup
⅔   cup uncooked wild
    rice, rinsed and
    drained
½   teaspoon dried
    thyme, crushed
¼   teaspoon salt
¼   teaspoon ground
    black pepper
3   cups chopped cooked
    chicken or turkey
    (about 1 pound)
2   cups shredded fresh
    spinach

1 In a 3½- or 4-quart slow cooker, combine water, broth, soup, wild rice, thyme, salt, and pepper.

2 Cover; cook on the low-heat setting for 7 to 8 hours or on high-heat setting for 3½ to 4 hours. Just before serving, stir in chicken and spinach.

Per serving: 479 cal., 25 g total fat (10 g sat. fat), 80 mg chol., 1,263 mg sodium, 40 g carbo., 10 g fiber, 31 g pro.

Never mind traditional pairings. Beefy onion soup mix and red wine combine with chicken for a succulent stew that's luscious on a cold night. Mop your bowl clean with crusty bread.

coq au vin stew

Prep: 20 minutes Cook: 5 to 6 hours (low) or 2½ to 3 hours (high)
Makes: 4 servings

Nonstick cooking
 spray
3 pounds chicken
 thighs, skinned
1 envelope (½ of a
 2.2-ounce package)
 beefy onion soup
 mix
1½ cups frozen small
 whole onions
2 cups fresh button or
 wild mushrooms,
 quartered
½ cup dry red wine

1 Lightly coat a large skillet with cooking spray; heat over medium heat. Brown several of the chicken thighs at a time on both sides. Place in a 3½- or 4-quart slow cooker. Repeat with remaining chicken thighs. Drain off fat.

2 Sprinkle chicken with soup mix. Add onions and mushrooms. Pour wine over all.

3 Cover and cook on low-heat setting for 5 to 6 hours or on high-heat setting for 2½ to 3 hours.

Per serving: 305 cal., 8 g total fat (2 g sat. fat), 161 mg chol., 759 mg sodium, 12 g carbo., 2 g fiber, 41 g pro.

Cream of chicken soup, cooked chicken, and chicken broth triple the chicken flavor of this no-fuss meal in a bowl.

wild rice & chicken stew

Prep: 15 minutes Cook: 6 to 8 hours (low) or 3 to 4 hours (high)
Makes: 8 to 10 servings

2½ cups chopped cooked
chicken (about
12 ounces)
2 cups sliced fresh
mushrooms
1 cup coarsely
shredded carrot
(2 medium)
1 cup sliced celery
(2 stalks)
1 10.75-ounce can
condensed cream of
chicken or cream of
mushroom soup
1 6-ounce package long
grain and wild rice
mix
5 cups chicken broth
5 cups water

1 In a 5- to 6-quart slow cooker, combine chicken, mushrooms, carrot, celery, soup, uncooked rice mix, and the contents of the rice seasoning packet. Gradually stir in broth and the water.

2 Cover and cook on low-heat setting for 6 to 8 hours or on high-heat setting for 3 to 4 hours.

Per serving: 221 cal., 7 g total fat (2 g sat. fat), 44 mg chol., 1,251 mg sodium, 23 g carbo., 2 g fiber, 18 g pro.

chicken tortilla soup

Prep: 10 minutes Cook: 6 to 7 hours (low) or 3 to 3½ hours (high)
Makes: 4 to 6 servings

2   14-ounce cans
    chicken broth with
    roasted garlic
1   14.5-ounce can
    Mexican-style
    stewed tomatoes,
    undrained
1   9-ounce package
    frozen diced cooked
    chicken breast
2   cups frozen pepper
    stir-fry vegetables
1   cup corn chips
    Sliced fresh jalapeño
    chile peppers (see
    note, page 126)
    (optional)

1 In a 3½- or 4-quart slow cooker, combine broth, undrained tomatoes, chicken, and frozen vegetables.

2 Cover and cook on low-heat setting for 6 to 7 hours or on high-heat setting for 3 to 3½ hours.

3 To serve, ladle soup into warm soup bowls. Serve with corn chips. If desired, top with jalapeño peppers.

Per serving: 189 cal., 5 g total fat (0 g sat. fat), 36 mg chol., 1,395 mg sodium, 19 g carbo., 1 g fiber, 18 g pro.

Thicken this slow cooker chili to spooning consistency by slightly mashing the beans.

fix-and-forget white chili

Prep: 25 minutes Cook: 7 to 8 hours (low) or 3½ to 4 hours (high) Makes: 6 servings

12	ounces skinless, boneless chicken breast halves, cubed
1	tablespoon cooking oil
3	15-ounce cans Great Northern beans, rinsed and drained
2	4-ounce cans diced green chile peppers, undrained
½	cup chopped onion (1 medium)
2½	cups chicken broth
1½	teaspoons cumin seeds
¼	to 1 teaspoon cayenne pepper
¼	teaspoon salt
3	cloves garlic, minced Dairy sour cream (optional) Avocado slices (optional) Fresh thyme sprigs (optional)

1 In a large skillet cook chicken in hot oil just until light brown. Place beans in a 3½- or 4-quart slow cooker; mash slightly with a potato masher.

2 Add chicken to slow cooker. Stir undrained chile peppers, onion, broth, cumin seeds, cayenne pepper, salt, and garlic into chicken mixture in slow cooker. Cover and cook on low-heat setting for 7 to 8 hours or on high-heat setting for 3½ to 4 hours.

3 If desired, serve with sour cream and avocado and garnish with thyme sprigs.

Per serving: 124 cal., 3 g total fat (1 g sat. fat), 16 mg chol., 319 mg sodium, 13 g carbo., 3 g fiber, 12 g pro.

When winter's wind chills your spirit, it's time for a bowl of this hearty south-of-the-border-style soup.

southwestern white chili

Prep: 20 minutes Cook: 7 to 8 hours (low) or 3½ to 4 hours (high)
Makes: 8 servings

1 cup chopped onion
  (1 large)
4 cloves garlic, minced
2 teaspoons ground
  cumin
1 teaspoon dried
  oregano, crushed
¼ teaspoon cayenne
  pepper
3 15.5-ounce cans
  Great Northern
  beans, rinsed and
  drained
2 4-ounce cans diced
  green chile peppers,
  undrained
4 cups chicken broth
  or reduced-sodium
  chicken broth
3 cups chopped cooked
  chicken (about
  1 pound)
2 cups shredded
  Monterey Jack
  cheese (8 ounces)
  Dairy sour cream
  (optional)
  Cilantro leaves
  (optional)

1 In a 3½- to 5-quart slow cooker, place the onion, garlic, cumin, oregano, cayenne pepper, drained beans, undrained chile peppers, broth, and cooked chicken. Stir to combine.

2 Cover and cook on low-heat setting for 7 to 8 hours or on high-heat setting for 3½ to 4 hours. Stir in the cheese until melted.

3 Ladle the chili into bowls. If desired, top servings with sour cream and cilantro.

Per serving: *431 cal., 14 g total fat (7 g sat. fat), 72 mg chol., 671 mg sodium, 39 g carbo., 9 g fiber, 38 g pro.*

Take 15 minutes in the morning to brown the roast, cut up the potatoes, and layer the ingredients in your slow cooker. At the end of the day, gather the family for a pot roast dinner complete with meat, potatoes, carrots, and gravy.

pot roast with
mushroom sauce

Prep: 15 minutes **Cook:** 10 to 12 hours (low) or 5 to 6 hours (high)
Makes: 5 servings

1 1½-pound boneless
   beef eye round
   roast or rump roast
   Nonstick cooking
   spray
4 medium potatoes,
   quartered
1 16-ounce package
   peeled baby carrots
1 10.75-ounce can
   condensed golden
   mushroom soup
½ teaspoon dried
   tarragon or basil,
   crushed

1 Trim fat from roast. Lightly coat a large skillet with cooking spray; heat over medium heat. Brown roast on all sides in hot skillet.

2 In a 3½- or 4-quart slow cooker place potatoes and carrots. Place roast on top of vegetables. In a small bowl stir together soup and tarragon; pour over roast in slow cooker.

3 Cover and cook on low-heat setting for 10 to 12 hours or on high-heat setting for 5 to 6 hours. Transfer roast and vegetables to a serving platter. Stir sauce; spoon over roast and vegetables.

Per serving: 391 cal., 13 g total fat (5 g sat. fat), 79 mg chol., 567 mg sodium, 33 g carbo., 5 g fiber, 33 g pro.

Fennel, tomatoes, olives, and Greek seasoning raise ordinary beef brisket to new flavor heights.

mediterranean pot roast

Prep: 25 minutes Cook: 10 to 11 hours (low) or 5 to 5½ hours (high) Makes: 8 servings

1 3-pound fresh beef brisket
3 teaspoons dried Greek or Italian seasoning, crushed
2 medium fennel bulbs, trimmed, cored, and cut into thick wedges
1 14.5-ounce can diced tomatoes with basil, garlic, and oregano, undrained
½ cup beef broth
¼ cup pitted green and/or ripe olives
¾ teaspoon salt
½ teaspoon finely shredded lemon peel
¼ teaspoon ground black pepper
¼ cup water
2 tablespoons all-purpose flour
Hot cooked noodles or rice (optional)

1 Trim fat from beef. If necessary, cut beef to fit into a 5- to 6-quart slow cooker. Sprinkle meat with 1 teaspoon of the Greek seasoning. Place beef in the slow cooker. Top with fennel wedges.

2 Combine undrained tomatoes, broth, olives, salt, lemon peel, pepper, and remaining 2 teaspoons Greek seasoning. Pour over beef and vegetables in cooker. Cover and cook on low-heat setting for 10 to 11 hours or on high-heat setting for 5 to 5½ hours.

3 Remove beef from slow cooker, reserving cooking liquid. Thinly slice meat. Arrange beef and vegetables on a platter. Cover beef and vegetables; keep warm. Pour cooking liquid into a glass measuring cup; skim off fat.

4 For sauce, if necessary, add water to cooking liquid to make 2 cups. Transfer to a small saucepan. In a small bowl combine the ¼ cup water and the flour; stir into liquid in saucepan. Cook and stir until thickened and bubbly. Cook and stir for 1 minute more. Serve sauce with beef and vegetables. If desired, serve with hot cooked noodles.

Per serving: 286 cal., 11 g total fat (3 g sat. fat), 82 mg chol., 754 mg sodium, 8 g carbo., 1 g fiber, 37 g pro.

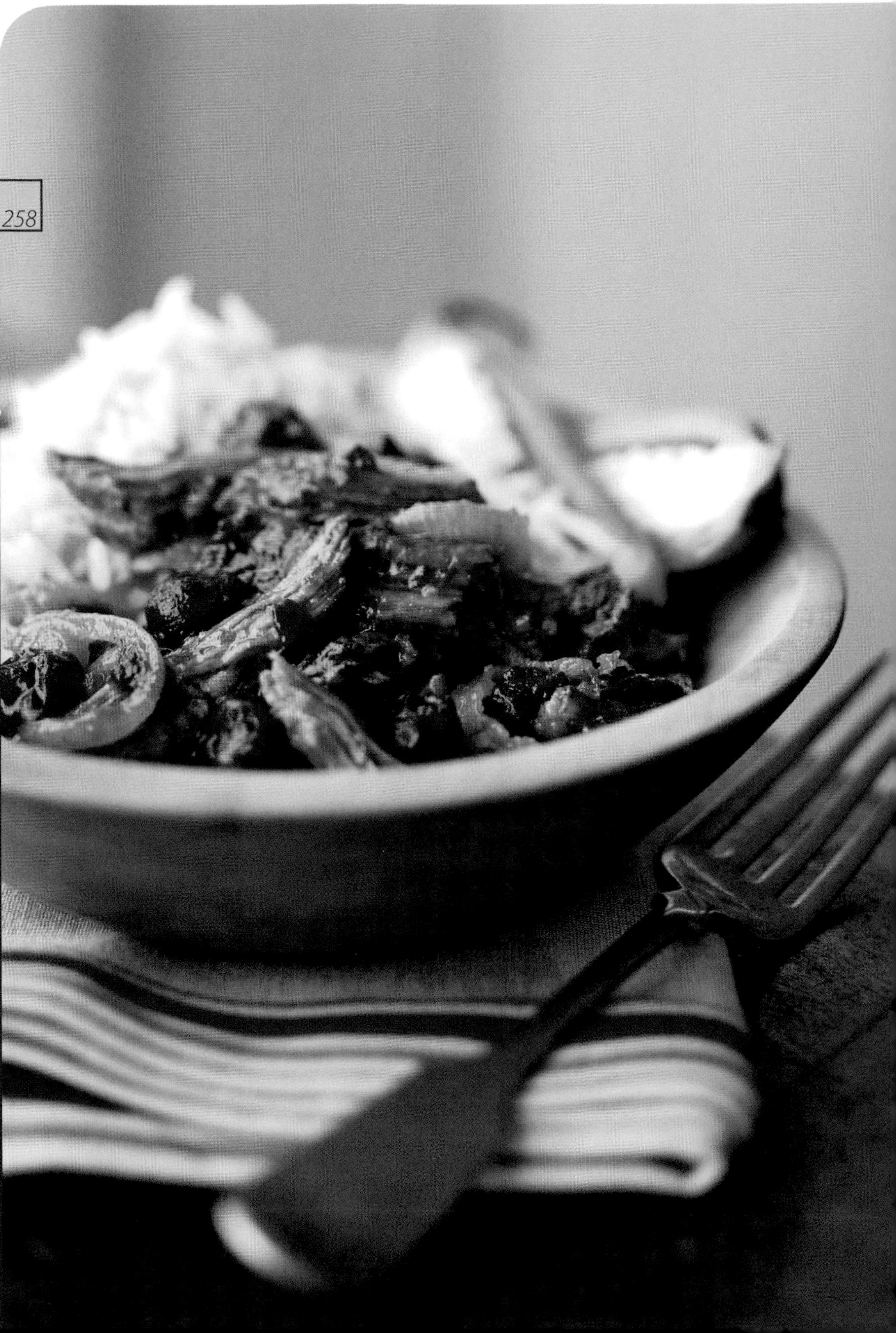

cranberry-chipotle
beef

Prep: 15 minutes Cook: 8 to 10 hours (low) or 4 to 5 hours (high)
Makes: 6 servings

1   2½- to 3-pound
       boneless beef chuck
       pot roast
1   medium onion, cut
       into thin wedges
¼   teaspoon salt
¼   teaspoon ground
       black pepper
3   cloves garlic, minced
1   16-ounce can whole
       cranberry sauce
2   to 3 teaspoons finely
       chopped canned
       chipotle chile
       peppers in adobo
       sauce
4   cups hot cooked
       brown rice
     Fresh jalapeño chile
       peppers, halved
       (optional) (see note,
       page 126)

1 Trim fat from beef. If necessary, cut beef to fit into a 3½- or 4- quart slow cooker. Place onion wedges and beef in slow cooker. Sprinkle with salt, black pepper, and garlic. In a small bowl stir together cranberry sauce and chipotle peppers. Pour over beef mixture in slow cooker.

2 Cover and cook on low-heat setting for 8 to 10 hours or on high-heat setting for 4 to 5 hours. Skim fat from pan juices.

3 Serve beef mixture with rice. If desired, garnish with jalapeño peppers.

Per serving: 419 cal., 6 g total fat (2 g sat. fat), 75 mg chol., 229 mg sodium, 61 g carbo., 4 g fiber, 30 g pro.

Thanks to ready-made stir-fry sauce and your slow cooker, this Asian classic has never been easier!

beef lo mein

Prep: 25 minutes Cook: 7 to 9 hours (low) or 3 to 4 hours (high) plus 30 minutes (high)
Makes: 8 servings

2   pounds boneless beef sirloin steak, cut 1 inch thick
1   tablespoon cooking oil
1   large onion, sliced
1   8-ounce can sliced water chestnuts, drained
1   4.5-ounce jar (drained weight) whole mushrooms, drained
1   12.1-ounce jar stir-fry sauce
1   tablespoon quick-cooking tapioca
1   16-ounce package frozen broccoli, cauliflower, and carrots
1/3 cup cashews
4   cups hot cooked lo mein noodles

1 Trim fat from meat. Cut steak into 1-inch pieces. In a large skillet brown steak, half at a time, in hot oil. Drain off fat. Set aside.

2 Place onion in a 3 1/2- or 4-quart slow cooker. Add steak, drained water chestnuts, and drained mushrooms. In a small bowl stir together stir-fry sauce and tapioca. Pour over steak mixture in slow cooker.

3 Cover and cook on low-heat setting for 7 to 9 hours or on high-heat setting for 3 to 4 hours.

4 If using low-heat setting, turn slow cooker to high-heat setting. Stir in frozen vegetables. Cover and cook for 30 to 40 minutes more or until vegetables are crisp-tender. Stir in cashews. Serve steak mixture over lo mein noodles.

Per serving: *447 cal., 11 g total fat (2 g sat. fat), 95 mg chol., 995 mg sodium, 52 g carbo., 4 g fiber, 35 g pro.*

really great chili

Prep: 25 minutes Cook: 10 to 12 hours (low) or 5 to 6 hours (high)
Makes: 6 servings

1½ pounds ground beef
1 16-ounce jar salsa
2 15-ounce cans kidney
    or red beans, rinsed
    and drained
2 14.5-ounce cans
    Mexican-style
    stewed tomatoes,
    undrained
1 cup chopped onion
    (1 large)
¾ cup chopped green
    sweet pepper
1 clove garlic, minced
    Shredded cheddar
    or Monterey Jack
    cheese, sliced green
    onion, chopped
    tomato, and broken
    tortilla chips
    (optional)

1 In a large skillet cook ground beef over medium heat until brown; drain off fat. Place beef in a 4- to 5-quart slow cooker. Add salsa, beans, undrained tomatoes, onion, sweet pepper, and garlic; stir to combine.

2 Cover and cook on low-heat setting for 10 to 12 hours or high-heat setting for 5 to 6 hours, if desired, serve with cheese, green onion, chopped tomato, and/or tortilla chips.

Per serving: 163 cal., 4 g total fat (2 g sat. fat), 30 mg chol., 724 mg sodium, 22 g carbo., 3 g fiber, 9 g pro.

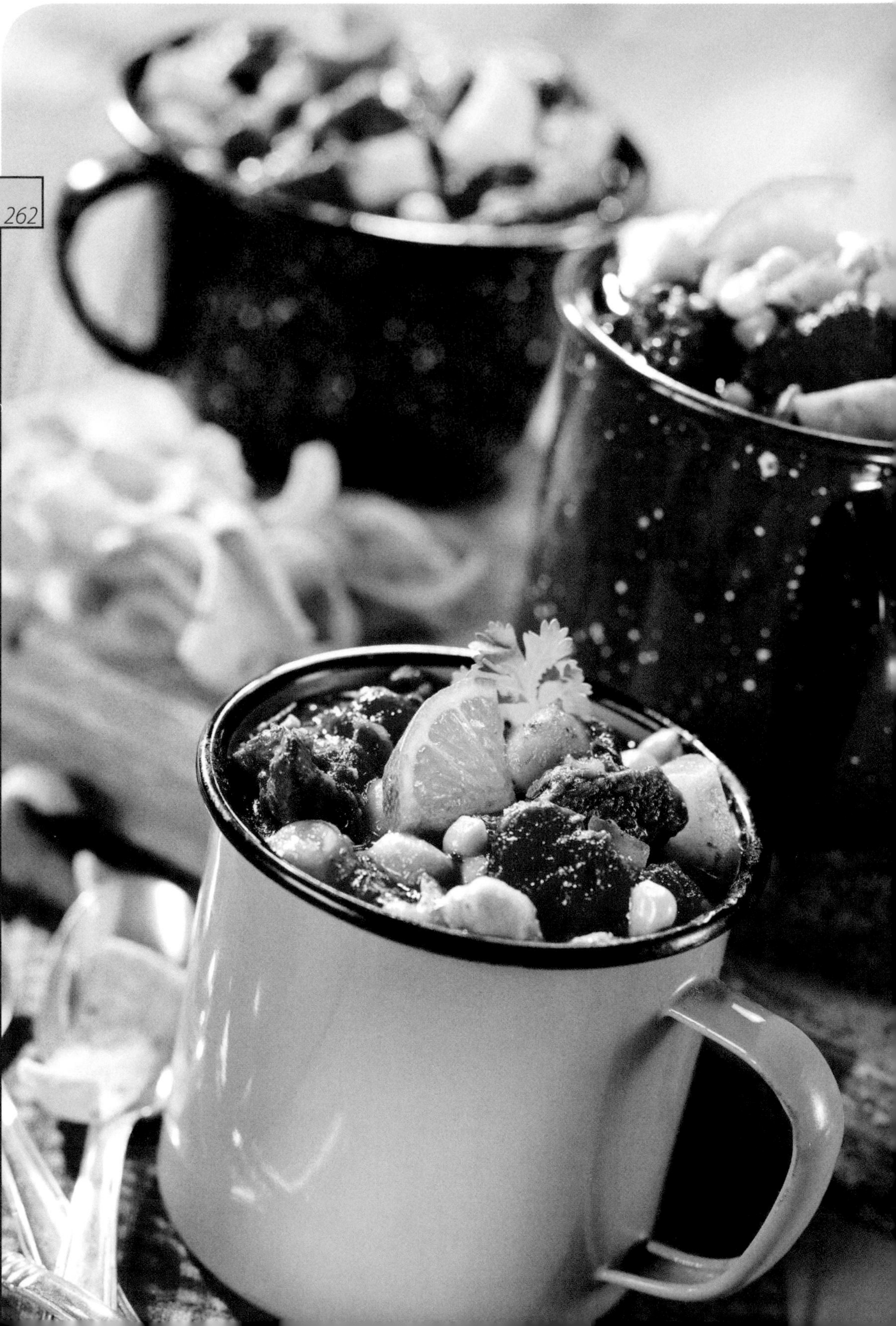

Chipotle peppers are dried, smoked jalapeño peppers, so they pack considerable heat. Canned in piquant adobo sauce, they're convenient for seasoning stews. You'll find them in the ethnic foods section of supermarkets or in Hispanic food markets.

new mexico beef stew

Prep: 30 minutes Cook: 12 to 14 hours (low) or 6 to 7 hours (high)
Makes: 6 servings

2 cups fresh corn
   kernels or one
   10-ounce package
   frozen whole kernel
   corn, thawed
1 15-ounce can
   chickpeas
   (garbanzo beans),
   rinsed and drained
2 cups chopped, peeled
   celery root, or 1 cup
   sliced celery
1 cup chopped onion
   (1 large)
3 cloves garlic, minced
2 to 3 canned chipotle
   peppers in adobo
   sauce, chopped
1½ pounds boneless
   beef chuck, cut into
   ¾-inch pieces
1 teaspoon salt
½ teaspoon ground
   black pepper
1 teaspoon dried
   thyme, crushed
1 28-ounce can
   whole tomatoes,
   undrained and cut
   up
   Lime slices,
   quartered (optional)

1 In a 4- to 5-quart slow cooker place corn, drained chickpeas, celery root, onion, garlic, and chipotle peppers. Add beef. Sprinkle with salt, ground black pepper, and thyme. Pour undrained tomatoes over all.

2 Cover and cook on low-heat setting for 12 to 14 hours or on high-heat setting for 6 to 7 hours. Stir before serving. Season to taste. If desired, garnish servings with lime slices.

Per serving: 367 cal., 8 g total fat (2 g sat. fat), 54 mg chol., 1,078 mg sodium, 42 g carbo., 7 g fiber, 33 g pro.

Because the meatballs are cooked before they're frozen, you can add them straight from the package.

meatball-vegetable stew

Prep: 10 minutes Cook: 6 to 8 hours (low) or 3 to 4 hours (high)
Makes: 4 servings

1   16- or 18-ounce
     package frozen
     cooked meatballs
1   16-ounce package
     frozen mixed
     vegetables
1   14.5-ounce can diced
     tomatoes with
     onion and garlic,
     undrained
1   12-ounce jar
     mushroom gravy
⅓   cup water
1½ teaspoons dried basil,
     crushed

1 In a 3½- or 4-quart slow cooker, combine meatballs and mixed vegetables. In a medium bowl stir together undrained tomatoes, gravy, water, and basil; pour over meatballs and vegetables.

2 Cover and cook on low-heat setting for 6 to 8 hours or on high-heat setting for 3 to 4 hours.

Per serving: 496 cal., 33 g total fat (12 g sat. fat), 40 mg chol., 1,930 mg sodium, 35 g carbo., 8 g fiber, 21 g pro.

pesto meatball stew

Prep: 10 minutes Cook: 5 to 7 hours (low) or 2½ to 3½ hours (high)
Makes: 6 servings

1   16-ounce package
    frozen cooked
    Italian-style
    meatballs (32),
    thawed
2   14.5-ounce cans
    Italian-style
    stewed tomatoes,
    undrained
1   15- to 19-ounce can
    cannellini (white
    kidney) beans,
    rinsed and drained
½   cup water
¼   cup purchased basil
    pesto
½   cup finely shredded
    Parmesan cheese
    (2 ounces)

1 In a 3½- or 4-quart slow cooker, combine meatballs, undrained tomatoes, drained beans, water, and pesto.

2 Cover and cook on low-heat setting for 5 to 7 hours or on high-heat setting for 2½ to 3½ hours. Ladle stew into bowls. Sprinkle with cheese.

Per serving: 408 cal., 27 g total fat (10 g sat. fat), 34 mg chol., 1,201 mg sodium, 24 g carbo., 6 g fiber, 17 g pro.

slow cooker pot roast stew

Prep: 40 minutes Cook: 6 hours (low) or 3 hours (high) plus 1¹⁄₂ to 2 hours (high)
Makes: 8 servings

2 large onions, cut into
   ¹⁄₂-inch wedges
1 3- to 3¹⁄₂-pound
   boneless beef chuck
   pot roast, cut into
   1-inch cubes
¾ cup dry red wine or
   lower-sodium beef
   broth
¼ cup tomato paste
3 tablespoons balsamic
   vinegar or cider
2 3-inch cinnamon
   sticks
1 teaspoon dried
   rosemary, crushed
1 teaspoon ground
   allspice
¾ teaspoon salt
¼ to ¹⁄₂ teaspoon
   crushed red pepper
1 2-pound butternut
   squash, peeled,
   seeded, and cut
   into 1¹⁄₂-inch pieces
   (about 4¹⁄₂ cups)
2 large cooking apples,
   cored and cut into
   ¹⁄₂-inch wedges
4 cups hot cooked
   couscous

1 Place onion wedges in a 5- to 6-quart
slow cooker. Place beef on top of onion.
In a small bowl combine wine, tomato paste,
vinegar, cinnamon, rosemary, allspice, salt,
and crushed red pepper; pour over beef in
slow cooker.

2 Cover and cook on low-heat setting
for 6 hours or on high-heat setting for
3 hours. If using low-heat setting turn slow
cooker to high-heat setting. Stir in squash.
Cover and cook for 1¹⁄₂ to 2 hours more or
until squash is tender. Add apple wedges to
slow cooker the last 30 minutes of cooking.
Remove and discard cinnamon. Serve
with couscous.

Per serving: 418 cal., 8 g total fat (2 g sat. fat), 101 mg chol.,
347 mg sodium, 36 g carbo., 4 g fiber, 41 g pro.

On a super-busy day, start this soup simmering before leaving home, and it will be ready to serve when dinner rolls around.

beef-vegetable soup

Prep: 25 minutes Cook: 8 to 10 hours (low) or 4 to 5 hours (high)
Makes: 4 or 5 servings

1   pound boneless beef
     chuck roast, cut into
     1-inch pieces
1   tablespoon cooking
     oil
2   14.5-ounce cans
     diced tomatoes,
     undrained
1   cup water
1½   cups sliced carrot
     (3 medium)
2   small potatoes,
     peeled if desired,
     cut into
     ½-inch cubes
     (1½ cups)
1   cup chopped onion
     (1 large)
1   teaspoon salt
½   teaspoon dried
     thyme, crushed
½   cup frozen peas,
     thawed

1 In a large skillet brown beef in hot oil over medium-high heat.

2 Transfer beef to a 3½- to 4½-quart slow cooker. Add undrained tomatoes, water, carrot, potato, onion, salt, and thyme to slow cooker.

3 Cover and cook on low-heat setting for 8 to 10 hours or on high-heat setting for 4 to 5 hours. Stir in peas.

Per serving: *335 cal., 8 g total fat (2 g sat. fat), 67 mg chol., 1,054 mg sodium, 35 g carbo., 5 g fiber, 29 g pro.*

This might remind you a little of one of those filling skillet dinners served at popular chain restaurants. This recipe, adapted for the slow cooker, lets you bring the specialty home.

pork chops o'brien

Prep: 20 minutes Cook: 7 to 9 hours (low) or 3½ to 4½ hours (high) Makes: 4 servings

Nonstick cooking
spray
5 cups loose-pack
frozen diced hash
brown potatoes
with onion and
peppers, thawed
1 10.75-ounce can
reduced-fat and
reduced-sodium
condensed cream of
mushroom soup
½ cup bottled roasted
red sweet peppers,
drained and
chopped
½ cup dairy sour cream
½ cup shredded Colby
and Monterey Jack
cheese (2 ounces)
¼ teaspoon ground
black pepper
4 pork loin chops, cut
¾ inch thick
1 tablespoon cooking
oil
1 2.8-ounce can french-
fried onions

1 Lightly coat a 3½- or 4-quart slow cooker with cooking spray; set aside. In a large bowl stir together thawed hash brown potatoes, soup, roasted sweet peppers, sour cream, cheese, and ground black pepper. Transfer potato mixture to prepared slow cooker.

2 Trim fat from chops. In a large skillet brown chops on both sides in hot oil over medium heat. Drain off fat. Place chops on top of potato mixture in slow cooker.

3 Cover and cook on low-heat setting for 7 to 9 hours or on high-heat setting for 3½ to 4½ hours. Sprinkle servings with french-fried onions.

Per serving: *670 cal., 29 g total fat (9 g sat. fat), 92 mg chol., 639 mg sodium, 64 g carbo., 4 g fiber, 37 g pro.*

By substituting brown lentils for the white beans used in a traditional French cassoulet, you skip the step of precooking and soaking the dried beans. Lentils are added to the slow cooker straight from the package. How easy is that?

pork & lentil cassoulet

Prep: 25 minutes Cook: 10 to 12 hours (low) or 4½ to 5½ hours (high)
Makes: 6 servings

1 pound boneless pork shoulder roast
1 large onion, cut into wedges
2 cloves garlic, minced
1 tablespoon cooking oil
2½ cups beef broth
1 14.5-ounce can diced tomatoes, undrained
4 medium carrots and/or parsnips, cut into ½-inch pieces
1 cup thinly sliced celery (2 stalks)
¾ cup brown lentils, rinsed and drained
1 teaspoon dried rosemary, crushed
¼ teaspoon ground black pepper

1 Trim fat from meat. Cut beef into ¾-inch pieces. In a very large skillet cook pork, onion, and garlic in hot oil over medium-high heat until beef is brown. Drain off fat.

2 Transfer pork mixture to a 3½- or 4-quart slow cooker. Stir in broth, undrained tomatoes, carrot and/or parsnips, celery, lentils, rosemary, and pepper.

3 Cover and cook on low-heat setting for 10 to 12 hours or on high-heat setting for 4½ to 5½ hours.

Per serving: 263 cal., 7 g total fat (2 g sat. fat), 49 mg chol., 586 mg sodium, 25 g carbo., 9 g fiber, 23 g pro.

Perfect for a meal on a blustery fall day, this pork dish gets its exceptional flavor from a port wine sauce that's loaded with garlic, rosemary, and thyme.

pork with parsnips & pears

Prep: 30 minutes Cook: 11 to 12 hours (low) or 5½ to 6 hours (high)
Makes: 8 to 10 servings

1 2½- to 3-pound boneless pork top loin roast (single loin)
1 tablespoon cooking oil
1½ pounds parsnips and/or carrots, peeled and cut into 1½- to 2-inch pieces*
2 medium pears, peeled, quartered, and cored (stems intact, if desired) (about 2 cups)
2 tablespoons quick-cooking tapioca
6 cloves garlic, minced
1 teaspoon dried rosemary, crushed
1 teaspoon dried thyme, crushed
½ teaspoon salt
¼ teaspoon ground black pepper
½ cup port wine or apple juice
   Salt
   Ground black pepper

1 In a large skillet brown pork on all sides in hot oil. In a 5- to 6-quart slow cooker, place parsnips and/or carrot pieces and pear quarters; sprinkle with tapioca. Place pork on top; sprinkle pork with garlic, rosemary, thyme, the ½ teaspoon salt, and the ¼ teaspoon pepper. Pour wine over all.

2 Cover and cook on low-heat setting for 11 to 12 hours or on high-heat setting for 5½ to 6 hours.

3 Transfer pork to serving platter, reserving cooking liquid; use a slotted spoon to transfer parsnips and/or carrots and pears to a serving platter.

4 Slice pork. Season sauce to taste with additional salt and pepper. Serve sauce with pork and vegetables.

*Tip: Cut any thick carrot or parsnip pieces in half lengthwise.

Per serving: 340 cal., 9 g total fat (3 g sat. fat), 78 mg chol., 292 mg sodium, 27 g carbo., 6 g fiber, 32 g pro.

Sweet-and-sour pork can be a lot of work to prepare because the pork is battered and fried. With this easy-fixing stew, you can enjoy all the same flavors but skip the kitchen time.

sweet-sour pork stew

Prep: 25 minutes Cook: 7 to 9 hours (low) or 3½ to 4½ hours (high)
Makes: 4 to 6 servings

1½ pounds lean pork
    stew meat
3   tablespoons all-
    purpose flour
½   teaspoon salt
¼   teaspoon ground
    black pepper
1   tablespoon cooking
    oil
1   cup chopped onion
    (1 large)
5   medium carrots, cut
    into ½-inch slices
    (2½ cups)
1   14.5-ounce can
    diced tomatoes,
    undrained
¼   cup packed brown
    sugar
¼   cup cider vinegar
2   tablespoons quick-
    cooking tapioca
1   tablespoon
    Worcestershire
    sauce

1 Cut meat into 1-inch pieces. In a resealable plastic bag combine flour, salt, and pepper. Add pork pieces, a few at a time, shaking to coat. In a large skillet cook half of the pork in hot oil until brown. Transfer pork to a 3½- or 4-quart slow cooker. Add remaining pork and the onion to skillet. Cook until pork is brown and onion is tender. Drain off fat. Transfer pork mixture to cooker. Add carrot.

2 In a medium bowl combine undrained tomatoes, brown sugar, vinegar, tapioca, and Worcestershire sauce. Pour over pork mixture in slow cooker.

3 Cover and cook on low-heat setting for 7 to 9 hours or on high-heat setting for 3½ to 4½ hours.

Per serving: 394 cal., 10 g total fat (3 g sat. fat), 95 mg chol., 619 mg sodium, 41 g carbo., 4 g fiber, 34 g pro.

pork, apricot & squash stew

Prep: 20 minutes Cook: 7 to 8 hours (low) or 3½ to 4 hours (high)
Makes: 4 to 5 servings

1½ pounds boneless pork
      shoulder roast
2   tablespoons cooking
      oil
1½ pounds winter
      squash (such as
      hubbard, butternut,
      or acorn), peeled
      and cut into 1-inch
      pieces
1   medium onion, sliced
½   cup dried apricots
2   tablespoons raisins
3   tablespoons instant
      flour (Wondra)
      or ¼ cup instant
      mashed potato
      flakes
2   tablespoons packed
      brown sugar
¾   teaspoon pumpkin
      pie spice
¼   teaspoon salt
1¼ cups chicken broth
1   tablespoon bottled
      steak sauce

1 Trim fat from pork. Cut pork into 1-inch pieces. In a large skillet brown pork, half at a time, in hot oil for about 5 minutes. Drain off fat.

2 In a 3½- or 4-quart slow cooker, place squash, onion, apricots, and raisins. Add pork. Sprinkle with flour, brown sugar, pumpkin pie spice, and salt. Combine broth and steak sauce; pour over all.

3 Cover and cook on low-heat setting for 7 to 8 hours or on high-heat setting for 3½ to 4 hours. Stir gently before serving.

Per serving: 469 cal., 21 g total fat (6 g sat. fat), 115 mg chol., 771 mg sodium, 33 g carbo., 2 g fiber, 38 g pro.

Apple cider gives this fix-and-forget stew a captivating hint of sweetness. Caraway seeds lend a savory twist.

cider pork stew

Prep: 20 minutes Cook: 10 to 12 hours (low) or 5 to 6 hours (high)
Makes: 8 servings

2 pounds pork shoulder roast
2½ cups cubed potato (3 medium)
3 medium carrots, cut into ½-inch pieces (about 1½ cups)
2 medium onions, sliced
1 cup coarsely chopped apple (1 large)
½ cup coarsely chopped celery (1 stalk)
2 cups apple juice or apple cider
3 tablespoons quick-cooking tapioca
1 teaspoon salt
1 teaspoon caraway seeds
¼ teaspoon ground black pepper
   Celery leaves (optional)

1 Cut meat into 1-inch cubes. In a 3½- to 5-quart slow cooker, combine pork, potato, carrot, onion, apple, and celery. In a medium bowl combine apple juice, tapioca, salt, caraway seeds, and pepper. Pour over pork mixture.

2 Cover and cook on low-heat setting for 10 to 12 hours or on high-heat setting for 5 to 6 hours. If desired, garnish servings with celery leaves.

Per serving: *272 cal., 7 g total fat (2 g sat. fat), 73 mg chol., 405 mg sodium, 27 g carbo., 3 g fiber, 24 g pro.*

If your supermarket doesn't routinely carry smoked pork hocks, ask the butcher to order some for you.

curried split pea soup

Prep: 25 minutes Cook: 9 to 11 hours (low) or 4½ to 5½ hours (high)
Makes: 6 servings

1 pound dry split peas, rinsed and drained
1 pound smoked pork hocks or meaty ham bone
1½ cups cubed cooked ham (about 8 ounces)
1½ cups coarsely chopped celery (3 stalks)
1 cup chopped onion (1 large)
1 cup coarsely chopped carrot (2 medium)
3 to 4 teaspoons curry powder
1 tablespoon dried marjoram, crushed
2 bay leaves
¼ teaspoon ground black pepper
6 cups water

1 In a 5- to 6-quart slow cooker, combine split peas, pork hocks, ham, celery, onion, carrot, curry powder, marjoram, bay leaves, and pepper. Stir in the water.

2 Cover and cook on low-heat setting for 9 to 11 hours or on high-heat setting for 4½ to 5½ hours.

3 Discard bay leaves. Remove pork hocks. When pork hocks are cool enough to handle, remove meat from bones; discard bones. Coarsely chop pork. Return pork to soup.

Per serving: 379 cal., 6 g total fat (2 g sat. fat), 32 mg chol., 788 mg sodium, 54 g carbo., 22 g fiber, 29 g pro.

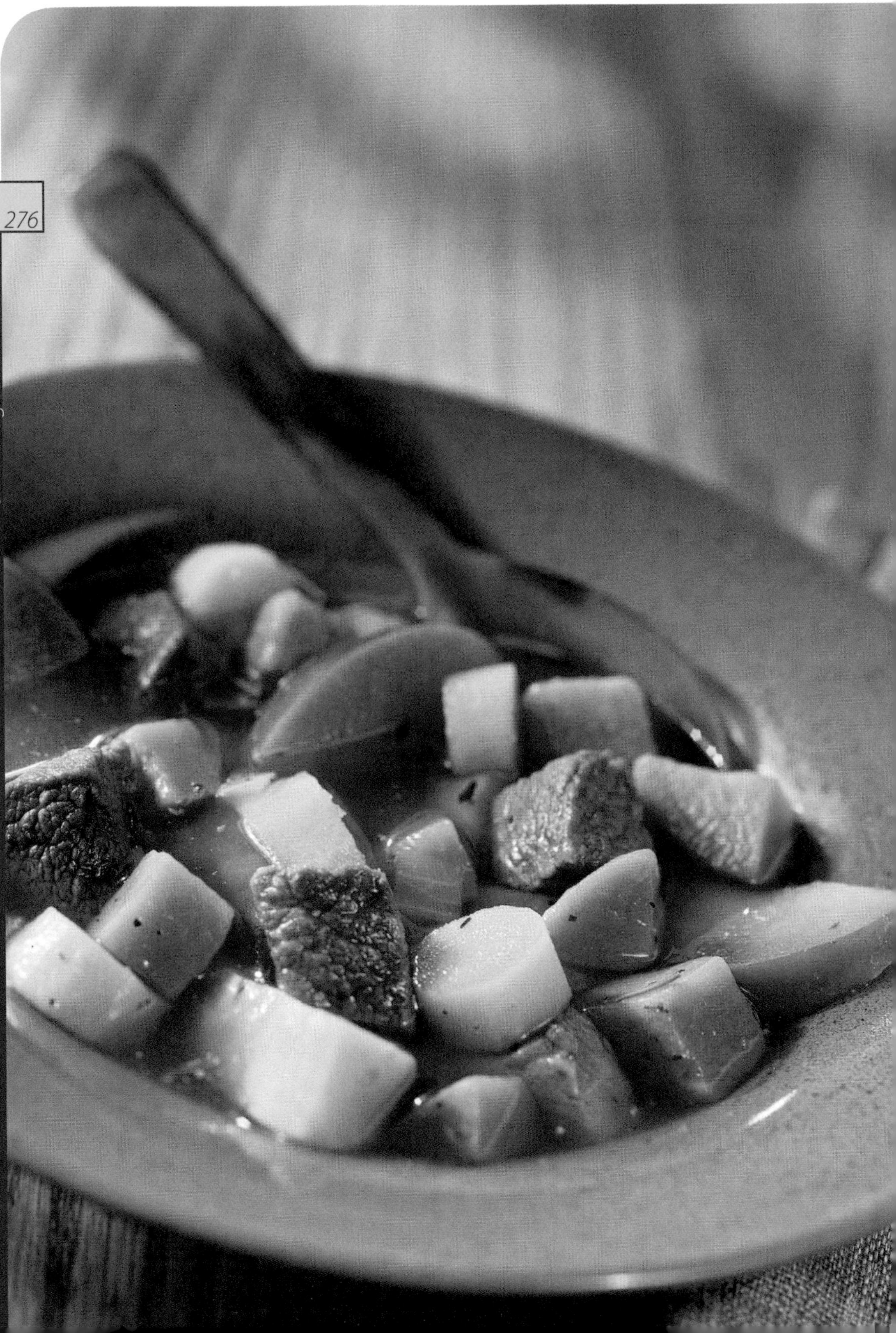

If you usually look past the parsnips to more familiar vegetables when you shop, it's time to give the sweet root vegetable a try. Look for small to firm medium-size parsnips with fairly smooth skin and few rootlets.

harvest stew

Prep: 20 minutes Cook: 7 to 8 hours (low) or 3½ to 4 hours (high)
Makes: 4 servings

1   pound boneless pork
      shoulder
2   cups cubed, peeled
      sweet potatoes
2   medium parsnips,
      peeled and cut into
      ½-inch pieces
      (1¾ cups)
2   small cooking apples,
      cored and cut into
      ¼-inch slices
      (1¾ cups)
½   cup chopped onion
      (1 medium)
¾   teaspoon dried
      thyme, crushed
½   teaspoon dried
      rosemary, crushed
½   teaspoon salt
¼   teaspoon ground
      black pepper
1   cup apple cider or
      apple juice
1   cup chicken or
      vegetable broth

1 Trim fat from pork. Cut pork into 1-inch cubes.

2 In a 3½- or 4-quart slow cooker, layer sweet potato, parsnip, apple, and onion. Add pork. Sprinkle with thyme, rosemary, salt, and pepper. Pour apple cider and broth over all.

3 Cover and cook on low-heat setting for 7 to 8 hours or on high-heat setting for 3½ to 4 hours.

Per serving: 336 cal., 8 g total fat (3 g sat. fat), 76 mg chol., 660 mg sodium, 40 g carbo., 7 g fiber, 25 g pro.

*Serve this German-style dish
with hearty dark rye bread, a
selection of mustards, cornichons,
and, if you like, cold beer. (Polka
music optional.)*

potatoes & sausage supper

Prep: 20 minutes Cook: 5 to 6 hours (low) or 2½ to 3 hours (high) plus 30 minutes (high)
Makes: 8 servings

1   20-ounce package
      refrigerated diced
      potatoes with
      onions
1   cup chopped carrot
      (2 medium)
1   cup chopped green
      sweet pepper
      (1 large)
1½ pounds cooked,
      smoked Polish
      sausage, cut into
      2-inch pieces
⅔   cup apple juice or
      apple cider
1   tablespoon cider
      vinegar
½   teaspoon caraway
      seeds
¼   teaspoon salt
¼   teaspoon ground
      black pepper
1   14-ounce can
      sauerkraut, rinsed
      and drained
2   tablespoons chopped
      fresh parsley

1 In a 4½- to 5½-quart slow cooker,
combine potatoes, carrot, and sweet
pepper. Add sausage.

2 In a small bowl combine apple juice,
vinegar, caraway seeds, salt, and ground
black pepper. Pour over vegetable mixture in
slow cooker.

3 Cover and cook on low-heat setting
for 5 to 6 hours or on high-heat setting
for 2½ to 3 hours.

4 If using low-heat setting, turn slow cooker
to high-heat setting. Stir in sauerkraut.
Cover and cook for 30 minutes.

5 To serve, transfer sausage mixture to a
serving dish. Sprinkle with parsley.

Per serving: *374 cal., 25 g total fat (9 g sat. fat), 60 mg chol.,
1,291 mg sodium, 24 g carbo., 4 g fiber, 14 g pro.*

Kielbasa, a smoked pork sausage, comes in chubby links and usually is precooked.

kielbasa stew

Prep: 20 minutes Cook: 7 to 9 hours (low) or 3½ to 4½ hours (high)
Makes: 4 or 5 servings

4 cups coarsely
   chopped cabbage
3 cups peeled, cubed
   potato (3 medium)
1½ cups sliced carrots
   (3 medium)
1 pound cooked
   kielbasa, sliced
½ teaspoon dried basil,
   crushed
½ teaspoon dried
   thyme, crushed
½ teaspoon ground
   black pepper
2 14-ounce cans
   reduced-sodium
   chicken broth

1 In a 4- to 5-quart slow cooker, combine cabbage, potato, and carrot. Top with kielbasa. Sprinkle basil, thyme, and pepper over kielbasa. Pour broth over all.

2 Cover and cook on low-heat setting for 7 to 9 hours or on high-heat setting for 3½ to 4½ hours.

Per serving: 522 cal., 34 g total fat (12 g sat. fat), 76 mg chol., 1,658 mg sodium, 34 g carbo., 5 g fiber, 23 g pro.

A chunky stew of smoked sausage, lentils, and veggies in broth is delicious with nutty-crunchy chopped fennel and a tangy splash of red wine vinegar. Set out wedges of rye bread for dunking or wiping the last of the broth from the bowl.

smoked sausage & lentil stew

Prep: 20 minutes Cook: 8 to 10 hours (low) or 4 to 5 hours (high) Makes: 6 servings

1 In a 3¹/₂- or 4-quart slow cooker, combine lentils, broth, water, sausage, fennel, onion, carrot, garlic, thyme, and pepper.

2 Cover and cook on low-heat setting for 8 to 10 hours or on high-heat setting for 4 to 5 hours.

3 Stir in vinegar before serving. If desired, garnish servings with reserved fennel tops.

Per serving: *322 cal., 13 g total fat (4 g sat. fat), 27 mg chol., 1,127 mg sodium, 31 g carbo., 14 g fiber, 20 g pro.*

1¹/₄ cups lentils, rinsed and drained
2 14-ounce cans chicken broth
1 cup water
8 ounces smoked sausage, cut into ¹/₂-inch pieces
1¹/₂ cups trimmed, coarsely chopped fennel (1 medium, tops reserved)
¹/₂ cup chopped onion (1 medium)
¹/₂ cup chopped carrot (1 medium)
4 cloves garlic, minced
1 teaspoon dried thyme, crushed
¹/₄ teaspoon black pepper
3 tablespoons red wine vinegar

For a traditional Italian trattoria presentation, purchase a wedge of Parmesan cheese and use a vegetable peeler to cut wide shavings of cheese to garnish the soup.

sausage-tortellini soup

Prep: 10 minutes Cook: 8 to 10 hours (low) or 4 to 5 hours (high) plus 15 minutes (high)
Makes: 6 servings

2 14.5-ounce cans Italian-style stewed tomatoes, undrained
3 cups water
2 cups loose-pack frozen cut green beans or Italian-style green beans
1 10.5-ounce can condensed French onion soup
8 ounces fully cooked smoked turkey sausage, halved lengthwise and cut into ½-inch slices
2 cups packaged shredded cabbage with carrot (coleslaw mix)
1 9-ounce package refrigerated cheese-filled tortellini
    Shaved or shredded Parmesan cheese

1 In a 4- to 5-quart slow cooker, combine undrained tomatoes, water, frozen green beans, soup, and turkey sausage.

2 Cover and cook on low-heat setting for 8 to 10 hours or on high-heat setting for 4 to 5 hours.

3 If using low-heat setting, turn slow cooker to high-heat setting. Stir cabbage and tortellini into soup. Cover and cook for 15 minutes more. Garnish servings with Parmesan cheese.

Per serving: *271 cal., 7 g total fat (3 g sat. fat), 51 mg chol., 1,207 mg sodium, 37 g carbo., 4 g fiber, 14 g pro.*

The exotic aromas of a North African spice market fill the kitchen as this dish cooks. For even more flavor, add ¼ to ½ teaspoon ground turmeric to the slow cooker along with the couscous.

moroccan-style lamb

Prep: 15 minutes Cook: 9 to 10 hours (low) or 4½ to 5½ hours (high) plus 5 minutes (high) Makes: 6 servings

2   pounds lean boneless lamb
2   large carrots, cut into 1-inch pieces
2   large onions, cut into wedges
2   cups chicken broth
1½ cups chopped tomato (3 medium)
1½ teaspoons ground cumin
½   teaspoon ground turmeric
¼   teaspoon crushed red pepper (optional)
1   10-ounce package quick-cooking couscous (1½ cups)
¼   cup currants, raisins, or golden raisins

1 Trim fat from meat. Cut lamb into ¾-inch cubes. In a 3½- or 4-quart slow cooker, combine lamb, carrot, onion, broth, tomato, cumin, turmeric, and, if desired, crushed red pepper.

2 Cover and cook on low-heat setting for 9 to 10 hours or on high-heat setting for 4½ to 5½ hours.

3 If using low-heat setting, turn slow cooker to high-heat setting. Using a slotted spoon, transfer lamb mixture to a serving bowl; keep warm. Skim fat from cooking juices; reserve juices in cooker. Stir couscous and currants into cooking juices. Cover and cook for 5 to 7 minutes.

4 With a fork, fluff couscous just before serving. Divide couscous among 8 shallow bowls or pasta dishes. Spoon lamb mixture over couscous.

Per serving: 440 cal., 7 g total fat (2 g sat. fat), 98 mg chol., 452 mg sodium, 52 g carbo., 5 g fiber, 39 g pro.

Assemble the ingredients in the slow cooker and set an electric timer to start the cooker while you're away. Add the chilled shrimp and let it heat while you set the table and toss a salad.

cajun shrimp & rice

Prep: 20 minutes Cook: 5 to 6 hours (low) or 3 to 3½ hours (high) plus 15 minutes on high
Makes: 6 servings

1   28-ounce can tomatoes, undrained and cut up
1   14-ounce can chicken broth
1   cup chopped onion (1 large)
1   cup chopped green sweet pepper (1 large)
1   6- to 6.25-ounce package long grain and wild rice mix
¼   cup water
2   cloves garlic, minced
½   teaspoon Cajun seasoning
1   pound cooked, peeled, and deveined shrimp
     Bottled hot pepper sauce (optional)

1 In a 3½- or 4-quart slow cooker, combine undrained tomatoes, broth, onion, sweet pepper, rice mix with seasoning packet, water, garlic, and Cajun seasoning.

2 Cover and cook on low-heat setting for 5 to 6 hours or on high-heat setting for 3 to 3½ hours.

3 If using low-heat setting, turn to high-heat setting. Stir shrimp into rice mixture in slow cooker. Cover and cook for 15 minutes more. If desired, pass hot pepper sauce.

Per serving: 223 cal., 2 g total fat (0 g sat. fat), 147 mg chol., 1,063 mg sodium, 32 g carbo., 3 g fiber, 21 g pro.

Rich and full-flavored, these curry-accented vegetables are best served with plain meats and poultry.

vegetable & garbanzo curry

Prep: 25 minutes Cook: 5 to 6 hours (low) or 2½ to 3 hours (high)
Makes: 4 to 6 servings

3   cups cauliflower
    florets
1   15-ounce can
    garbanzo beans
    (chickpeas), rinsed
    and drained
1   cup frozen cut green
    beans
1   cup sliced carrot
    (2 medium)
½   cup chopped onion
    (1 medium)
1   14-ounce can
    vegetable broth
2   to 3 teaspoons curry
    powder
1   14-ounce can light
    coconut milk
¼   cup shredded fresh
    basil leaves

1 In a 3½- or 4-quart slow cooker, combine cauliflower, drained garbanzo beans, green beans, carrot, and onion. Stir in broth and curry powder.

2 Cover and cook on low-heat setting for 5 to 6 hours or on high-heat setting for 2½ to 3 hours. Stir in coconut milk and basil.

Per serving: 219 cal., 7 g total fat (4 g sat. fat), 0 mg chol., 805 mg sodium, 32 g carbo., 9 g fiber, 8 g pro.

This hearty chili for two features black beans and a multitude of vegetables.

vegetable chili

Prep: 20 minutes Cook: 6 to 8 hours (low) or 3 to 4 hours (high)
Makes: 4 servings

2   15-ounce cans black
     beans, rinsed and
     drained
3   cups low-sodium
     tomato juice
2   cups frozen whole
     kernel corn
1½ cups coarsely
     chopped zucchini
     or yellow summer
     squash
¾   cup coarsely chopped
     red or yellow sweet
     pepper (1 medium)
½   cup chopped onion
     (1 medium)
2   teaspoons chili
     powder
½   teaspoon dried
     oregano, crushed
¼   teaspoon salt
2   cloves garlic, minced

1 In a 3½- or 4-quart slow cooker, combine
drained beans, tomato juice, corn,
zucchini, sweet pepper, onion, chili powder,
oregano, salt, and garlic.

2 Cover and cook on low-heat setting
for 6 to 8 hours or on high-heat setting
for 3 to 4 hours.

Per serving: *271 cal., 2 g total fat (0 g sat. fat), 0 mg chol.,
790 mg sodium, 59 g carbo., 14 g fiber, 19 g pro.*

The hearty barley grain adds bulk and staying power to savory vegetable soup—which means that you'll feel full and satisfied long after enjoying it.

barley vegetable soup

Prep: 25 minutes Cook: 8 to 10 hours (low) or 4 to 5 hours (high)
Makes: 6 servings

1   15-ounce can red
    beans, rinsed and
    drained
1   10-ounce package
    frozen whole kernel
    corn
½   cup medium pearl
    barley
1   14.5-ounce can
    stewed tomatoes,
    undrained
2   cups sliced fresh
    mushrooms
1   cup chopped onion
    (1 large)
½   cup coarsely chopped
    carrot (1 medium)
½   cup coarsely chopped
    celery (1 stalk)
3   cloves garlic, minced
2   teaspoons dried
    Italian seasoning,
    crushed
¼   teaspoon ground
    black pepper
5   cups vegetable broth
    or chicken broth

1 In a 3½- to 5-quart slow cooker, place drained beans, corn, barley, undrained tomatoes, mushrooms, onion, carrot, celery, garlic, Italian seasoning, and pepper. Pour broth over all.

2 Cover and cook on low-heat setting for 8 to 10 hours or on high-heat setting for 4 to 5 hours.

Per serving: 220 cal., 2 g total fat (0 g sat. fat), 0 mg chol., 1,167 mg sodium, 47 g carbo., 9 g fiber, 12 g pro.

Potatoes blend with cheddar cheese, cream, and roasted garlic in this chunky good-to-the-last-spoonful soup.

smashed potato soup

Prep: 25 minutes Cook: 8 to 10 hours (low) or 4 to 5 hours (high) Makes: 8 servings

3½ pounds potatoes, peeled and cut into ¾-inch cubes

½ cup chopped yellow and/or red sweet pepper

1½ teaspoons bottled roasted garlic

½ teaspoon ground black pepper

4½ cups chicken broth

½ cup whipping cream, half-and-half, or light cream

1 cup shredded cheddar cheese (4 ounces)

½ cup thinly sliced green onion (4) Sliced green onion (optional)

1 In a 4- to 6-quart slow cooker, combine potatoes, sweet pepper, garlic, and ground black pepper. Pour broth over all.

2 Cover and cook on low-heat setting for 8 to 10 hours or on high-heat setting for 4 to 5 hours.

3 Mash potatoes slightly with a potato masher. Stir in whipping cream, cheddar cheese, and the ½ cup thinly sliced green onions. If desired, top servings with additional sliced green onion.

Per serving: 243 cal., 11 g total fat (6 g sat. fat), 37 mg chol., 644 mg sodium, 30 g carbo., 3 g fiber, 8 g pro.

7

fresh salads

Complete each meal with some satisfying salads
and sides. These recipes will round out every
meal perfectly!

& sides

*Hungry fans cheer this portable
rice salad flavored with feta cheese
and veggies. If you transport it to a
game, pack it with an ice pack in an
insulated cooler.*

tuscan chicken-rice salad

Prep: 30 minutes Chill: 4 hours Makes: 6 servings

2 cups water
1 cup long grain rice
1 2.25-ounce can sliced
   ripe olives, drained
½ cup bottled roasted
   red sweet peppers,
   drained and
   chopped
½ cup cooked or
   canned chickpeas
   (garbanzo beans),
   drained
¼ cup thinly sliced
   green onion (2)
1 6- or 6.5-ounce jar
   marinated artichoke
   hearts
12 ounces skinless,
   boneless chicken
   breast halves, cut
   into bite-size strips
2 teaspoons chili
   powder
½ teaspoon dried
   rosemary, crushed
½ cup crumbled feta
   cheese with basil
   and tomato or
   crumbled plain feta
   (2 ounces)

1 In a medium saucepan combine water
and rice. Bring to boiling; reduce heat.
Simmer, covered, for about 15 minutes or until
water is absorbed. Place rice in colander; rinse
with cold water. Set aside to drain.

2 In a large bowl combine olives, roasted
peppers, drained chickpeas, and green
onion. Drain artichokes, reserving marinade.
Chop artichokes; add to olive mixture. Stir in
cooked rice.

3 Sprinkle chicken with chili powder
and rosemary. In a large nonstick skillet
heat 1 tablespoon of the reserved artichoke
marinade over medium heat; add chicken.
Cook for 3 to 4 minutes or until chicken is
no longer pink. Add chicken and remaining
artichoke marinade to rice mixture. Add feta
cheese; toss gently to combine. Cover and chill
for 4 to 24 hours.

*Per serving: 261 cal., 6 g total fat (2 g sat. fat), 41 mg chol.,
401 mg sodium, 33 g carbo., 2 g fiber, 18 g pro.*

cool-as-a-cucumber
chicken salad

Start to Finish: 25 minutes Makes: 4 to 6 servings

2   cups shredded
      cooked chicken
      (10 ounces)
2   cups purchased
      cut-up cantaloupe
      or halved seedless
      red grapes
1   cup chopped
      cucumber
⅓   cup orange juice
3   tablespoons salad oil
1   tablespoon snipped
      fresh mint or
      cilantro
      Salt
      Ground black pepper
4   cups shredded
      romaine or leaf
      lettuce

1 In a large bowl toss together chicken, cantaloupe, and cucumber.

2 For dressing, in a screw-top jar combine orange juice, oil, and mint. Cover and shake well. Season to taste with salt and pepper. Drizzle dressing over chicken mixture; toss lightly to coat.

3 Arrange lettuce on 4 salad plates. Top with chicken mixture.

Per serving: *269 cal., 16 g total fat (3 g sat. fat), 62 mg chol., 114 mg sodium, 11 g carbo., 1 g fiber, 22 g pro.*

asian chicken salad

Start to Finish: 15 minutes Makes: 4 servings

1 10-ounce package
torn mixed salad
greens
1½ cups chopped cooked
chicken (8 ounces)
⅓ cup bottled Asian
vinaigrette salad
dressing
1 11-ounce can
mandarin orange
sections, drained
3 tablespoons sliced
almonds, toasted

1 In a large bowl combine salad greens and
chicken. Add salad dressing; toss to coat.
Divide greens mixture among 4 salad plates.
Top with orange sections and almonds.

Per serving: 218 cal., 9 g total fat (1 g sat. fat), 50 mg chol.,
502 mg sodium, 15 g carbo., 2 g fiber, 19 g pro.

smoked turkey & tortellini salad

Start to Finish: 25 minutes Makes: 4 servings

1 7- to 8-ounce package
   dried cheese-filled
   tortellini
1 cup chopped cooked,
   smoked turkey,*
   ham, or chicken
   (5 ounces)
8 cherry tomatoes,
   quartered
½ cup coarsely chopped
   green sweet pepper
¼ cup sliced pitted ripe
   olives (optional)
¼ cup bottled Italian
   vinaigrette or
   balsamic vinaigrette
   salad dressing
   Ground black pepper

1 Cook tortellini according to package directions; drain. Rinse with cold water; drain again.

2 In a large bowl combine tortellini, turkey, tomatoes, sweet pepper, and, if desired, olives. Drizzle salad dressing over mixture; toss to coat. Season to taste with pepper.

*Tip: For a vegetarian salad, replace the turkey with 1 cup chopped fresh broccoli or cauliflower.

Per serving: 330 cal., 15 g total fat (2 g sat. fat), 20 mg chol., 897 mg sodium, 32 g carbo., 1 g fiber, 17 g pro.

italian wedding salad

Start to Finish: 25 minutes Makes: 4 servings

6   ounces dried orzo
     pasta
1   16-ounce package
     frozen cooked
     meatballs (32),
     thawed
½   cup bottled Italian
     salad dressing
1   6-ounce package
     prewashed baby
     spinach
1   6-ounce jar marinated
     artichoke hearts,
     drained and
     chopped
¼   cup chopped walnuts,
     toasted
     Salt
     Ground black pepper
     Finely shredded
       Parmesan or
       Romano cheese
       (optional)

1 Cook orzo according to package
directions; drain well.

2 Meanwhile, in a 4-quart Dutch oven
combine meatballs and salad dressing.
Cook over medium heat until meatballs are
heated through, stirring occasionally. Stir
in drained orzo, spinach, drained artichoke
hearts, and walnuts. Heat and stir just until
spinach is wilted. Season to taste with salt and
pepper. If desired, sprinkle with cheese.

Per serving: 730 cal., 52 g total fat (15 g sat. fat), 40 mg chol.,
1,383 mg sodium, 48 g carbo., 8 g fiber, 23 g pro.

beef & three-cheese tortellini salad

Start to Finish: 30 minutes Makes: 4 servings

2 cups refrigerated or frozen cheese-filled tortellini (about 9 ounces)
8 ounces cooked beef or cooked ham, cut into thin strips (1½ cups)
1 cup packaged Colby and Monterey Jack cheese or cheddar cheese cubes
1 cup small broccoli florets
1 small yellow summer squash or zucchini, halved lengthwise and sliced (1 cup)
½ cup bottled Parmesan Italian salad dressing
Leaf lettuce
Cherry tomatoes, halved (optional)

1 Cook tortellini according to package directions. Drain tortellini. Rinse with cold water; drain again.

2 In a large bowl combine tortellini, beef strips, cheese, broccoli, and squash. Drizzle salad dressing over beef mixture; toss gently to coat. Quick-chill in the freezer for 10 minutes or until ready to serve (or chill in the refrigerator for 4 to 24 hours).

3 To serve, line 4 salad plates with leaf lettuce. Divide beef mixture among plates. If desired, garnish with cherry tomatoes.

Per serving: 498 cal., 28 g total fat (12 g sat. fat), 97 mg chol., 822 mg sodium, 30 g carbo., 3 g fiber, 31 g pro.

smoked pork salad

Prep: 15 minutes   Cook: 8 minutes   Makes: 4 servings

1 In a large skillet cook chops in hot oil for 8 to 10 minutes or until hot, turning once.

2 Meanwhile, divide lettuce, tomatoes, and cheese among 4 salad plates. Thinly slice chops; add to lettuce mixture. For dressing, in a small bowl whisk together salad dressing, mustard, and thyme. Drizzle some of the dressing over salad; serve with remaining dressing.

Per serving: 386 cal., 29 g total fat (8 g sat. fat), 77 mg chol., 1,629 mg sodium, 5 g carbo., 1 g fiber, 26 g pro.

4   boneless cooked smoked pork chops, cut ¾ inch thick
1   tablespoon cooking oil
6   cups torn Boston or Bibb lettuce
8   pear or grape tomatoes, halved
2   ounces Gouda or white cheddar cheese, cut into bite-size pieces
½   cup bottled oil-and-vinegar salad dressing
2   teaspoons Dijon-style mustard
1   teaspoon snipped fresh thyme

bacon & spinach salad

Start to Finish: 20 minutes Makes: 6 servings

6 cups baby spinach
½ cup sliced
    mushrooms*
4 slices thick-sliced
    peppered bacon,
    cut into 1-inch
    pieces
1 tablespoon chopped
    shallot
½ cup bottled oil and
    vinegar salad
    dressing
6 hard-cooked eggs,
    quartered

1 In a large heatproof bowl combine spinach and mushrooms; set aside.

2 For dressing, in a large skillet cook bacon over medium heat until crisp. Using a slotted spoon, remove bacon, reserving 1 tablespoon drippings in skillet. Drain bacon on paper towels; set aside.

3 Add shallot to drippings in skillet. Cook and stir over medium heat until tender. Stir in dressing; bring to boiling. Drizzle dressing over spinach mixture; toss to coat. Top with cooked bacon and hard-cooked eggs. Divide mixture among 6 dishes or salad plates.

*Note: If desired, add the mushrooms to the skillet along with the shallots and cook until tender.

Per serving: 219 cal., 19 g total fat (4 g sat. fat), 217 mg chol., 271 mg sodium, 3 g carbo., 1 g fiber, 9 g pro.

Just about any shape of pasta works in this salad, including spaghetti.

shrimp pasta salad

Prep: 30 minutes Chill: 2 hours Makes: 5 or 6 servings

5 ounces dried campanelle or bow tie pasta (about 1½ cups)

12 ounces cooked, peeled, and deveined shrimp

½ cup chopped celery (1 stalk)

¼ cup chopped red onion

¼ cup chopped green sweet pepper

¼ cup sliced pitted ripe olives

2 plum tomatoes, cut into thin wedges

⅔ cup bottled Italian salad dressing

1 Cook pasta according to package directions; drain. Rinse with cold water; drain again.

2 In a very large bowl combine pasta, shrimp, celery, onion, sweet pepper, and olives. Stir in tomato wedges. Pour salad dressing over pasta mixture; toss gently to coat. Cover and chill for 2 to 24 hours. Stir before serving.

Per serving: 308 cal., 13 g total fat (2 g sat. fat), 133 mg chol., 280 mg sodium, 29 g carbo., 2 g fiber, 18 g pro.

The right mix of a few basic ingredients and you've created a gourmet salad.

spinach-apricot salad

Start to Finish: 20 minutes Makes: 4 servings

8   cups torn fresh prewashed baby spinach
⅓   cup dried apricots, snipped
1   tablespoon olive oil
1   clove garlic, thinly sliced or minced
4   teaspoons balsamic vinegar
    Salt
    Freshly ground black pepper
2   tablespoons slivered almonds, toasted

1 If desired, remove stems from spinach. In a large bowl combine spinach and apricots; set aside.

2 In a very large skillet heat oil over medium heat. Cook and stir garlic in hot oil until golden. Stir in the balsamic vinegar. Bring to boiling; remove from heat.

3 Add the spinach mixture to skillet. Return to heat and toss spinach mixture in skillet for about 1 minute or just until spinach is wilted.

4 Transfer spinach mixture to a serving dish. Season to taste with salt and pepper. Sprinkle with almonds. Serve salad immediately.

Per serving: *91 cal., 6 g total fat (1 g sat. fat), 0 mg chol., 146 mg sodium, 9 g carbo., 7 g fiber, 3 g pro.*

The succulent juiciness and exotic flavor of mangoes help make this a salad you'll want time and time again.

mango-broccoli salad

Start to Finish: 30 minutes Makes: 8 servings

4 cups chopped fresh broccoli
1 large ripe mango, peeled, pitted, and diced
½ cup cashews
½ cup finely chopped red onion (1 medium)
¾ cup bottled buttermilk ranch salad dressing
3 tablespoons orange juice
1 tablespoon prepared horseradish
1 11-ounce can mandarin orange sections, drained

1 In a large bowl combine broccoli, mango, cashews, and onion. In a small bowl combine salad dressing, orange juice, and horseradish. Add to broccoli mixture; toss to mix. Top with drained orange sections.

Per serving: 207 cal., 16 g total fat (3 g sat. fat), 1 mg chol., 284 mg sodium, 16 g carbo., 3 g fiber, 3 g pro.

asparagus-squash
salad

Start to Finish: 25 minutes Makes: 8 servings

8   ounces asparagus,
    cut into 1-inch
    pieces
8   ounces yellow
    summer squash, cut
    in half lengthwise
    and sliced
3   tablespoons white
    wine vinegar
1   tablespoon snipped
    fresh tarragon or
    1 teaspoon dried
    tarragon, crushed
1   tablespoon Dijon-
    style mustard
    Dash freshly ground
    black pepper
⅓   cup salad oil
8   cups packaged baby
    salad greens (about
    10 ounces)

1 In a small saucepan cook asparagus,
covered, in a small amount of boiling
salted water for about 4 minutes or until
crisp-tender. (Or steam asparagus for about
4 minutes.) Immediately drain and plunge into
ice water. Drain.

2 In a small saucepan cook squash, covered,
in a small amount of boiling salted water
for about 3 minutes or until crisp-tender.
(Or steam squash for about 3 minutes.)
Immediately drain and plunge into ice
water. Drain again.

3 For dressing, in a blender combine
vinegar, tarragon, mustard, and pepper.
With blender running, add oil in a thin, steady
stream. Continue blending until dressing
mixture is thick.

4 In a salad bowl combine salad greens,
asparagus, and squash. Toss with dressing
to coat.

Per serving: *98 cal., 9 g total fat (1 g sat. fat), 0 mg chol.,
51 mg sodium, 2 g carbo., 1 g fiber, 1 g pro.*

green bean salad

Prep: 15 minutes Chill: 1 hour Makes: 6 servings

12 ounces fresh green
    beans, trimmed
⅓ cup snipped fresh
    basil
3   tablespoons red wine
    vinegar
2   tablespoons snipped
    dried tomatoes
1   tablespoon olive oil
2   cloves garlic, minced
¼ teaspoon salt
¼ teaspoon ground
    black pepper
8   ounces yellow
    and/or red cherry
    tomatoes, halved
½ of a small red onion,
    thinly sliced

1 In a medium saucepan cook green beans, covered, in a small amount of boiling lightly salted water for about 8 minutes or just until crisp-tender. Drain; rinse with cold water and drain again.

2 Meanwhile, for dressing, in a small bowl stir together basil, vinegar, dried tomatoes, oil, garlic, salt, and pepper.

3 In a large bowl combine cooked beans, cherry tomatoes, and red onion. Drizzle with dressing; toss gently to coat. Cover and chill for 1 to 4 hours before serving.

Per serving: 53 cal., 2 g total fat (0 g sat. fat), 0 mg chol., 126 mg sodium, 8 g carbo., 3 g fiber, 2 g pro.

strawberry spinach toss

Start to Finish: 25 minutes   Makes: 6 servings

5   cups torn spinach
1   cup sliced
      strawberries
1   cup honeydew melon
      or cantaloupe balls
2   ounces Gouda or
      Edam cheese, cut
      into thin bite-size
      strips
⅓   cup coarsely chopped
      pecans, toasted
2   tablespoons lime
      juice
2   tablespoons honey
1   tablespoon salad oil
½   teaspoon fresh ginger
      or ¼ teaspoon
      ground ginger

1 In a salad bowl toss together spinach, strawberries, melon, cheese, and pecans.

2 For dressing, in a screw-top jar combine lime juice, honey, oil, and ginger. Cover; shake well. Pour some dressing over spinach mixture. Toss to coat. Pass remaining dressing.

Per serving: 145 cal., 9 g total fat (2 g sat. fat), 11 mg chol., 119 mg sodium, 13 g carbo., 2 g fiber, 4 g pro.

Insalata mista means "mixed salad" in Italian. Create a mixture of your own using the best selections from your grocery store. Or if you're short on time, buy mesclun, a blend of young, small salad greens.

insalata mista

Start to Finish: 25 minutes Makes: 4 servings

2　tablespoons olive oil or salad oil
2　tablespoons balsamic vinegar
2　teaspoons snipped fresh oregano or basil
⅛　teaspoon salt
⅛　teaspoon ground black pepper
4　cups torn mixed salad greens (such as radicchio, spinach, arugula, and/or chicory)
1　cup yellow and/or red cherry tomatoes, halved
¼　cup snipped fresh oregano or basil
½　cup pitted black olives
3　ounces thinly sliced fresh mozzarella cheese

1 For dressing, in a screw-top jar combine oil, balsamic vinegar, the 2 teaspoons oregano, the salt, and pepper. Cover and shake well to combine.

2 In a large serving bowl toss together salad greens, cherry tomatoes, the ¼ cup oregano, and the olives. Shake dressing again and drizzle over salad; toss to coat. Top with mozzarella cheese.

Per serving: 166 cal., 13 g total fat (4 g sat. fat), 15 mg chol., 298 mg sodium, 7 g carbo., 1 g fiber, 5 g pro.

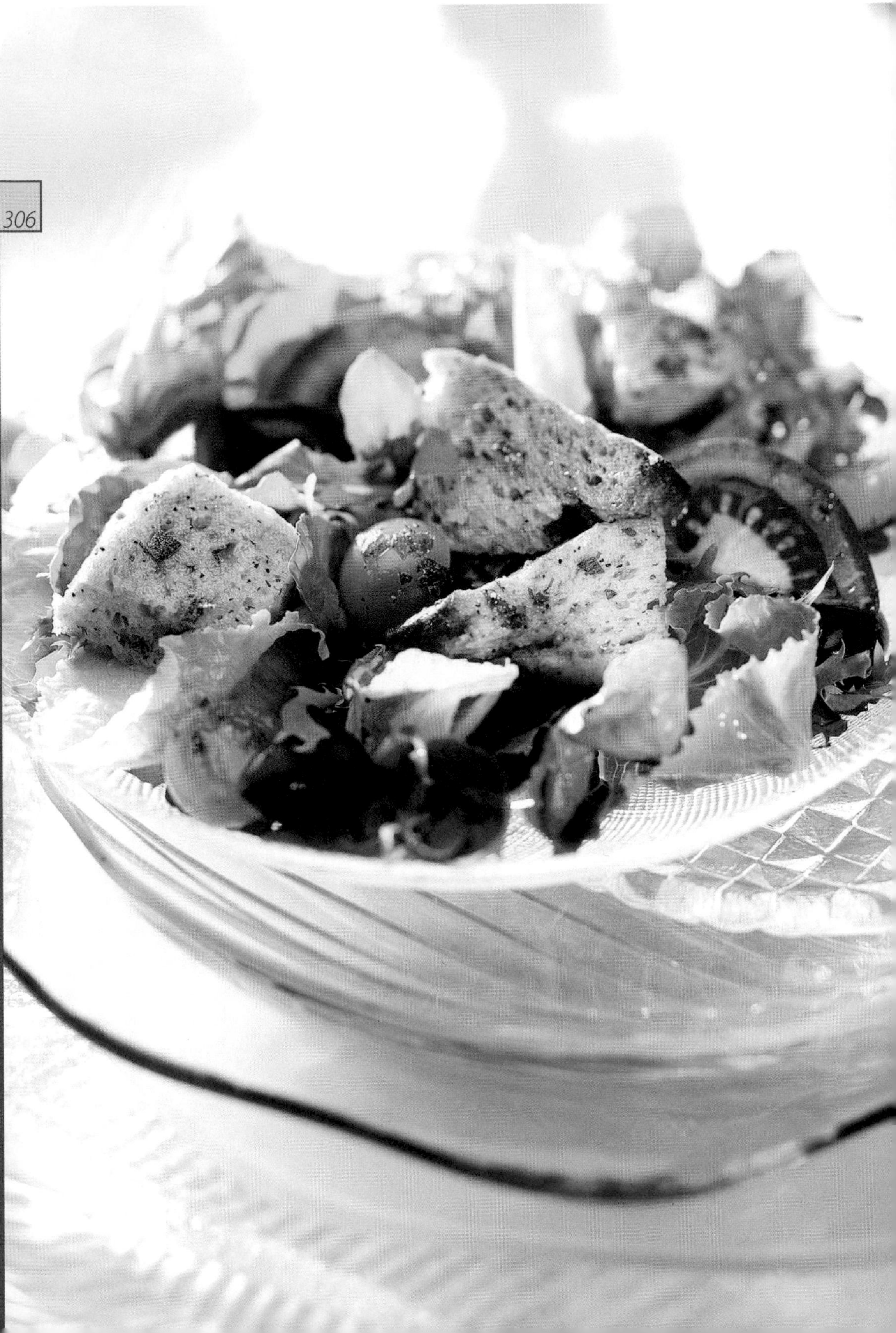

Bread salad—called panzanella in Italy—is a great use for day-old bread. Serve the salad alongside platters of fresh cheeses and pickled vegetables for an easy-going supper.

quick bread salad

Start to Finish: 20 minutes Makes: 6 servings

¼ cup olive oil
3 tablespoons red wine
  vinegar
3 tablespoons snipped
  fresh oregano
½ teaspoon sugar
¼ teaspoon salt
¼ teaspoon ground
  black pepper
4 ounces whole wheat
  sourdough or other
  country-style bread,
  cut into 1½-inch
  cubes
½ of a 10-ounce
  package Italian-
  style torn mixed
  salad greens (about
  5 cups)
1 medium tomato, cut
  into thin wedges
¼ cup halved yellow
  cherry tomatoes
  or yellow sweet
  pepper cut into
  ½-inch pieces
½ cup pitted black
  olives (such as
  kalamata)

1 For dressing, in a screw-top jar combine oil, wine vinegar, oregano, sugar, salt, and black pepper. Cover and shake well.

2 In a large salad bowl combine bread cubes, salad greens, tomato wedges, cherry tomatoes, and olives. Add dressing; toss gently to coat. Serve immediately.

Per serving: 151 cal., 11 g total fat (1 g sat. fat), 0 mg chol., 238 mg sodium, 13 g carbo., 1 g fiber, 2 g pro.

greens & berries salad

Start to Finish: 15 minutes Makes: 4 to 6 servings

1 8-ounce package torn
mixed salad greens
(about 8 cups)
½ cup crumbled blue
cheese (optional)
2 ¼-inch slices red
onion, separated
into rings
1 cup fresh raspberries
or sliced fresh
strawberries
1 2-ounce package
slivered almonds,
toasted (⅓ cup)
¼ cup bottled balsamic
vinaigrette salad
dressing
1 teaspoon Dijon-style
mustard

1 In a large salad bowl combine salad greens, blue cheese (if desired), red onion, raspberries, and almonds.

2 For dressing, in a small bowl whisk together the salad dressing and mustard. Pour dressing over the salad ingredients. Toss well to combine; serve immediately.

Per serving: *157 cal., 12 g total fat (1 g sat. fat), 0 mg chol., 215 mg sodium, 11 g carbo., 5 g fiber, 5 g pro.*

Dunking the asparagus in ice water after cooking it allows the asparagus to maintain a bright green color and cools it quickly to serve on this refreshing salad.

chilled asparagus salad

Prep: 20 minutes Cook: 3 minutes Makes: 4 to 6 servings

½ cup mayonnaise or salad dressing
¼ cup plain yogurt
½ teaspoon finely shredded orange peel
⅓ cup orange juice
⅛ teaspoon lemon-pepper seasoning
1 pound fresh asparagus spears
6 cups torn butterhead (Boston or Bibb) lettuce
1 small red onion, cut into thin wedges
1 11-ounce can mandarin orange sections, drained

1 For dressing, in a small bowl stir together mayonnaise, yogurt, orange peel, orange juice, and lemon-pepper seasoning; set aside.

2 Snap off and discard woody bases from asparagus. Cook, covered, in a large saucepan in a small amount of lightly salted boiling water for 3 to 5 minutes or until crisp-tender. Drain asparagus. Immediately plunge cooked asparagus into ice water. When chilled, drain.

3 Arrange lettuce, asparagus, onion wedges, and drained orange sections on serving plates. Drizzle dressing over salads.

Per serving: *277 cal., 23 g total fat (4 g sat. fat), 11 mg chol., 180 mg sodium, 16 g carbo., 3 g fiber, 1 g pro.*

black bean slaw with soy ginger dressing

Prep: 25 minutes Chill: 8 hours Makes: 4 servings

1 15-ounce can black
   beans, rinsed and
   drained
6 cups shredded
   cabbage with carrot
   (coleslaw mix)
1⅓ cups chopped green
   apple (2 medium)
1 cup chopped red
   sweet pepper
   (1 large)
¼ cup cider vinegar
2 tablespoons reduced-
   sodium soy sauce
2 tablespoons peanut
   oil
2 teaspoons grated
   fresh ginger
2 teaspoons honey
¼ teaspoon ground
   black pepper

1 In a large bowl combine drained black
beans, shredded cabbage with carrot,
apple, and sweet pepper.

2 For dressing, in a screw-top jar combine
vinegar, soy sauce, oil, ginger, honey,
and black pepper; cover and shake well. Pour
dressing over cabbage mixture; toss to coat.
Cover and chill for 8 hours or overnight.

Per serving: 217 cal., 7 g total fat (1 g sat. fat), 0 mg chol.,
577 mg sodium, 36 g carbo., 9 g fiber, 9 g pro.

napa cabbage slaw

Start to Finish: 15 minutes Makes: 6 servings

3   cups finely shredded
    Chinese (napa)
    cabbage
1   cup finely shredded
    bok choy
¼   of a small red sweet
    pepper, cut into
    very thin strips
    (about ¼ cup)
¼   cup rice vinegar or
    white wine vinegar
1   tablespoon salad oil
½   teaspoon toasted
    sesame oil

1 In a large bowl combine cabbage, bok
choy, and sweet pepper strips.

2 For dressing, in a small bowl stir together
vinegar, salad oil, and sesame oil. Pour
dressing over cabbage mixture; toss gently
to coat. If desired, cover and chill for up to
2 hours.

Per serving: 40 cal., 3 g total fat (0 g sat. fat), 0 mg chol.,
81 mg sodium, 2 g carbo., 2 g fiber, 1 g pro.

new potato salad

Prep: 25 minutes Chill: 6 hours Makes: 8 servings

1 pound tiny new
potatoes
½ cup mayonnaise or
salad dressing
½ cup chopped celery
(1 stalk)
½ cup chopped onion
(1 medium)
3 tablespoons chopped
sweet pickles
¼ teaspoon salt
⅛ teaspoon coarsely
ground black
pepper
1 hard-cooked egg,
chopped
2 to 3 teaspoons pickle
juice or milk
Salt
Coarsely ground
black pepper

1 In a large saucepan combine potatoes
and enough water to cover potatoes.
Bring to boiling; reduce heat. Simmer, covered,
for 15 to 20 minutes or just until tender. Drain
well; cool potatoes. Cut potatoes into quarters.

2 In a large bowl combine mayonnaise,
celery, onion, pickles, the ¼ teaspoon salt,
and the ⅛ teaspoon pepper. Add the potatoes
and egg; toss gently to coat. Cover and chill for
6 to 24 hours.

3 To serve, stir pickle juice into salad to
reach desired consistency. Season to
taste with additional salt and coarsely ground
black pepper.

Per serving: 161 cal., 12 g total fat (2 g sat. fat), 32 mg chol.,
196 mg sodium, 12 g carbo., 1 g fiber, 2 g pro.

Just before serving, sprinkle with sliced green onions, lemon zest, and parsley for added freshness and flavor.

maple-glazed new potatoes

Prep: 20 minutes Roast: 55 minutes Oven: 325°F Makes: 6 servings

3 pounds tiny new potatoes
¼ cup butter or margarine, melted
Salt and cracked black pepper
3 tablespoons white balsamic vinegar
2 tablespoons pure maple syrup
3 cloves garlic, thinly sliced
¼ cup chopped green onion (2)
2 tablespoons chopped fresh Italian (flat-leaf) parsley
1 tablespoon finely shredded lemon peel

1 Preheat oven to 325°F. Halve or quarter any large potatoes. In a shallow dish large enough to hold potatoes in a single layer, toss potatoes with butter; season with salt and pepper. Spread in a single layer. Roast potatoes, uncovered, in the preheated oven for 45 minutes, stirring once or twice during roasting.

2 Meanwhile, in a small bowl stir together vinegar, maple syrup, and garlic. Drizzle potatoes with vinegar mixture, gently tossing to coat. Roast potatoes about 10 to 20 minutes more or until potatoes are tender and glazed, stirring once or twice.

3 To serve, sprinkle potatoes with green onion, parsley, and lemon peel.

Per serving: 275 cal., 8 g total fat (5 g sat. fat), 20 mg chol., 265 mg sodium, 47 g carbo., 5 g fiber, 3 g pro.

fresh **salads & sides**

sweet potato casserole

Prep: 20 minutes Bake: 20 minutes Oven: 350°F Makes: 8 servings

2 eggs, beaten
½ cup granulated sugar
¼ cup butter, melted and cooled slightly
1 teaspoon vanilla
4 cups mashed, cooked sweet potatoes* (about 3 pounds)
½ cup raisins
½ cup packed brown sugar
¼ cup all-purpose flour
2 tablespoons cold butter
½ cup chopped pecans

1 Preheat oven to 350°F. In a large bowl stir together eggs, granulated sugar, melted butter, and vanilla. Stir in cooked sweet potatoes and raisins. Spread sweet potato mixture evenly into an ungreased 2-quart square baking dish.

2 For topping, in a small bowl combine brown sugar and flour. Cut in butter until mixture resembles coarse crumbs. Stir in pecans. Sprinkle topping over sweet potato mixture.

3 Bake, uncovered, in the preheated oven for about 20 minutes or until heated through.

*Tip: To make these quicker, use two 24-ounce packages of refrigerated mashed sweet potatoes, available seasonally at many grocery stores.

Per serving: 458 cal., 16 g total fat (7 g sat. fat), 78 mg chol., 137 mg sodium, 77 g carbo., 4 g fiber, 6 g pro.

Skip a step! Here you add the vegetables to the pasta during the last three minutes of cooking; just heat up a little Alfredo sauce, add a touch of tarragon, and you've got an Italian classic at its fresh-and-simple best.

pasta-vegetable
primavera

Start to Finish: 25 minutes Makes: 4 servings

1   pound asparagus spears
8   ounces dried cavatappi (corkscrews) or rotini pasta (about 2½ cups)
1   cup mixed sweet pepper chunks from salad bar or 1 large red or yellow sweet pepper, cut into 1-inch pieces
4   baby sunburst squash, halved (½ cup)
½   of a medium yellow summer squash or zucchini, sliced (½ cup)
1   10-ounce container refrigerated light Alfredo sauce
2   tablespoons snipped fresh tarragon or thyme

1 Snap off and discard woody bases from asparagus. Bias-slice asparagus into 1-inch pieces (you should have about 2½ cups).

2 Cook pasta according to package directions, adding asparagus, sweet pepper, and squash to pasta during the last 3 minutes of cooking; drain. Return pasta and vegetables to hot saucepan.

3 Add Alfredo sauce and tarragon to pasta mixture. Toss gently over medium heat about 5 minutes or until mixture is heated through.

Per serving: *335 cal., 7 g total fat (5 g sat. fat), 24 mg chol., 467 mg sodium, 54 g carbo., 4 g fiber, 14 g pro.*

This classic sauce (pronounced poot-tah-NES-kah) sings with the sharp flavors of olives and anchovies. It's a great dish for a weeknight supper because it cooks quickly.

pasta puttanesca

Prep: 20 minutes Cook: 5 minutes Makes: 6 servings

6   ounces dried thin
       spaghetti
1   clove garlic, minced
2   tablespoons olive oil
2   cups chopped,
       seeded, peeled
       tomato (3 or 4)
½   cup chopped pitted
       black olives (such
       as kalamata)
4   or 5 anchovy fillets,
       chopped
1   teaspoon drained
       capers, chopped
½   teaspoon ground
       black pepper
½   teaspoon crushed red
       pepper (optional)
¼   cup snipped fresh
       Italian (flat-leaf)
       parsley

1 In a Dutch oven cook spaghetti according to package directions; drain and return to pan.

2 Meanwhile, in a large skillet cook garlic in hot olive oil for 30 seconds. Add tomato, olives, anchovy fillets, capers, black pepper, and, if desired, crushed red pepper.

3 Bring just to boiling; reduce heat to medium-low. Cook, uncovered, for 5 to 6 minutes or until slightly thickened, stirring occasionally.

4 Add tomato mixture to pasta; toss to coat. Sprinkle with parsley.

Per serving: 179 cal., 7 g total fat (1 g sat. fat), 2 mg chol., 222 mg sodium, 25 g carbo., 2 g fiber, 5 g pro.

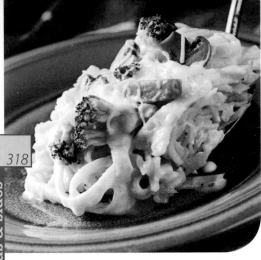

broccoli-cauliflower
tetrazzini

Prep: 35 minutes **Bake:** 15 minutes **Oven:** 400°F **Makes:** 8 servings

8 ounces dried fettuccine or spaghetti, broken
1 16-ounce package frozen broccoli, carrots, and cauliflower
2 tablespoons butter or margarine
3 tablespoons all-purpose flour
2½ cups milk
½ cup grated Parmesan cheese
¼ teaspoon salt
¼ teaspoon ground black pepper
1 4.5-ounce jar (drained weight) sliced mushrooms, drained
2 tablespoons grated Parmesan cheese

1 Preheat oven to 400°F. Lightly grease a 3-quart rectangular baking dish; set aside. Cook pasta according to package directions; drain. Cook vegetables according to package directions; drain and set aside.

2 Meanwhile, for cheese sauce, in a large saucepan melt butter. Stir in flour. Add milk. Cook and stir over medium heat until slightly thickened and bubbly. Cook and stir for 1 minute more. Remove from heat. Stir in the ½ cup Parmesan cheese, the salt, and pepper.

3 Toss pasta with ½ cup of the cheese sauce. Spread pasta evenly in prepared dish. Top with vegetables and mushrooms. Pour remaining cheese sauce over all. Sprinkle with the 2 tablespoons Parmesan cheese.

4 Bake, uncovered, in the preheated oven for 15 minutes or until heated through.

Make-Ahead Directions: Prepare and assemble as above. Cover; chill up to 24 hours. To serve, bake, covered, in a preheated 400°F oven for 15 minutes. Uncover and bake for 10 to 15 minutes more.

Per serving: 239 cal., 7 g total fat (3 g sat. fat), 12 mg chol., 500 mg sodium, 33 g carbo., 3 g fiber, 11 g pro.

bow ties with mushrooms & spinach

Prep: 10 minutes Cook: 10 minutes Makes: 4 servings

6   ounces dried bow tie
    pasta
½   cup chopped onion
    (1 medium)
1   cup sliced portobello
    or other fresh
    mushrooms
2   cloves garlic, minced
1   tablespoon olive oil
4   cups thinly sliced
    fresh spinach
1   teaspoon snipped
    fresh thyme
⅛   teaspoon ground
    black pepper
2   tablespoons shredded
    Parmesan cheese

1 Cook pasta according to package directions. Drain well.

2 Meanwhile, in a large skillet cook and stir onion, mushrooms, and garlic in hot oil over medium heat for 2 to 3 minutes or until mushrooms are nearly tender. Stir in spinach, thyme, and pepper; cook for 1 minute or until heated through and spinach is slightly wilted. Stir in cooked pasta; toss gently to mix. Sprinkle with cheese.

Per serving: 219 cal., 5 g total fat (1 g sat. fat), 2 mg chol., 86 mg sodium, 35 g carbo., 4 g fiber, 9 g pro.

broccoli kugel

Prep: 15 minutes Bake: 35 minutes Oven: 350°F Makes: 8 servings

1   10-ounce package
    frozen chopped
    broccoli
1   cup half-and-half or
    light cream
3   eggs, slightly beaten
¼   cup butter or
    margarine, melted
1   envelope onion
    soup mix (½ of a
    2½-ounce box)
8   ounces cooked pasta

1 Preheat oven to 350°F. Cook broccoli according to package directions; drain well. Combine broccoli, half-and-half, eggs, butter, and soup mix. Stir in cooked pasta. Spoon into a 2-quart square baking dish.

2 Bake in the preheated oven for about 35 minutes or until heated through.

Per serving: 180 cal., 12 g total fat (4 g sat. fat), 91 mg chol., 507 mg sodium, 14 g carbo., 2 g fiber, 6 g pro.

Think rice is boring? You'll change your mind after tasting this savory version.

festive rice

Prep: 25 minutes   Bake: 20 minutes   Oven: 350°F   Makes: 8 servings

1   cup chopped red, yellow, or green sweet pepper (1 large)
½   cup chopped onion (1 medium)
2   to 3 medium jalapeño peppers, seeded and finely chopped (see note, page 126)
2   cloves garlic, minced
1   tablespoon cooking oil
1½   cups chopped plum tomatoes
2   to 3 tablespoons snipped fresh cilantro
¼   teaspoon salt
2   cups cooked brown rice (⅔ cup uncooked rice)
1   15-ounce can garbanzo beans, rinsed and drained
1   cup shredded Monterey Jack cheese (4 ounces)

1 Preheat oven to 350°F. In a large saucepan cook sweet pepper, onion, jalapeño pepper, and garlic in hot oil for about 5 minutes or until tender, stirring occasionally. Stir in tomato, cilantro, and salt. Bring to boiling; reduce heat. Simmer, uncovered, for 5 minutes. Add cooked rice, drained garbanzo beans, and ½ cup of the cheese, stirring gently to combine. Turn into a 1½-quart casserole. Sprinkle with remaining ½ cup cheese.

2 Bake, covered, in the preheated oven for about 20 minutes or until heated through.

Per serving: *189 cal., 8 g total fat (3 g sat. fat), 13 mg chol., 347 mg sodium, 24 g carbo., 4 g fiber, 8 g pro.*

For classic risotto, the rice is cooked slowly, allowing the outside to become soft while the inside remains firm. In this shortcut version, the rice is uniformly tender and the risotto's texture is less creamy.

risotto with peas

Start to Finish: 35 minutes Makes: 4 to 6 servings

2   tablespoons olive oil
½   cup chopped onion
     (1 medium)
2   cloves garlic, minced
1   cup Arborio rice
2   14-ounce cans
     vegetable broth
     or chicken broth
     (3½ cups)
1   cup frozen tiny or
     regular-size peas
¼   cup coarsely
     shredded carrot
2   cups fresh spinach,
     shredded
¼   cup grated Parmesan
     cheese (1 ounce)
1   tablespoon snipped
     fresh thyme

1 In a large saucepan heat oil over medium heat. Add onion and garlic; cook until onion is tender. Add the uncooked rice. Cook and stir for about 2 minutes.

2 Carefully stir in all of the broth. Bring to boiling; reduce heat. Cover and simmer for 20 minutes (do not lift lid). Remove from heat. Stir in peas and carrot. Cover and let stand for 5 minutes. Rice should be tender and the mixture should be slightly creamy. (If necessary, stir in a little water to reach desired consistency.)

3 Stir in spinach, Parmesan cheese, and thyme; heat through. Serve immediately.

Per serving: *252 cal., 8 g total fat (2 g sat. fat), 4 mg chol., 912 mg sodium, 38 g carbo., 2 g fiber, 7 g pro.*

For just-right creaminess, use Arborio or medium-grain rice and don't peek during cooking. You'll find Arborio rice in Italian specialty food shops or in the rice section of some supermarkets.

fennel-mushroom
risotto

Prep: 20 minutes Cook: 20 minutes Stand: 5 minutes Makes: 4 servings

1 cup sliced fresh mushrooms (such as shiitake, oyster, morel, or porcini)
1 cup sliced fennel bulb
½ teaspoon fennel seeds, crushed
1 tablespoon olive oil
⅔ cup Arborio or medium-grain rice
2 cups water
½ teaspoon salt
⅛ teaspoon ground black pepper
4 asparagus spears,* trimmed and cut into 1-inch pieces (about ¼ cup)
⅓ cup thinly sliced green onion
1 tablespoon snipped fennel leaves
 Fennel leaves (optional)

1 In a medium saucepan cook mushrooms, sliced fennel bulb, and fennel seeds in hot oil until tender. Stir in uncooked rice. Cook and stir for 2 minutes more.

2 Carefully stir in water, salt, and pepper. Bring to boiling; reduce heat. Simmer, covered, for 20 minutes (do not lift lid).

3 Remove from heat. Stir in asparagus and green onion. Let stand, covered, for 5 minutes. The rice should be tender but slightly firm, and the mixture should be creamy. If necessary, stir in a little water to reach the desired consistency.

4 Stir in snipped fennel leaves. If desired, garnish risotto with additional fennel leaves.

*Note: If using thick asparagus spears, halve the spears lengthwise and cook in a small amount of boiling water until crisp-tender before stirring into risotto.

Per serving: 160 cal., 4 g total fat (1 g sat. fat), 4 mg chol., 285 mg sodium, 28 g carbo., 1 g fiber, 3 g pro.

fresh corn skillet

Prep: 25 minutes   Chill: 1 hour   Makes: 6 servings

4   fresh ears of corn
     or one 10-ounce
     package frozen
     whole kernel corn,
     thawed
2   tablespoons olive oil
1½ teaspoons instant
     chicken bouillon
     granules
1   teaspoon snipped
     fresh thyme or
     rosemary
1   teaspoon sugar
     (optional)
1   cup fresh pea pods
1   medium red sweet
     pepper, cut into
     thin, bite-size strips
¼   cup sliced green
     onion (2)
     Freshly ground black
     pepper

1 If using fresh corn, remove husks. Scrub with a stiff brush to remove the silks. Rinse. Use a sharp knife to cut corn from the cob at three-quarters depth of kernels; do not scrape. (You should have about 2 cups corn.) Set aside.

2 In a large skillet combine oil, bouillon granules, thyme, and, if desired, sugar. Cook for 30 seconds over medium-high heat. Stir in corn, pea pods, sweet pepper, and green onion. Cook over medium-high heat for 4 minutes or until the vegetables are crisp-tender, stirring occasionally. Transfer to a serving bowl. Chill for 1 to 24 hours. Sprinkle with black pepper before serving.

Per serving: 108 cal., 5 g total fat (1 g sat. fat), 0 mg chol., 227 mg sodium, 15 g carbo., 3 g fiber, 3 g pro.

No need to peel and chop vegetables with this recipe—it starts with an easy-to-use bag of frozen broccoli, cauliflower, and carrots.

vegetable medley
au gratin

Prep: 20 minutes Bake: 60 minutes Oven: 325°F/375°F Makes: 10 servings

1 10.75-ounce can condensed cream of chicken or cream of mushroom soup
½ cup dairy sour cream
½ teaspoon dried dill
2 16-ounce packages frozen broccoli, cauliflower, and carrots, thawed
⅔ cup crushed stone-ground wheat crackers (about 15 crackers)
⅓ cup finely chopped walnuts or pecans
¼ cup finely shredded Parmesan cheese
2 tablespoons butter, melted

1 Preheat oven to 325°F. In a very large bowl combine soup, sour cream, and dill; stir in thawed vegetables. Transfer to a 2-quart rectangular baking dish. Bake, covered, in the preheated oven for 45 minutes.

2 In a small bowl combine crackers, walnuts, cheese, and butter. Uncover baking dish; sprinkle cracker mixture over vegetable mixture. Increase oven temperature to 375°F. Bake, uncovered, for about 15 minutes more or until heated through and topping is brown.

Per serving: 157 cal., 10 g total fat (4 g sat. fat), 16 mg chol., 452 mg sodium, 11 g carbo., 3 g fiber, 5 g pro.

golden green bean crunch

Prep: 15 minutes Bake: 30 minutes Oven: 350°F Makes: 4 to 6 servings

1 16-ounce package
   frozen French-cut
   green beans
1 10.75-ounce can
   condensed golden
   mushroom soup
1 8-ounce can sliced
   water chestnuts,
   drained (optional)
1 cup chow mein
   noodles or ½ of
   a 2.8-ounce can
   french-fried onions
   (about ¾ cup)

1 Preheat oven to 350°F. Cook frozen beans according to package directions; drain well. In a 1½-quart casserole combine the cooked beans, soup, and, if desired, drained water chestnuts.

2 Bake, uncovered, in the preheated oven for 25 minutes or until bubbly around edges. Sprinkle with chow mein noodles. Bake for about 5 minutes more or until heated through.

Per serving: 188 cal., 6 g total fat (1 g sat. fat), 3 mg chol., 719 mg sodium, 27 g carbo., 5 g fiber, 5 g pro.

summer vegetable gratin

Prep: 15 minutes Bake: 20 minutes Oven: 425°F Makes: 4 servings

Nonstick cooking
   spray
2 large leeks, cut
    into ¼-inch slices
    (1 cup)
1 medium zucchini, cut
    into ¼-inch slices
    (1¼ cups)
1 medium yellow
    summer squash, cut
    into ¼-inch slices
    (1¼ cups)
2 tablespoons olive oil
    Salt
    Ground black pepper
2 tablespoons fine dry
    bread crumbs
2 tablespoons finely
    shredded Parmesan
    cheese
2 teaspoons snipped
    fresh thyme
1 clove garlic, minced

1 Preheat oven to 425°F. Coat a shallow 2-quart baking dish with cooking spray; set aside. Rinse and trim leeks; pat dry with paper towel. In a medium bowl combine leeks, zucchini, yellow squash, and 1 tablespoon of the oil. Sprinkle with salt and pepper. Transfer vegetables to prepared baking dish.

2 In a small bowl stir together bread crumbs, cheese, thyme, garlic, and the remaining oil. Sprinkle crumb mixture evenly over vegetables.

3 Bake, uncovered, in the preheated oven for 20 to 25 minutes or until vegetables are tender.

Per serving: 117 cal, 8 g total fat (1 g sat fat), 2 mg chol, 104 mg sodium, 10 g carbo., 3 g fiber, 3 g pro.

Green beans and Brussels sprouts are a delectable pair when roasted with aromatic rosemary and smoky bacon.

rosemary roasted vegetables

Prep: 30 minutes Roast: 20 minutes Oven: 425°F Makes: 12 servings

1 pound fresh Brussels
sprouts
12 ounces fresh green
beans
1 bunch green onions
(6), trimmed and
cut up
12 fresh rosemary sprigs
8 slices pancetta or
bacon, partially
cooked, drained,
and cut up
2 tablespoons olive oil
Salt
Freshly ground black
pepper
1 lemon, halved

1 Preheat oven to 425°F. Wash Brussels sprouts and green beans; drain. Halve any large Brussels sprouts. In a covered large saucepan cook Brussels sprouts in a small amount of lightly salted boiling water for 3 minutes; add green beans and cook 5 minutes more. Drain.

2 Transfer Brussels sprouts and green beans to an ungreased 13×9×2-inch baking dish. Add green onion and rosemary sprigs; toss to combine. Top with partially cooked pancetta. Drizzle vegetable mixture with oil. Sprinkle with salt and pepper.

3 Roast, uncovered, in the preheated oven for about 20 minutes or until vegetables are crisp-tender and pancetta is crisp. Transfer to a serving platter. Squeeze juice from lemon over vegetables.

Per serving: 143 cal., 10 g total fat (4 g sat. fat), 10 mg chol., 275 mg sodium, 6 g carbo., 3 g fiber, 4 g pro.

If you like mushrooms, you'll love this Asian-inspired dish.

spicy teriyaki mushrooms

Start to Finish: 15 minutes Makes: 4 servings

2 tablespoons sugar
2 tablespoons soy
sauce
1 tablespoon white
wine vinegar
1 tablespoon cooking
oil
¼ to ½ teaspoon
crushed red pepper
flakes
¼ to ½ teaspoon ground
ginger
⅛ to ¼ teaspoon garlic
powder
24 small mushrooms
(about 8 ounces),
quartered
2 tablespoons sliced
green onion (1)

1 In a medium saucepan combine sugar,
soy sauce, vinegar, oil, red pepper flakes,
ginger, and garlic powder. Add mushrooms
and green onion. Cook and stir over medium
heat until heated through.

Per serving: 178 cal., 4 g total fat (1 g sat. fat), 0 mg chol.,
518 mg sodium, 33 g carbo., 1 g fiber, 4 g pro.

bonus

8

sweet & simple

des

And now for a little something sweet! Whether it's fruit, chocolate, cake, or custard, you are guaranteed to find a one-dish treat to finish the meal off right. Enjoy!

serts

mississippi mud cake

Prep: 15 minutes Bake: 30 minutes Oven: 350°F Makes: 12 to 16 servings

1   package 2-layer-size
    chocolate cake mix
1¼ cups water
⅓   cup cooking oil
⅓   cup creamy peanut
    butter
3   eggs
1   cup semisweet
    chocolate pieces
    (6 ounces)
1   16-ounce can
    chocolate fudge
    frosting
1   cup tiny
    marshmallows
1   cup chopped peanuts

1 Preheat the oven to 350°F. Grease and lightly flour a 13×9×2-inch baking pan; set aside.

2 In a large mixing bowl combine cake mix, water, oil, peanut butter, and eggs. Beat with an electric mixer on low speed until moistened. Beat on medium speed for 2 minutes. Stir in chocolate pieces. Pour into the prepared pan.

3 Bake in the preheated oven for 30 to 35 minutes or until a wooden toothpick inserted in center comes out clean. Cool in pan on a wire rack.

4 Drop spoonfuls of frosting over cake; spread evenly. Sprinkle with marshmallows and peanuts.

Per serving: 591 cal., 30 g total fat (8 g sat. fat), 53 mg chol., 456 mg sodium, 76 g carbo., 3 g fiber, 9 g pro.

chocolate chip ice cream cake

Prep: 20 minutes Freeze: 6 hours Makes: 10 to 12 servings

1   3-ounce package
      cream cheese,
      softened
1   tablespoon sugar
1½ cups chocolate chip,
      strawberry, or
      vanilla ice cream
1   8- or 9-inch
      purchased angel
      food cake (15 or
      16 ounces)
⅓   cup sliced fresh
      strawberries
⅓   cup chocolate fudge
      or strawberry ice
      cream topping

1 For filling, in a small bowl stir together cream cheese and sugar. In a medium bowl use a wooden spoon to stir ice cream just until it begins to soften; fold cream cheese mixture into ice cream. Place in freezer while preparing the cake.

2 Use a serrated knife to cut off the top ½ inch of the cake; set aside. Hold the knife parallel to the center hole of the cake and cut around the hole, leaving about ¾-inch thickness of cake around the hole and cutting within 1 inch of bottom of cake. Cut around the outer edge of the cake, leaving an outer cake wall about ¾ inch thick. Use a spoon to remove center of cake, leaving about a ¾-inch-thick base. (Reserve scooped-out cake for another use.)

3 Spoon filling into hollowed cake. Arrange sliced strawberries on the filling. Replace the top of the cake. Cover and freeze for at least 6 hours or for up to 24 hours.

4 To serve, in a small saucepan heat ice cream topping until drizzling consistency; drizzle over cake. Slice cake with a serrated knife.

Per serving: 219 cal., 7 g total fat (4 g sat. fat), 18 mg chol., 265 mg sodium, 37 g carbo., 0 g fiber, 5 g pro.

A coconut-pecan topping gets toasty as it bakes and makes this super-moist pineapple cake a standout. Serve warm with a little whipped cream.

pineapple cake

Prep: 25 minutes Bake: 30 minutes Oven: 350°F Makes: 16 servings

1	20-ounce can crushed pineapple
2½	cups all-purpose flour
1½	teaspoons baking powder
½	teaspoon baking soda
¼	teaspoon salt
½	cup butter, softened
1	cup granulated sugar
2	eggs
¾	cup packed brown sugar
¾	cup chopped pecans
¾	cup flaked or shredded coconut

1 Preheat oven to 350°F. Grease a 13×9×2-inch baking pan; set aside. Drain pineapple, reserving juice. In a medium bowl combine flour, baking powder, baking soda, and salt; set aside.

2 In a large bowl beat butter with an electric mixer on medium to high speed for 30 seconds. Add granulated sugar; beat until fluffy. Add eggs; beat until smooth. Alternately add flour mixture and reserved pineapple juice to beaten mixture, beating on low speed after each addition just until combined. Fold in drained pineapple. Spread batter evenly in prepared pan.

3 In a small bowl combine brown sugar, pecans, and coconut; sprinkle over batter. Bake in the preheated oven for 30 to 35 minutes or until a toothpick inserted in center comes out clean. Serve warm.

Per serving: *285 cal., 12 g total fat (5 g sat. fat), 43 mg chol., 189 mg sodium, 43 g carbo., 1 g fiber, 3 g pro.*

almond snack cake

Prep: 20 minutes Bake: 30 minutes Oven: 350°F Makes: 8 servings

1   1-layer-size chocolate
     or yellow cake mix
¼   cup packed brown
     sugar
½   cup almond butter or
     peanut butter
½   cup water
1   egg
½   cup almond toffee
     pieces
¼   cup chopped almonds
     or peanuts

1 Preheat oven to 350°F. Grease and flour an 8×8×2-inch baking pan; set aside. In a large bowl combine cake mix and brown sugar; add almond butter. Beat with an electric mixer on low speed just until crumbly. Set aside ⅓ cup of the crumb mixture. Add the water and egg to remaining crumb mixture; beat on low speed for 30 seconds, scraping sides of bowl constantly. Beat on high speed for 2 minutes. Stir in ¼ cup of the almond toffee pieces. Pour into prepared baking pan.

2 Bake in the preheated oven for 20 minutes. Stir remaining ¼ cup almond toffee pieces and the almonds into the reserved crumb mixture; carefully sprinkle over cake. Bake for 10 to 20 minutes more or until a toothpick inserted into center comes out clean. Cool in pan on a wire rack.

Per serving: 366 cal., 22 g total fat (5 g sat. fat), 37 mg chol., 406 mg sodium, 41 g carbo., 2 g fiber, 6 g pro.

mocha-chip cheesecake

Prep: 15 minutes Chill: 1 hour Makes: 9 servings

1   11.1-ounce package
      cheesecake mix
⅓   cup butter, melted
1¼ cups milk
2   teaspoons instant
      coffee crystals
½   cup dairy sour cream
½   cup miniature
      semisweet
      chocolate pieces

1 In a small bowl stir together crust crumbs from the cheesecake mix and the melted butter. Press crumb mixture into the bottom of an 8×8×2-inch baking pan.

2 In a large mixing bowl combine milk and instant coffee crystals; stir to dissolve coffee crystals. Add filling mix from the cheesecake mix. Beat with an electric mixer on medium speed just until combined. Add sour cream; beat on high speed for 3 minutes.

3 Stir in ¼ cup of the chocolate pieces. Spread cheesecake mixture over crumb layer in baking pan. Sprinkle remaining ¼ cup chocolate pieces on top. Cover and chill for at least 1 hour or up to 24 hours. To serve, cut into squares.

Per serving: 323 cal., 17 g total fat (10 g sat. fat), 27 mg chol., 351 mg sodium, 37 g carbo., 1 g fiber, 5 g pro.

sour cream-blueberry pie

Prep: 15 minutes   Bake: 40 minutes   Chill: 4 hours   Oven: 400°F
Makes: 8 servings

1	egg, beaten
1	8-ounce carton dairy sour cream
¾	cup sugar
2	tablespoons all-purpose flour
1	teaspoon vanilla
¼	teaspoon salt
2½	cups fresh blueberries
1	unbaked 9-inch pastry shell*
¼	cup all-purpose flour
¼	cup butter, softened
¼	cup chopped pecans or walnuts

1 Preheat oven to 400°F. For filling, in a large bowl combine egg, sour cream, sugar, the 2 tablespoons flour, the vanilla, and salt; stir until smooth. Fold in blueberries. Pour filling into unbaked pastry shell.

2 Bake in the preheated oven for 25 minutes. Meanwhile, in a small bowl thoroughly combine the ¼ cup flour, butter, and nuts. Pinch off small bits of flour mixture and sprinkle on top of pie. Bake for 15 minutes more. Cool on a wire rack. Chill at least 4 hours before serving.

*Note: If you do not wish to prepare your own pastry shell, use 1 rolled refrigerated unbaked piecrust (½ of a 15-ounce package), or use one 9-inch frozen deep-dish pastry shell. (If you use a frozen pastry shell, a deep-dish one is essential to hold all of the filling.)

Per serving: *397 cal., 24 g total fat (10 g sat. fat), 54 mg chol., 211 mg sodium, 42 g carbo., 3 g fiber, 5 g pro.*

Your secret to a great pie is refrigerated piecrust with a free-form, no-crimp edge. No pie-making experience necessary.

easy-as-peach pie

Prep: 20 minutes Bake: 1 hour Stand: 45 minutes Oven: 350°F
Makes: 6 to 8 servings

½ of a 15-ounce
   package rolled
   refrigerated
   unbaked piecrust
   (1 crust)
1 cup sugar
3 tablespoons
   cornstarch
4 cups sliced, peeled
   peaches, or one
   16-ounce package
   frozen unsweetened
   peach slices
1 cup fresh or frozen
   red raspberries
1 9-inch disposable foil
   pie pan
   Vanilla ice cream
   (optional)

1 Bring piecrust to room temperature according to package directions. Preheat oven to 350°F. Meanwhile, in a large bowl combine sugar and cornstarch. Add peaches and raspberries; toss to coat. (If using frozen fruit, let stand for 15 to 30 minutes or until partially thawed.)

2 Ease crust into pie pan, allowing edges of crust to hang over edges of pan. (Or use a 9-inch pie plate.) Spoon peach mixture into pastry-lined pan. Fold crust edges over filling (crust will not totally cover fruit mixture).

3 Place pie pan in a foil-lined shallow baking pan. Bake on the bottom rack of the preheated oven for 60 to 70 minutes or until pastry is golden brown and filling is bubbly.

4 Remove pan from oven and let stand for 45 minutes before serving. If desired, serve warm with ice cream.

Per serving: *401 cal., 11 g total fat (2 g sat. fat), 0 mg chol., 205 mg sodium, 76 g carbo., 5 g fiber, 4 g pro.*

luscious lemon squares

Prep: 25 minutes Bake: 33 minutes Oven: 350°F Makes: 36 bars

2 cups all-purpose flour
½ cup sifted powdered
  sugar
2 tablespoons
  cornstarch
¼ teaspoon salt
¾ cup butter
4 eggs, slightly beaten
1½ cups granulated
  sugar
3 tablespoons all-
  purpose flour
1 teaspoon finely
  shredded lemon
  peel
¾ cup lemon juice
¼ cup half-and-half,
  light cream, or milk
  Powdered sugar

1 Preheat oven to 350°F. Line a 13×9×2-inch baking pan with foil; grease foil and set aside. In a large bowl combine the 2 cups flour, the ½ cup powdered sugar, cornstarch, and salt. Using a pastry blender, cut in butter until mixture resembles coarse crumbs. Press flour mixture into the bottom of the prepared pan. Bake in the preheated oven for 18 to 20 minutes or until edges are golden brown.

2 Meanwhile, for filling, in a medium bowl stir together eggs, the granulated sugar, the 3 tablespoons flour, lemon peel, lemon juice, and half-and-half. Pour filling over hot crust. Bake in the 350°F oven for 15 to 20 minutes more or until center is set. Cool on a wire rack. Sift powdered sugar over top. Cut into bars. Cover and store in the refrigerator.

Per bar: *114 cal., 5 g total fat (3 g sat. fat), 35 mg chol., 65 mg sodium, 16 g carbo., 0 g fiber, 2 g pro.*

streusel strawberry bars

Prep: 20 minutes Bake: 45 minutes Oven: 350°F Makes: 24 bars

1 cup butter, softened
1 cup granulated sugar
1 egg
2 cups all-purpose flour
¾ cup pecans, coarsely
   chopped
1 10-ounce jar
   strawberry or
   raspberry preserves
1 recipe Powdered
   Sugar Icing (see
   recipe, below) or
   powdered sugar

1 Preheat oven to 350°F. In a medium mixing bowl beat butter and granulated sugar with an electric mixer on medium speed until combined, scraping side of bowl occasionally. Beat in egg.

2 Beat in as much of the flour as you can with the mixer. Stir in any remaining flour. Stir in pecans. Set aside 1 cup of the pecan mixture.

3 Press the remaining pecan mixture into the bottom of an ungreased 9×9×2-inch baking pan. Spread preserves to within ½ inch of the edges of the bottom crust. Dot the 1 cup reserved pecan mixture on top of preserves.

4 Bake in the preheated oven for about 45 minutes or until top is golden brown. Cool on a wire rack. Drizzle with Powdered Sugar Icing or sprinkle with powdered sugar. Cut into bars.

Per bar: 209 cal., 11 g total fat (5 g sat. fat), 31 mg chol., 91 mg sodium, 28 g carbo., 1 g fiber, 2 g pro.

Powdered Sugar Icing: In a small bowl combine 1 cup powdered sugar, 1 tablespoon milk, and ¼ teaspoon vanilla. Stir in additional milk, 1 teaspoon at a time, until icing is of drizzling consistency.

Keep just six ingredients on hand for those spur-of-the-moment potlucks.

raspberry-pecan bars

Prep: 15 minutes Bake: 45 minutes Oven: 350°F Makes: 16 bars

1   cup butter (no
      substitutes),
      softened
1   cup sugar
1   egg
2¼   cups all-purpose flour
1   cup chopped pecans
1   10-ounce jar
      raspberry preserves

1 Preheat oven to 350°F. In a large mixing bowl beat butter with an electric mixer on medium to high speed for 30 seconds. Add sugar; beat until combined. Add the egg; beat until combined. Beat in flour until crumbly. Stir in pecans. Measure 1½ cups of the mixture. Set aside.

2 Press the remaining flour mixture into the bottom of an ungreased 8×8×2-inch baking pan. Spread raspberry preserves evenly over crust, leaving a ½-inch border around sides. Crumble reserved mixture over the top.

3 Bake in the preheated oven for 45 to 50 minutes until top is brown. Cool in pan on a wire rack. Cut into bars.

Per bar: 308 cal., 17 g total fat (8 g sat. fat), 44 mg chol., 92 mg sodium, 38 g carbo., 1 g fiber, 3 g pro.

These all-time favorite bars can be made with a fraction of the effort using refrigerated oatmeal chocolate chip cookie dough.

shortcut chocolate revel bars

Prep: 20 minutes Bake: 25 minutes Oven: 350°F Makes: 30 bars

1½ cups semisweet
    chocolate pieces
1 14-ounce can
    sweetened
    condensed milk
    (1¼ cups)
2 tablespoons butter
½ cup chopped walnuts
    or pecans
2 teaspoons vanilla
2 18-ounce rolls
    refrigerated
    oatmeal chocolate
    chip cookie dough

1 Preheat oven to 350°F. In a small saucepan combine chocolate pieces, condensed milk, and butter. Cook and stir over low heat until chocolate is melted. Remove from heat. Stir in nuts and vanilla.

2 Press two-thirds (1⅓ rolls) of the cookie dough into the bottom of an ungreased 15×10×1-inch baking pan. Spread chocolate mixture evenly over the cookie dough. Dot remaining cookie dough on top of chocolate mixture.

3 Bake in the preheated oven for about 25 minutes or until top is light brown (chocolate will still look moist). Cool on a wire rack. Cut into bars. To store, cover and chill for up to 3 days or freeze up to 1 month.

Per bar: 255 cal., 13 g total fat (5 g sat. fat), 13 mg chol., 136 mg sodium, 33 g carbo., 1 g fiber, 3 g pro.

bonus: sweet & simple **desserts**

layered bars

Prep: 25 minutes Chill: 2 hours Makes: 24 bars

½ cup butter (no substitutes)
¼ cup granulated sugar
¼ cup unsweetened cocoa powder
1 egg, beaten
1 teaspoon vanilla
1¾ cups graham cracker crumbs
1 cup coconut
½ cup chopped nuts, toasted
¼ cup butter (no substitutes), softened
¼ cup half-and-half, light cream, or milk
3 tablespoons custard-flavor dessert mix (half of a 2.9-ounce package)
2 cups sifted powdered sugar
6 ounces semisweet chocolate, cut up
4 teaspoons butter (no substitutes)

1 For crust, in a medium saucepan combine the ½ cup butter, the granulated sugar, cocoa powder, egg, and vanilla. Cook and stir until butter is melted and mixture is thoroughly combined and just starts to bubble. Remove from heat. Stir in graham cracker crumbs, coconut, and nuts. Press into the bottom of a 9×9×2-inch baking pan. Set aside.

2 For filling, in a medium mixing bowl combine the ¼ cup softened butter, the half-and-half, and dessert mix. Beat with an electric mixer on medium speed until combined. Beat in powdered sugar until light in texture. Carefully spread filling evenly over crust. Cover and chill until firm (about 1 hour).

3 For topping, in a small saucepan heat and stir semisweet chocolate and the 4 teaspoons butter over low heat until combined. Spread over filling. Cover and chill until firm. Cut into bars.

Per bar: 212 cal., 13 g total fat (7 g sat. fat), 27 mg chol., 95 mg sodium, 24 g carbo., 1 g fiber, 2 g pro.

Peanut butter cookie dough, peanut butter pieces, and peanut butter icing create these rich bars.

triple peanut bars

Prep: 25 minutes Bake: 25 minutes Oven: 350°F Makes: 72 bars

Nonstick cooking
   spray
1 18-ounce package
   refrigerated peanut
   butter cookie dough
1 12-ounce package
   semisweet
   chocolate pieces
   (2 cups)
1 14-ounce can
   sweetened
   condensed milk
1½ cups dry-roasted
   peanuts
1 10-ounce package
   peanut butter-flavor
   pieces
¼ cup peanut butter
1 cup sifted powdered
   sugar
   Milk

1 Preheat oven to 350°F. Lightly coat a 15×10×1-inch baking pan with cooking spray. With floured hands press cookie dough into bottom of prepared pan. Sprinkle chocolate pieces evenly over dough. Drizzle sweetened condensed milk over chips; top with peanuts and peanut butter pieces. Press down firmly. Bake in the preheated oven for about 25 minutes or until edges are firm. Cool in pan on a wire rack.

2 For icing, in a small bowl beat together peanut butter, powdered sugar, and 1 tablespoon milk. Add additional milk, 1 teaspoon at a time, until drizzling consistency. Drizzle icing over bars. Cover pan and store in the refrigerator up to 3 days.

Per bar: 122 cal., 7 g total fat (2 g sat. fat), 4 mg chol., 49 mg sodium, 12 g carbo., 1 g fiber, 3 g pro.

chocolate goody bars

Prep: 20 minutes Bake: 28 minutes Oven: 350°F Makes: 36 bars

1   19.8-ounce package
    fudge brownie mix
½   cup cooking oil
2   eggs
¼   cup water
1   16-ounce can vanilla
    frosting
¾   cup chopped peanuts
3   cups crisp rice cereal
1   cup creamy peanut
    butter
1   12-ounce package
    semisweet
    chocolate pieces

1 Preheat oven to 350°F. Grease a 13×9×2-inch baking pan; set aside.

2 In a large bowl stir together the brownie mix, oil, eggs, and water until well mixed. Spread brownie mixture into prepared pan.

3 Bake in the preheated oven for 28 to 30 minutes or until toothpick inserted 2 inches from sides of pan comes out clean. Cool completely on wire rack.

4 Spread frosting over cooled brownies. Sprinkle with peanuts. Cover; chill.

5 Meanwhile, place rice cereal in a medium bowl. In a small saucepan combine peanut butter and chocolate pieces. Heat and stir over low heat until chocolate is melted. Pour over cereal. Stir to coat evenly. Spread over frosting. Cover; chill until chocolate layer is set. Cover and refrigerate leftover bars.

Per bar: 261 cal., 14 g total fat (2 g sat. fat), 12 mg chol., 150 mg sodium, 33 g carbo., 1 g fiber, 4 g pro.

chocolate-peanut
butter crunch bars

Prep: 15 minutes Bake: 15 minutes Oven: 350°F Makes: 36 bars

1   cup butter, softened
1   cup granulated sugar
1   cup packed brown
      sugar
4   cups quick-cooking
      rolled oats
1   cup semisweet
      chocolate pieces
      (6 ounces)
¾   cup creamy peanut
      butter
      Chopped peanuts
      (optional)

1 Preheat oven to 350°F. In a large bowl beat butter with an electric mixer on medium speed for 30 seconds. Beat in granulated sugar and brown sugar until fluffy. Stir in oats. Press into an ungreased 13×9×2-inch baking pan.

2 Bake in the preheated oven for about 15 minutes or until edges just begin to brown. Place pan on a wire rack.

3 In a medium saucepan heat and stir in chocolate pieces and peanut butter over medium-low heat until melted and smooth. Spread chocolate mixture over crust. If desired, sprinkle with peanuts. Cool until set. Cut into bars.

Per bar: 178 cal., 10 g total fat (2 g sat. fat), 0 mg chol., 88 mg sodium, 22 g carbo., 1 g fiber, 3 g pro.

polka-dot cookie bars

Prep: 10 minutes Bake: 20 minutes Oven: 350°F Makes: 24 bars

1 cup all-purpose flour
⅔ cup packed brown sugar
⅓ cup whole wheat flour
½ teaspoon baking powder
⅛ teaspoon baking soda
    Dash salt
½ cup shortening
2 eggs, slightly beaten
⅓ cup milk
½ cup miniature candy-coated semisweet or milk chocolate pieces

1 Preheat oven to 350°F. Grease an 11×7×1½-inch baking pan; set aside. In a large bowl combine all-purpose flour, brown sugar, whole wheat flour, baking powder, baking soda, and salt. Using a pastry blender, cut in shortening until mixture resembles fine crumbs. Stir in eggs and milk until combined. Spread batter evenly in the prepared pan.

2 Bake in the preheated oven for 10 minutes. Sprinkle chocolate pieces evenly over top of partially baked bars. Bake for 10 to 15 minutes more or until golden brown and firm around edges. Cool in pan on a wire rack. Cut into bars.

Per bar: *111 cal., 5 g total fat (2 g sat. fat), 18 mg chol., 29 mg sodium, 14 g carbo., 0 g fiber, 2 g pro.*

rain forest bars

Prep: 25 minutes Bake: 30 minutes Oven: 350°F Makes: 40 bars

¾ cup butter (no
   substitutes)
½ cup packed brown
   sugar
1 egg yolk
1 teaspoon vanilla
2 cups all-purpose flour
1 cup packed brown
   sugar
3 eggs
1 teaspoon vanilla
3 tablespoons
   all-purpose flour
¼ teaspoon salt
2 cups chopped Brazil
   nuts
1 cup flaked or
   shredded coconut

1 Preheat oven to 350°F. In a medium mixing bowl beat butter with an electric mixer on medium to high speed for 30 seconds. Add the ½ cup brown sugar; beat until combined, scraping sides of bowl occasionally. Beat in egg yolk and 1 teaspoon vanilla until combined. Beat in the 2 cups flour until combined. Pat dough evenly into the bottom of a 13×9×2-inch baking pan. Bake in the preheated oven for 10 minutes. Cool in pan on a wire rack for 5 minutes.

2 Meanwhile, in a large bowl stir together the 1 cup brown sugar, the eggs, and 1 teaspoon vanilla. Beat at medium speed until combined. Beat in the 3 tablespoons flour and the salt until combined. Stir in nuts and coconut. Spread evenly over baked crust. Bake in the preheated oven for about 20 minutes more or until set. Cool in pan on wire rack. Cut into bars. Cover and refrigerate to store.

Per bar: 154 cal., 10 g total fat (4 g sat. fat), 30 mg chol., 55 mg sodium, 15 g carbo., 1 g fiber, 2 g pro.

mixed nut bars

Prep: 20 minutes Bake: 35 minutes Oven: 350°F Makes: 32 bars

¾ cup butter (no
     substitutes),
     softened
⅓ cup packed brown
     sugar
1¾ cups all-purpose flour
1⅔ cups granulated
     sugar
¼ cup all-purpose flour
1 cup buttermilk
3 eggs
¼ cup butter (no
     substitutes), melted
1½ teaspoons vanilla
2 cups coarsely
     chopped mixed nuts
     (no peanuts)
     Sifted powdered
     sugar (optional)

1 Preheat oven to 350°F. In a medium bowl beat the ¾ cup butter, brown sugar, and the 1¾ cups flour on medium speed until well combined (mixture will be crumbly). Pat mixture into the bottom and ½ inch up the sides of an ungreased 13×9×2-inch baking pan. Bake in the preheated oven for 10 minutes.

2 Meanwhile, in a medium mixing bowl combine together granulated sugar, the ¼ cup flour, buttermilk, eggs, the ¼ cup melted butter, and vanilla. Beat with an electric mixer on low speed until combined. Stir in nuts. Pour into crust.

3 Bake in the preheated oven for 25 minutes more or until golden brown and center is set. Cool in pan on a wire rack. Store in the refrigerator. To serve, cut into bars and sprinkle with powdered sugar, if desired.

Per bar: 194 cal., 11 g total fat (5 g sat. fat), 35 mg chol., 57 mg sodium, 21 g carbo., 1 g fiber, 3 g pro.

You can store these fudgy brownies for up to three days. Place them in a tightly covered container to keep them from drying out.

top-of-the-world
brownies

Prep: 20 minutes Bake: 1 hour Cool: 1 hour Oven: 350°F
Makes: 16 brownies

¾ cup butter (no substitutes)
3 ounces unsweetened chocolate, cut up
1⅓ cups sugar
2 teaspoons vanilla
3 eggs
1 cup all-purpose flour
2 tablespoons unsweetened cocoa powder
½ cup coarsely chopped hazelnuts (filberts) or pecans
2 egg whites
⅔ cup sugar
1 tablespoon unsweetened cocoa powder

1 Preheat oven to 350°F. Line bottom and sides of an 8×8×2-inch baking pan with heavy foil; grease foil and set aside.

2 In a medium saucepan stir butter and the cut-up chocolate over low heat just until melted. Remove from heat. Using a wooden spoon, stir in the 1⅓ cups sugar and the vanilla. Cool about 5 minutes.

3 Add eggs, one at a time, beating after each just until combined. Stir in flour and the 2 tablespoons cocoa. Spread batter evenly in prepared pan. Sprinkle with nuts; set aside.

4 In a small mixing bowl beat egg whites with an electric mixer on medium to high speed for 1 minute or until soft peaks form (tips curl). Gradually add the ⅔ cup sugar, beating on high speed until stiff peaks form (tips stand straight) and sugar is almost dissolved. Reduce speed to low; beat in the 1 tablespoon cocoa.

5 Using a tablespoon, carefully dollop the meringue in 16 even mounds on top of the brownie batter, leaving about ½ of an inch of space between them.

6 Bake in the preheated oven for about 1 hour or until a wooden toothpick inserted near the center of the brownie portion comes out clean. Cool brownies in pan on a wire rack at least 1 hour. To serve, before cutting, lift whole brownie from pan using foil. Cut into 16 pieces.

Per brownie: 269 cal., 15 g total fat (7 g sat. fat), 63 mg chol., 107 mg sodium, 34 g carbo., 1 g fiber, 4 g pro.

White baking pieces and semisweet chocolate pieces dress up a packaged brownie mix in this easy recipe. Frost the bars with chocolate icing and sprinkle with pecans.

black & white brownies

Prep: 25 minutes Bake: 31 minutes Cool: 1½ hours Oven: 350°F
Makes: 36 brownies

1	19- to 21-ounce package fudge brownie mix
1	10- to 12-ounce package white baking pieces
1	cup semisweet chocolate pieces
½	cup pecan pieces
¼	cup butter, melted
3	tablespoons hot water
2	cups powdered sugar
¼	cup unsweetened cocoa powder
1	teaspoon vanilla
¾	cup pecan pieces

1 Preheat oven to 350°F. Grease bottom of a 13×9×2-inch baking pan; set aside. Prepare brownie mix according to package directions. Stir in half of the white baking pieces, all of the semisweet chocolate pieces, and the ½ cup pecans. Spread batter evenly in the prepared pan.

2 Bake in the preheated oven for about 30 minutes or until center is set. Sprinkle with the remaining white baking pieces; return to oven for 1 minute. Cool in pan or dish on a wire rack.

3 For frosting, in a medium bowl combine melted butter and hot water; stir in powdered sugar, cocoa powder, and vanilla. Using a wooden spoon, beat by hand until smooth; spoon over brownies. Sprinkle with the ¾ cup pecans. Cool about 1½ hours or until frosting is set. Cut into bars.

Per brownie: 221 cal., 12 g total fat (4 g sat. fat), 18 mg chol., 67 mg sodium, 25 g carbo., 1 g fiber, 2 g pro.

raspberry & white
chocolate brownies

Prep: 30 minutes Bake: 30 minutes Oven: 350°F Makes: 20 brownies

½ cup butter (no
   substitutes)
2 ounces white
   chocolate baking
   bar or squares,
   cut up
2 eggs
⅔ cup sugar
1 teaspoon vanilla
1 cup all-purpose flour
½ cup chopped toasted
   almonds
½ teaspoon baking
   powder
   Dash salt
1 cup fresh raspberries
2 ounces white
   chocolate baking
   bar or squares,
   melted

1 Preheat oven to 350°F. Line an 8×8×2-inch baking pan with foil. Grease foil; set pan aside.

2 In a medium saucepan melt butter and white chocolate over low heat, stirring frequently. Remove from heat. Stir in eggs, sugar, and vanilla. Beat lightly with a wooden spoon just until combined. Stir in flour, almonds, baking powder, and salt. Spread batter in the prepared pan. Sprinkle with raspberries.

3 Bake in the preheated oven for 30 to 35 minutes or until golden brown. Cool in pan on a wire rack. Remove from pan by lifting foil. Cut with a 2-inch round cutter or cut into bars. Drizzle cutouts or bars with melted white chocolate.

Per brownie: 146 cal., 8 g total fat (4 g sat. fat), 35 mg chol., 62 mg sodium, 16 g carbo., 1 g fiber, 2 g pro.

Crème de menthe, a favorite mid-20th-century flavoring, appeared in mile-high cream pies, luscious desserts, and grasshoppers, the classic cocktail. The elegant liqueur makes a comeback in an easy brownie, with chocolate as its co-star.

crème de menthe brownies

Prep: 20 minutes Bake: 20 minutes Cool: 1 hour Oven: 375°F
Makes: 16 to 20 brownies

½ cup butter
2 ounces unsweetened chocolate
1 cup granulated sugar
2 eggs
¼ teaspoon mint extract
⅔ cup all-purpose flour
¼ cup butter, softened
1½ cups sifted powdered sugar
2 tablespoons green crème de menthe
1 ounce semisweet chocolate
Layered chocolate-mint candies, chopped (optional)

1 Preheat oven to 375°F. Grease an 8×8×2-inch baking pan; set aside.

2 In a medium heavy saucepan place the ½ cup butter and the unsweetened chocolate. Heat and stir over low heat until melted. Remove from heat. Stir in granulated sugar, eggs, and mint extract. Beat lightly by hand until just combined. Stir in flour.

3 Spread batter in the prepared pan. Bake in the preheated oven for 20 minutes. Cool completely in pan on a wire rack.

4 In a medium mixing bowl beat the ¼ cup butter with an electric mixer on medium to high speed for 30 seconds. Gradually add 1 cup of the powdered sugar. Beat in crème de menthe. Gradually beat in enough of the remaining ½ cup powdered sugar to make frosting of spreading consistency.

5 Spread crème de menthe mixture over brownies. In a small heavy saucepan melt semisweet chocolate over low heat. Drizzle chocolate over brownies. If desired, sprinkle with chopped layered chocolate-mint candies. Cut into triangles or bars.

To Store: Cover and store in the refrigerator up to 3 days or freeze plain brownies up to 3 months. Thaw, then spread with crème de menthe mixture.

Per brownie: 231 cal., 12 g total fat (7 g sat. fat), 49 mg chol., 71 mg sodium, 31 g carbo., 1 g fiber, 2 g pro.

fudgy brownies

Prep: 20 minutes Bake: 25 minutes Oven: 350°F Makes: 16 brownies

½ cup butter (no
    substitutes)
3   ounces unsweetened
    chocolate, coarsely
    chopped
1   cup sugar
2   eggs
1   teaspoon vanilla
⅔ cup all-purpose flour
¼ teaspoon baking soda
½ cup chopped nuts
    (optional)
1   recipe Chocolate-
    Cream Cheese
    Frosting (see recipe,
    below) (optional)

1 In a medium saucepan melt butter and unsweetened chocolate over low heat, stirring constantly. Remove from heat; cool.

2 Meanwhile, preheat oven to 350°F. Grease an 8×8×2-inch or 9×9×2-inch baking pan; set aside. Stir sugar into cooled chocolate mixture in saucepan. Add the eggs, one at a time, beating with a wooden spoon just until combined. Stir in the vanilla.

3 In a small bowl stir together the flour and baking soda. Add flour mixture to chocolate mixture; stir just until combined. If desired, stir in nuts. Spread the batter into the prepared pan.

4 Bake in the preheated oven for 30 minutes for 8-inch pan or 25 minutes for 9-inch pan. Cool on a wire rack. If desired, frost with Chocolate-Cream Cheese Frosting. Cut into bars.

Per brownie: 157 cal., 10 g total fat (6 g sat. fat), 43 mg chol., 90 mg sodium, 18 g carbo., 1 g fiber, 2 g pro.

Chocolate-Cream Cheese Frosting: In a small saucepan melt 1 cup semisweet chocolate pieces over low heat, stirring constantly. Remove from heat; cool. In a small bowl stir together two 3-ounce packages softened cream cheese and ½ cup powdered sugar. Stir in melted chocolate until smooth.

almond brittle brownies

Prep: 30 minutes Bake: 37 minutes Oven: 350°F Makes: 36 brownies

⅓ cup slivered almonds
¼ cup sugar
1 tablespoon butter
   (no substitutes)
½ cup butter (no
   substitutes)
½ cup sugar
1 cup all-purpose flour
¾ cup butter (no
   substitutes)
4 ounces unsweetened
   chocolate, cut up
2 cups sugar
2 teaspoons vanilla
4 eggs
1½ cups all-purpose flour

1 Preheat oven to 350°F. Line a baking sheet with foil; grease foil and set aside. In a medium heavy skillet combine almonds, the ¼ cup sugar, and the 1 tablespoon butter. Place over medium-high heat. Cook, shaking skillet occasionally, until sugar begins to melt. Do not stir. Reduce heat to low and continue cooking until sugar is golden brown, stirring occasionally with a wooden spoon. Remove from heat. Spread almond mixture onto the prepared baking sheet; cool completely.

2 Place almond mixture in a heavy plastic bag; use a rolling pin or meat mallet to coarsely crush the almond mixture; set aside.

3 For crust, in a medium mixing bowl beat the ½ cup butter and the ½ cup sugar with an electric mixer on medium to high speed until combined. Stir in the 1 cup flour with a wooden spoon. Press into the bottom of a greased and floured 13×9×2-inch baking pan. Bake about 10 minutes or until edges are light brown.

4 Meanwhile, in a medium saucepan melt the ¾ cup butter and the chocolate over low heat. Remove from heat. Stir in the 2 cups sugar and the vanilla. Add eggs, one at a time, beating lightly with a wooden spoon just until combined. Stir in the 1½ cups flour. Spread batter over hot crust.

5 Bake in the preheated oven for 15 minutes. Sprinkle with crushed almond mixture; press almond mixture lightly into chocolate layer. Bake for 12 to 15 minutes more or until set. Cool in pan on a wire rack. Cut into diamonds or bars.

Per brownie: 164 cal., 10 g total fat (5 g sat. fat), 41 mg chol., 56 mg sodium, 20 g carbo., 1 g fiber, 2 g pro.

easy fruit cobbler

Prep: 15 minutes Bake: 25 minutes Oven: 400°F Makes: 6 servings

6 cups desired frozen
   fruit, such as
   sliced peaches,
   raspberries, and/or
   blueberries, thawed
¼ cup sugar
2 tablespoons quick-
   cooking tapioca
2 cups packaged
   biscuit mix
2 tablespoons sugar
½ cup milk
   Cinnamon-sugar
   (optional)

1 Preheat oven to 400°F. In a large bowl stir together undrained fruit, the ¼ cup sugar, and the tapioca. Divide fruit mixture among six 10-ounce ramekins or custard cups. Place ramekins in a shallow baking pan.

2 In a medium bowl stir together biscuit mix, the 2 tablespoons sugar, and the milk until combined. Spoon batter over fruit mixture. If desired, sprinkle tops lightly with cinnamon-sugar.

3 Bake in the preheated oven for about 25 minutes or until filling is bubbly and topping is golden brown. Serve warm.

Per serving: 307 cal., 6 g total fat (2 g sat. fat), 2 mg chol., 503 mg sodium, 62 g carbo., 3 g fiber, 5 g pro.

rhubarb crunch

Prep: 15 minutes Bake: 1 hour Cool: 30 minutes
Oven: 350°F Makes: 9 servings

1 cup all-purpose flour
1 cup quick-cooking
   oats
1 cup packed brown
   sugar
1 teaspoon ground
   cinnamon
½ cup butter
4 cups diced rhubarb
1 cup granulated sugar
2 tablespoons
   cornstarch
1 cup water
1 teaspoon vanilla
   Few drops red food
   coloring (optional)
   Vanilla ice cream or
   whipped cream
   (optional)

1 Preheat oven to 350°F. In a large bowl stir together the flour, oats, brown sugar, and cinnamon. Using a pastry blender or two knives, cut in butter until mixture resembles fine crumbs. Press half of the mixture into the bottom of a 9×9×2-inch baking pan. Sprinkle rhubarb evenly over crust; set aside.

2 In a small saucepan stir together granulated sugar and cornstarch; add the water. Cook and stir until mixture is thickened and bubbly. Stir in vanilla and, if desired, red food coloring. Pour evenly over rhubarb. Sprinkle with remaining crumb mixture.

3 Bake, uncovered, in the preheated oven for about 1 hour or until topping is brown and filling is bubbly. Cool about 30 minutes. Serve warm. If desired, serve with ice cream.

Per serving: 379 cal., 12 g total fat (7 g sat. fat), 29 mg chol., 124 mg sodium, 67 g carbo., 3 g fiber, 4 g pro.

Dried fruit adds variety to this easy recipe, and granola makes a super-simple topper.

quick fruit crisp

Prep: 5 minutes Bake: 25 minutes Oven: 375°F Makes: 6 servings

2 21-ounce cans apple
   pie filling
¼ cup dried cherries,
   cranberries, or
   mixed dried fruit
   bits
1½ cups granola
   Vanilla ice cream
   (optional)

1 Preheat oven to 375°F. In a 2-quart square baking dish stir together the pie filling and dried fruit; sprinkle with granola.

2 Bake, uncovered, in the preheated oven for 20 to 25 minutes or until heated through. If desired, serve warm with ice cream.

Per serving: 326 cal., 3 g total fat (2 g sat. fat), 0 mg chol., 107 mg sodium, 75 g carbo., 4 g fiber, 3 g pro.

warm apple spice crumble

Prep: 10 minutes Bake: 12 minutes Oven: 375°F Makes: 4 servings

1   20-ounce can sliced
     apples, undrained
¼   cup golden raisins or
     mixed dried fruit
     bits
1   teaspoon vanilla
2   to 3 tablespoons
     sugar
1   teaspoon apple pie
     spice or ground
     cinnamon
3   tablespoons butter,
     cut into small
     pieces
1½   cups low-fat granola
¼   cup flaked coconut
     Vanilla ice cream
     (optional)

1 Preheat oven to 375°F. In 2-quart square baking dish combine undrained apples, raisins, and vanilla. Sprinkle with sugar and apple pie spice; top with butter. Sprinkle evenly with granola and coconut.

2 Bake in the preheated oven for 12 to 15 minutes or until apples are heated through and topping is golden brown. Serve warm. If desired, serve with ice cream.

Per serving: 423 cal., 14 g total fat (8 g sat. fat), 23 mg chol., 188 mg sodium, 74 g carbo., 6 g fiber, 5 g pro.

strawberries with
cannoli cream

Start to Finish: 10 minutes Makes: 8 servings

1   cup ricotta cheese
      (about ½ of a
      15-ounce carton)
¼   cup sugar
1½ teaspoons vanilla
½   cup whipping cream
⅓   cup miniature
      semisweet
      chocolate pieces
6   cups fresh
      strawberries,
      halved

1 For cannoli cream, in a medium bowl stir together ricotta cheese, sugar, and vanilla; set aside. In a small chilled bowl beat whipping cream with an electric mixer on medium speed until soft peaks form. (Do not overbeat.) By hand, gently stir whipped cream and about half of chocolate pieces into ricotta mixture. (If desired, cover and chill for up to 24 hours.)

2 To serve, divide berries among 8 dessert dishes. Spoon cannoli cream over berries. Sprinkle with remaining chocolate pieces.

Per serving: *198 cal., 12 g total fat (7 g sat. fat), 36 mg chol., 36 mg sodium, 20 g carbo., 3 g fiber, 5 g pro.*

Surprise! Who'd think of serving basil in dessert? You, especially after you see how delicious it tastes with fresh peaches.

sweet basil peaches

Start to Finish: 25 minutes Makes: 4 servings

5   medium peaches or
      nectarines
½   cup sweet white
      wine, such as
      Gewürztraminer or
      Riesling, or apple
      juice
⅓   cup fresh basil leaves
1   to 2 tablespoons
      sugar (optional)
      Snipped and/or whole
      fresh basil leaves

1 Remove pits from 2 unpeeled peaches; chop. Set remaining whole peaches aside.

2 In a medium saucepan combine chopped peaches, wine, the ⅓ cup basil, and, if desired, sugar. Bring to boiling; reduce heat. Simmer, uncovered, for 12 to 15 minutes or until sauce is slightly thickened.

3 Remove and discard the basil. Pour peach mixture into a blender or food processor; cover and blend or process until smooth.

4 Remove pits from remaining peaches and cut into wedges. Serve with peach mixture. Garnish with additional basil.

Per serving: *73 cal., 0 g total fat (0 g sat. fat), 0 mg chol., 0 mg sodium, 13 g carbo., 2 g fiber, 1 g pro.*

Look for glazed almond salad toppers in the produce section of your supermarket.

almond poached pears

Start to Finish: 15 minutes   Makes: 6 servings

1   29-ounce can pear halves in syrup
2   tablespoons packed brown sugar
½   teaspoon ground nutmeg
½   teaspoon almond extract
⅓   cup sliced almonds, toasted, or purchased glazed sliced almonds (salad toppers)
    Vanilla yogurt or ice cream (optional)

1 Drain pear halves, reserving liquid; set pears aside. In a large skillet stir together pear liquid, brown sugar, and nutmeg. Bring to boiling, stirring until sugar is dissolved. Add pears and almond extract, turning pears to coat. Remove from heat; cover and set aside for 5 minutes.

2 Serve pears with some of the poaching liquid and sprinkle with almonds. If desired, serve with vanilla yogurt or ice cream.

Per serving: *174 cal., 4 g total fat (0 g sat. fat), 0 mg chol., 13 mg sodium, 33 g carbo., 2 g fiber, 2 g pro.*

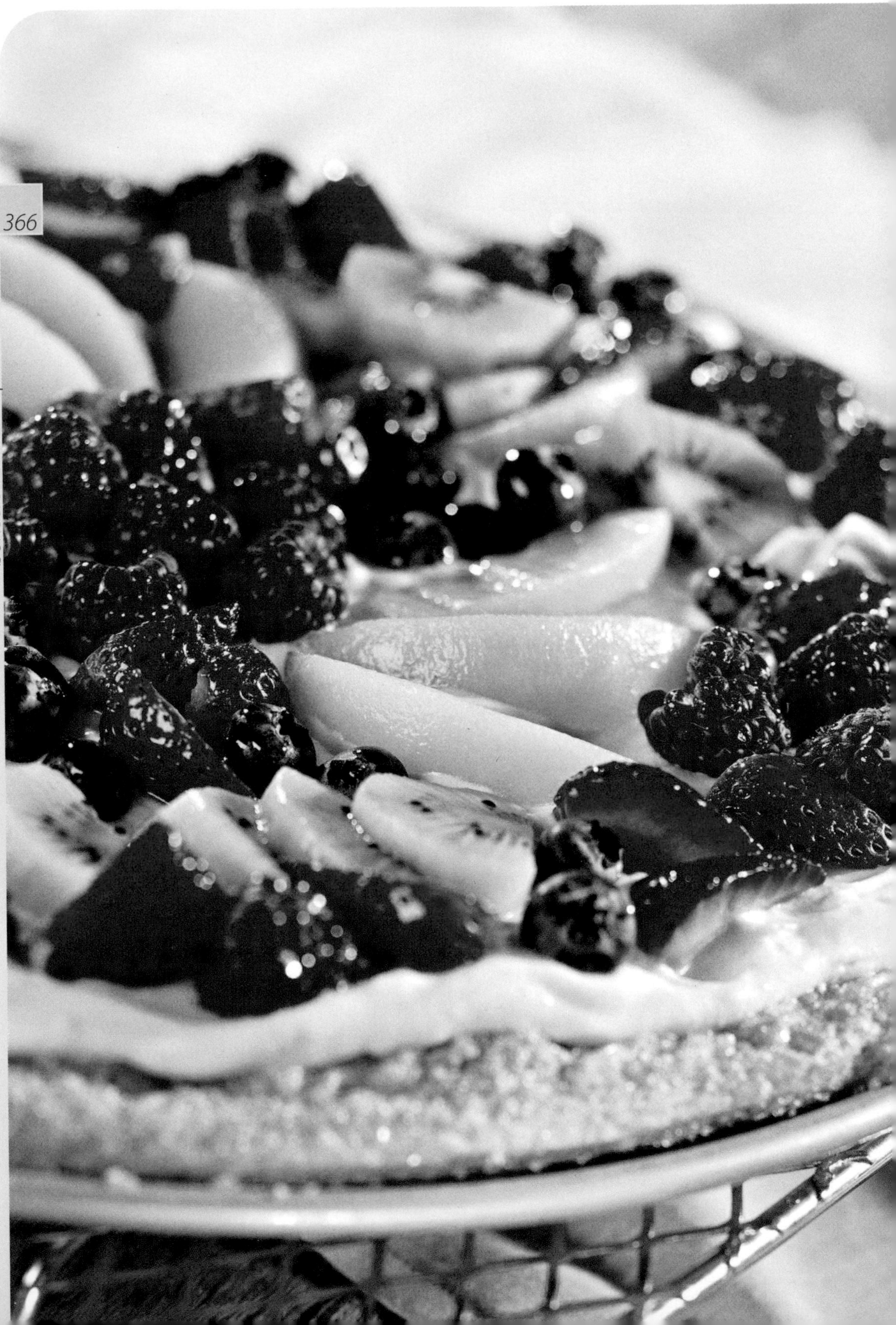

The best way to tote this along to a potluck is to pack the crust, filling, and fruit separately and assemble the tart on site.

crescent fruit pizza

Prep: 30 minutes Bake: 11 minutes Chill: 1 hour Oven: 375°F
Makes: 8 servings

1   8-ounce package
    refrigerated
    crescent rolls
1   tablespoon butter,
    melted
½   teaspoon almond
    extract
4   teaspoons sugar
1   4-serving-size
    package instant
    vanilla pudding mix
1½ cups milk
1   teaspoon finely
    shredded orange
    peel
¼   of an 8-ounce
    container frozen
    whipped dessert
    topping, thawed
3   cups fresh fruit (such
    as blueberries,
    raspberries, sliced
    strawberries, sliced
    peeled kiwifruits,
    and/or sliced peeled
    peaches)

1 Preheat oven to 375°F. Press crescent roll dough into the bottom of a 12-inch pizza pan or 13x9x2-inch baking pan. In a small bowl combine melted butter and almond extract; brush over dough. Sprinkle with sugar. Bake in the preheated oven for 11 to 13 minutes or until golden brown. Cool in pan on a wire rack.

2 Meanwhile, in a medium mixing bowl combine pudding mix and milk. Beat with an electric mixer on low speed for 2 minutes. Stir in orange peel. Cover and chill for 10 minutes. Fold in whipped topping.

3 Spread pudding mixture over crust. Arrange fruit on pudding mixture. Cover and chill for 1 to 3 hours.

Per serving: 235 cal., 10 g total fat (4 g sat. fat), 8 mg chol., 445 mg sodium, 34 g carbo., 2 g fiber, 4 g pro.

berry pudding cakes

Prep: 20 minutes Bake: 20 minutes Oven: 400°F Makes: 6 servings

Nonstick cooking
spray
2   eggs, slightly beaten
¼   cup granulated sugar
1   teaspoon vanilla
Dash salt
1   cup milk
½   cup all-purpose flour
½   teaspoon baking
powder
3   cups fresh
berries (such
as raspberries,
blueberries, and/or
sliced strawberries)
2   teaspoons powdered
sugar (optional)

1 Preheat oven to 400°F. Lightly coat six
6-ounce quiche dishes with cooking spray.
Arrange dishes in a 15×10×1-inch baking pan;
set aside. In a medium bowl combine eggs,
granulated sugar, vanilla, and salt; whisk until
light and frothy. Whisk in milk until combined.
Add flour and baking powder; whisk
until smooth.

2 Divide berries among prepared quiche
dishes. Pour batter over berries. (Batter
will not cover berries completely.)

3 Bake in the preheated oven for about
20 minutes or until puffed and golden
brown. Serve warm. If desired, sift powdered
sugar over each serving.

Per serving: *141 cal., 2 g total fat (1 g sat. fat), 71 mg chol.,
86 mg sodium, 26 g carbo., 3 g fiber, 5 g pro.*

warm chocolate bread pudding

Prep: 15 minutes Bake: 15 minutes Oven: 350°F Makes: 4 servings

Nonstick cooking
   spray
2 cups firm-textured
   white bread cubes
⅔ cup milk
¼ cup granulated sugar
¼ cup miniature
   semisweet
   chocolate pieces
3 eggs
1 teaspoon finely
   shredded orange
   peel or tangerine
   peel
½ teaspoon vanilla
   Powdered sugar or
   frozen whipped
   dessert topping
   (optional)

1 Preheat oven to 350°F. Lightly coat four ¾-cup soufflé dishes or 6-ounce custard cups with cooking spray. Place the bread cubes in the soufflé dishes.

2 In a small saucepan combine milk, granulated sugar, and chocolate. Cook and stir over low heat until chocolate is melted; remove from heat. If necessary, beat with a wire whisk until smooth.

3 In a small bowl lightly beat eggs; gradually stir in the chocolate mixture. Stir in orange peel and vanilla. Pour egg mixture over bread cubes; press bread with the back of a spoon to be sure it is all moistened.

4 Bake in the preheated oven for 15 to 20 minutes or until tops appear firm and a knife inserted near the centers comes out clean. Cool slightly on a wire rack. If desired, sprinkle with powdered sugar or top with whipped topping.

Per serving: 170 cal., 4 g total fat (2 g sat. fat), 1 mg chol., 143 mg sodium, 26 g carbo., 2 g fiber, 5 g pro.

index

Note: Boldfaced page references indicate photographs.

W

Z

Metric Information

The charts on this page provide a guide for converting measurements from the U.S. customary system, which is used throughout this book, to the metric system.

Product Differences

Most of the ingredients called for in the recipes in this book are available in most countries. However, some are known by different names. Here are some common American ingredients and their possible counterparts:
- Sugar (white) is granulated, fine granulated, or castor sugar.
- Powdered sugar is icing sugar.
- All-purpose flour is enriched, bleached or unbleached white household flour. When self-rising flour is used in place of all-purpose flour in a recipe that calls for leavening, omit the leavening agent (baking soda or baking powder) and salt.
- Light-colored corn syrup is golden syrup.
- Cornstarch is cornflour.
- Baking soda is bicarbonate of soda.
- Vanilla or vanilla extract is vanilla essence.
- Green, red, or yellow sweet peppers are capsicums or bell peppers.
- Golden raisins are sultanas.

Volume and Weight

The United States traditionally uses cup measures for liquid and solid ingredients. The chart below shows the approximate imperial and metric equivalents. If you are accustomed to weighing solid ingredients, the following approximate equivalents will be helpful.
- 1 cup butter, castor sugar, or rice = 8 ounces = $1/2$ pound = 250 grams
- 1 cup flour = 4 ounces = $1/4$ pound = 125 grams
- 1 cup icing sugar = 5 ounces = 150 grams
- Canadian and U.S. volume for a cup measure is 8 fluid ounces (237 ml), but the standard metric equivalent is 250 ml.
- 1 British imperial cup is 10 fluid ounces.
- In Australia, 1 tablespoon equals 20 ml, and there are 4 teaspoons in the Australian tablespoon.
- Spoon measures are used for smaller amounts of ingredients. Although the size of the tablespoon varies slightly in different countries, for practical purposes and for recipes in this book, a straight substitution is all that's necessary. Measurements made using cups or spoons always should be level unless stated otherwise.

Common Weight Range Replacements

Imperial / U.S.	Metric
$1/2$ ounce	15 g
1 ounce	25 g or 30 g
4 ounces ($1/4$ pound)	115 g or 125 g
8 ounces ($1/2$ pound)	225 g or 250 g
16 ounces (1 pound)	450 g or 500 g
$1 1/4$ pounds	625 g
$1 1/2$ pounds	750 g
2 pounds or $2 1/4$ pounds	1,000 g or 1 Kg

Oven Temperature Equivalents

Fahrenheit Setting	Celsius Setting	Gas Setting
300°F	150°C	Gas Mark 2 (very low)
325°F	160°C	Gas Mark 3 (low)
350°F	180°C	Gas Mark 4 (moderate)
375°F	190°C	Gas Mark 5 (moderate)
400°F	200°C	Gas Mark 6 (hot)
425°F	220°C	Gas Mark 7 (hot)
450°F	230°C	Gas Mark 8 (very hot)
475°F	240°C	Gas Mark 9 (very hot)
500°F	260°C	Gas Mark 10 (extremely hot)
Broil	Broil	Grill

*Electric and gas ovens may be calibrated using celsius. However, for an electric oven, increase celsius setting 10 to 20 degrees when cooking above 160°C. For convection or forced air ovens (gas or electric), lower the temperature setting 25°F/10°C when cooking at all heat levels.

Baking Pan Sizes

Imperial / U.S.	Metric
$9×1 1/2$-inch round cake pan	22- or 23×4-cm (1.5 L)
$9×1 1/2$-inch pie plate	22- or 23×4-cm (1 L)
8×8×2-inch square cake pan	20×5-cm (2 L)
9×9×2-inch square cake pan	22- or 23×4.5-cm (2.5 L)
$11×7×1 1/2$-inch baking pan	28×17×4-cm (2 L)
2-quart rectangular baking pan	30×19×4.5-cm (3 L)
13×9×2-inch baking pan	34×22×4.5-cm (3.5 L)
15×10×1-inch jelly roll pan	40×25×2-cm
9×5×3-inch loaf pan	23×13×8-cm (2 L)
2-quart casserole	2 L

U.S. / Standard Metric Equivalents

$1/8$ teaspoon = 0.5 ml	
$1/4$ teaspoon = 1 ml	
$1/2$ teaspoon = 2 ml	
1 teaspoon = 5 ml	
1 tablespoon = 15 ml	
2 tablespoons = 25 ml	
$1/4$ cup = 2 fluid ounces = 50 ml	
$1/3$ cup = 3 fluid ounces = 75 ml	
$1/2$ cup = 4 fluid ounces = 125 ml	
$2/3$ cup = 5 fluid ounces = 150 ml	
$3/4$ cup = 6 fluid ounces = 175 ml	
1 cup = 8 fluid ounces = 250 ml	
2 cups = 1 pint = 500 ml	
1 quart = 1 litre	